难以置信的实用职场英语

薛咏文 著

北京理工大学出版社
BEIJING INSTITUTE OF TECHNOLOGY PRESS

Introduction 内容简介

完美呈现商务英语培训课程

本书整理自商务精英英语培训课程，
将长达半年的课程去芜存菁成最精华的重点，完美呈现于书中！
作者拥有资深商务英语教学经验，加上 6 次新托业满分，
认真为你打造黄金课程。
篇章页中的前言都饱含着作者丰富的实战经验，
职场上的技巧一点都马虎不得。

3 个专为职场技巧应用设计的章节
开启你步步为营的人生布局

CH1 "简历及面试"让你成为职场达人，本章节教你如何漂亮地推销自己。

CH5 "商务会议"教你如何成功举办一场商务会议，从议程准备到结束致词毫不马虎。

▶ 职场上会使用到的格式、流程和职场秘密全收录！

3个专为职场应对设计的章节
开启你长袖善舞的职场生涯

CH2 "跨文化社交技巧"让你与老外谈笑风生。

CH3 "商务电话与电邮"让你无论电话还是邮件都能完美应对。

CH6 "协商及谈判"让你无论跟对手还是合作伙伴都能轻松建立良好的合作关系。

▶ 除了提供情境对话之外，还能充实职场应对思维，让你不会盲目地踩了一堆地雷自己却不知道。

User's Guide 使用说明

在职场中，英语重要，商务思维更重要

真正的职场英语，绝不是把场景换成"办公室"而已！
本书作者在多年商务英语教学实践中发现，
很多人在学生时期埋头苦背英语单词、英语会话，
但走入职场，马上使用不恰当的英语却把老外惹恼！
不是因为这个人太没有礼貌，而是因为有些句子只能用在朋友之间，
再加上跨文化差异，会让彼此的误会加深，阻碍双方的合作。

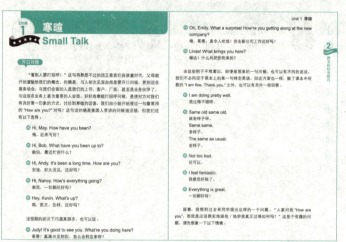

▶ 每个单元一开始，作者一定会将教学重点辅以中文，条理清晰地将每一个单元想强调的重要商务思维写出来。让你在学习职场英语之余，更能够将之融入实际中，达到现学现卖。

▶ 看完前面的教学重点，接着就是扎实的英语训练。职场英语绝对不会只有会话而已，也包含各种表格、格式的实际应用！你不必等到踏入办公室出糗后才开始学习，预先在书中预习，才能知己知彼、百战百胜！

User's Guide

阅读完内文，
立即学会单词及句型！

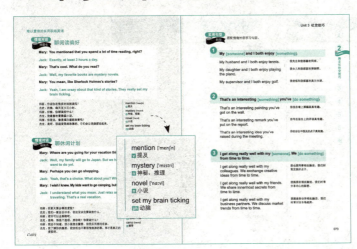

每一篇均细心挑选实用单词，看一次不会，多看几次就记住了！词汇重复率越高代表这个词越重要。基础功夫做扎实，在职场上才能步步高升。

除了单词之外，也整理了实用句型以及例句。随便背一句，在日常生活中应用就会让大家觉得你的英语超地道。

美式英语 MP3，
训练听力也训练口语

本书邀请美籍专业录音员，录制本书中所有英语情境对话及讲稿。只要多听、多读、多练习，那么，当你看到老外，就不会再手心冒汗，而是能够对答如流、谈笑风生。

附赠"单词总整理"

本书收录适用面试的实义动词（Action Verbs）、常用商务英语缩写（Abbreviation），以及全书单词总整理。单词表也标出该单词的同义词或变化词，这样更容易记忆，增加词汇量！

图示	代表意思
n n	名词
v v	动词
a a	形容词
ad ad	副词
ph ph	短语
同	同义词
变	变化词

"地球是平的"的时代已经来临！

如果你不能掌握新时代浪潮，
浪潮就会将你淘汰！
如果无法走出中国、迈向国际，
你如何和全世界的人做生意？

目录 Contents

Chapter 1 简历及面试 001
Resume Writing and Interviews

Chapter 2 跨文化社交技巧 051
Cross Culture and Socializing

Chapter 3 商务电话与电邮 085
Telephoning & E-mail

Chapter 4 简报及演说技巧 125
Presentations and Speeches

Chapter 5 商务会议 159
Business Conference

Chapter 6 协商及谈判 213
Negotiation

附录. 常用商务英语缩写、单词表 241

Resume Writing and Interviews
简历及面试

前言

  我在商务英语教学行业工作的近二十年中，时常被问及"一场成功的英语面试有什么秘诀？"事实上，各行各业的工作内容不尽相同，老板性格千百种、工作申请者的性格也各不相同，没有什么特别的"秘诀"或"固定公式"可以直接套用。但我还是可以整理出准备面试的基本心态，如何写出有效的英语简历，英语面试常见问题与参考答案和后续追踪信件等主题让读者们参考。以期读者们在准备英语面试前，有方向可以依循。

  首先，要养成"明确地"表达意见的习惯。英语系国家的文化和其国民人格特质都是偏向较"直接与开放"的，英美人士使用语言的习惯也是较偏向"要清楚明确地表达"。

  请看这个模糊的句子："Someone will contact you soon."（有人很快会跟你联络。）听到此话的人可能会有后续疑问：Who? 有人是指谁呀；How? 要如何联络呢，是会打我手机吗，还是要发邮件；When? 是何时会联络呢，很快是指明天吗，还是三天后呢。由此可看出，听这句话的人并没有得到明确的信息，难怪会产生后续的疑虑了。

  我们应该清楚地表达："My assistant will fax you the agreement Monday morning by 10."（我的秘书周一十点前会将合约传真给你。）此句内的信息是不是就清楚多了呢？在了解了"明确地表达"的重要性之后，今后在英语面试中就应注意。与其讲这样模糊的句子："I've been working for quite a long time."（我已工作很久了。）更应该明确地表达："I've been working in the IT Industry for three years."（我已在 IT 产业界工作三年了。）

  好的，这只是面试技巧中的一个小要点。以下就让我们全面地讨论英语面试的准备工作吧！

高品质简历
Curriculum Vitae

> 简历格式

日前我和加拿大朋友在书店闲逛,她看到简历表是表格形式的,并列出一些空格给工作申请者填写。我便顺口说"这样很方便吧",加拿大朋友表示"但看起来是要给想去速食店或加油站打工的人写的"。

陈大明的简历			
姓名	陈大明	年龄	23 岁
性别	男	婚姻状态	未婚
身高	170cm	体重	58kg
血型	B 型		
学历	高中毕业		
工作经验	1. 加油站打工 2. 速食店收银	家庭状况	1. 父母退休 2. 弟弟读高中

职场上老板注重的是申请者是否有能力帮公司开拓市场、服务客户、让客户满意,进而增加公司利润,而非申请者的外貌或家庭状况等信息。因此,如果申请者的简历表像上表一样,填一些与"是否会帮公司赚钱"无关的内容,企业老板自然提不起兴趣,也就不会想花时间了解了。

的确,职场上专业的商务简历表有其格式,不是画格子填些年龄、性别、结婚与否等内容。我们先不说简历表内容具体是什么,其较专业的格式如下所示:

Unit 1 高品质简历

简历表参考格式

Your Full Name
[Address]
[Phone Number]
[Email Address]

EDUCATION
    [University]
    [Period / Graduation Month and Year]
    [Major / Subjects]

EXPERIENCE
    [Organization Name]
    [Period]
    [Position Title]
    [Job Responsibilities]
    [Organization Name]
    [Period]
    [Position Title]
    [Job Responsibilities]

SKILLS
    [Language]
    [Computer]
    [Social Media]

ADDITIONAL ACHIEVEMENTS
    [Certifications]
    [Awards]
    [Paper / Book Published]

由此可以看出，一份专业的简历表应包括申请者基本联络方式、工作经验、学历背景、专业训练和人格特质等部分。有了这些内容之后，可以让面试官短时间内清楚明白地了解内容，文字不要使用创意、草书或可爱卡通等字体，更不要使用过大或过小的字体。为了突显重点，某些重点字使用粗体或加下划线是可以接受的。但不要在文字段落中间加插图、贴照片，或画笑脸等，如此便会显得不够专业。

除了上述的格式之外，内容与语句表达更是重要的一环。请想象一位桌前堆满简历的面试官的处境，他／她必须在短时间内浏览完数百份简历表，抓到重点，进而选出适当的人选来做初步面试。面试官会有这么多时间吗？为了工作效率，面试官用于浏览单份简历表的时间平均仅约六秒。仅有"重点明确，令人印象深刻"的简历表可以在六秒内抓住面试官的目光。为了要让自己的简历表有"重点马上跳出来"的效果，如同在"前言"处提及的，语句的描述自然是要非"明确又清楚"不可的。

比方说，要提到自己的工作表现很亮眼，便写了这样的句子：

例 My previous working performance was very good.
我前一份工作的表现非常好。

这样模糊的句子会引起人更多的疑虑。

What performance?
表现是指哪方面的表现？是业务吗？还是客服呢？

How good?
很好是代表多好？标准是什么？

如此还要别人花时间去想的内容，是不可能让面试官在六秒之内就抓到重点的。但是，若将此句修改为"明确的"描述便会成为：

例 I have completed two major projects within a year including ERP System Integration and Inventory Tracking System.
我在一年内完成了包括 ERP 系统整合和库存追踪系统的两个大项目。

或是

例 I have increased profits by 25% within a quarter.
在一季内我的业绩就增加了百分之二十五。

如此，明确地将自己的成就"量化"，才有机会让面试官在第一时间就抓到要点。以下，一起来看各种专业领域可使用的简历表格式吧！

EXERCISE

1. 写简历时，使用何种字型及字体大小最保险？
   A. Times New Roman，12pt
   B. Castellar，12pt
   C. Century Gothic，24pt
   D. Comic Sans MS，8pt

   答案：A

2. 一份简历上最显眼的信息应该是？
   A. 婚姻状态
   B. 生活照片
   C. 申请人信息
   D. 家庭背景

   答案：C

资深销售人员

Sandra Anderson
111 5th Ave.
New York, NY, 88888
(123) 555-7777

Summary of Qualifications
- More than ten years of sales experience
- Received numerous sales awards and achievements
- Strong leadership skills through participating in seminars
- Experience and skills in developing database systems

Experience

High-Tech Systems, Teaneck, NJ

Senior Account Manager — 1998 to Present
- Responsible for the sales and lease of ABC system products in New Jersey.
- Acquired computer skills and working knowledge of network connectivity.

Professional Accomplishments
- Recipient of 3 General Manager's Awards
- Sales Representative of The Year Award — two years
- President's Award for Sales Excellence — four-time recipient

Education

Roman University, New York, NY: Bachelor of Business Administration, 1996

Personal Interests
- Swimming, foreign travel, world history study
- Member of Peace Yoga Association

Unit 1 高品质简历

资深销售人员 ▶ 中译

珊卓·安德森
第五大道 111 号
纽约，纽约 88888
(123) 555-7777

资质概述
- 超过十年的销售经验
- 获得了多项销售奖励和成就
- 通过参加研讨会获得了强大的领导能力
- 有开发资料库系统的经验和技能

工作经验
新泽西 Teaneck 高科技系统公司
高级客户经理——1998 年至今
- 新泽西州 ABC 系统产品销售和租赁负责人。
- 获得了计算机技能和有关网络连接的专业知识。

专业成就
- 三项总经理奖得主
- 连续两年获得年度销售代表奖
- 总裁销售精英奖——第四次获得此奖励

学历
1996 年获纽约州纽约市罗曼大学商业管理学士学位

个人兴趣爱好
- 游泳、旅游、研究世界历史
- Peace Yoga 协会成员

---

award [ə'cɔ:rd]
n 奖励，奖项

leadership ['li:dərʃɪp]
n 领导才能

participate [pɑ:r'tɪsɪpeɪt]
v 参与

acquire [ə'kwaɪər]
v 取得，获得

recipient [rɪ'sɪpɪənt]
n 接受者

association [ə,soʊʃi'eɪʃn]
n 协会

难以置信的实用职场英语

简历范本 范例二 **百货公司管理阶层**

Tiffany Liu
2020 Fu-Hsing Rd.
A City, B Province 10411
(886) 2-2555-7000

WORK EXPERIENCE

8/2012 – Present *Sales Manager, Worth-Buys, A City, B Province*
Manage three shoe departments and two dress departments. Supervise 22 associates. Maintain excellent customer service. Ensure proper merchandise presentation on selling floor. Review and react to merchandise information reports. Communicate with vendors, as well as store managers and selling personnel. Control individual department inventory.

12/2010 – 7/2012 *Sales Coordinator, Best-Fashion, A City, B Province*
Maintain efficient vendor and branch store communication. Ensure accuracy of paperwork and inventory control. Review stock levels and merchandise assortment.

1/2008 – 11/2017 *Secretary, Formosa Dress, A City, B Province*
Work closely with store managers assistant. Familiar with compensation and insurance plans, payroll procedures, employee reviews, and customer service.

EDUCATION

7/2001 – 5/2005 Roman University, NY: Bachelor of Business Administration

Unit 1 高品质简历

百货公司管理阶层 ▶ 中译

蒂芬妮·刘
复兴路 2020 号
A 市，B 省 10411
(886) 2-2555-7000

工作经验

2012 年 8 月至今　　　　　　B 省 A 市好好买百货公司　销售经理

管理三个鞋具店面和两个服装店面。监督二十二名员工。维持良好的客户服务。确保销售店面的商品摆放正确。评估并回应商品信息报告。与供应商、店铺经理和销售人员进行沟通。控制每个店面的商品库存。

2010 年 12 月至 2012 年 7 月　　B 省 A 市完美时尚公司　销售协调员

与供应商和分店保持有效沟通。确保文件和库存控制的准确性。审查库存水准以及商品分类。

2008 年 1 月至 2017 年 11 月　　B 省 A 市服装公司　秘书

与店面经理助理进行紧密合作。熟悉薪酬和保险计划、工资处理程序、员工评估和客户服务等工作。

学历

2001 年 7 月至 2005 年 5 月　　纽约市罗曼大学商业管理学士

---

supervise ['suːpərvaɪz]
v 监督，领导

merchandise ['mɜːrtʃəndaɪs]
n 商品

inventory ['ɪnvəntɔːri]
n 库存

maintain [meɪn'teɪn]
v 保持，维持

accuracy ['ækjərəsi]
n 正确性

compensation [ˌkɑːmpen'seɪʃn]
n 补偿，报酬

 软件公司主管

Linda Chang
29 Central Street
A City, B Province, 80228
(886) 2-2895-5236

EXPERIENCE HIGHLIGHTS:

Best Software, A City, 2011 – Present

Data Analysis Supervisor: In charge of overseeing the work of 11 subordinates. Coordinated and controlled the use, and maintenance of Data Analysis software. Ensured accuracy and security of all data analysis and output.

Technical Programmer: Responsible for the operation of Data Center. Design applications to meet enterprise clients' Big Data analysis.

EDUCATION:

University of A City — A City, B Province, B.A. Computer Science

Major: Technology Management with emphasis on computer programming languages

PERSONAL ATTRIBUTES:

I am accustomed to assuming responsibility and delegating authority, and I am capable of working with people at all levels. I am able to plan, organize, develop, implement, and supervise complex programs and special projects.

REFERENCE:

Mr. Jacky Lee, GM of Scientific Software Inc.
Tel: 886-2-4736-7070 / Email: jacky-lee@scisoft.com

Unit 1 高品质简历

软件公司主管 ▶ 中译

琳达·张
中央街 29 号
A 市，B 省 80228
(886) 2-2895-5236

工作经验概要：

2011 年至今，A 市最佳软件公司

资料分析主管：负责督导十一名同事的工作。对资料分析软件的使用和维持进行协调和控制。确保各种资料分析和输出的准确性和安全性。

技术程序设计员：负责资料中心的运行。设计满足企业客户大数据分析的应用程序。

学历：

B 省 A 市—— A 市大学计算机科学学士
专业：侧重于计算机程序语言的技术管理专业

个人特点：

本人习惯于承担责任和授权他人，而且能够与各个层次的人合作。能够对复杂的程序和特殊专案进行规划、组织、开发、执行和督导。

推荐人：

杰克·李先生，科学软件公司总经理
电话：886-2-4736-7070 / Email: jacky-lee@scisoft.com

---

oversee [ˌoʊvərˈsiː]
v 监督

subordinate [səˈbɔːrdɪnət]
n 部属，属下

coordinate [koʊˈɔːrdɪneɪt]
v 协调，整合

analysis [əˈnæləsɪs]
n 分析

authority [əˈθɔːrəti]
n 授权，威信

implement [ˈɪmplɪmənt]
v 执行，部署

软件营销经理

Mark Chen
333 12th Street
A City, B Province, 38438
(886) 3-328-8462

Job Target: Product Manager

Experience

12/2013 — Present   Big-Byte Software Inc., A City, B Province
- ☑ Senior Marketing Manager
- ☑ Duties include: Establish partnership with software vendors and act as the main coordinator for marketing and sales plans

12/2010 — 11/2013   SoftTech B Province Corporation, A City, B Province
- ☑ Assistant Partner Development Manager
- ☑ Duties include:
  — In charge of channel marketing activities including product brand and value proposition.
  — Responsible for partners conference, partner kick-off, and major events.
  — Design partner incentive programs & activities.

Education

8/2005 — 5/2009   **University of A City, A City, B Province**
📖 Master of Science / Major: Computer Science

On-Job Training

- Microsoft network systems related technical training courses.
- Information Systems related products sales / marketing trainings.
- Advanced English writing, reading, and critical reasoning trainings.
- Professional English speech / presentation skills trainings.

软件营销经理 ▶ 中译

马克·陈
12 街 333 号
A 市，B 省 38438
(886) 3-328-8462

求职目标：产品经理

工作经验

2013 年 12 月至今　　　　　　　　　B 省 A 市，Big-Byte 软件公司
　☑ 高级营销经理
　☑ 职责包括：与软件供应商建立合作关系并担任营销和销售计划的主要协调人。

2010 年 12 月至 2013 年 11 月　　　　B 省 A 市，SoftTech B 省有限公司
　☑ 合作伙伴开发助理经理
　☑ 职责包括：
　　－负责渠道营销活动，包括产品品牌和价值建议。
　　－负责管理合作伙伴会议、合作启动和重大事件。
　　－设计合作伙伴激励项目和活动。

学历

2005 年 8 月至 2009 年 5 月　　　　　B 省 A 市，A 市大学
　📖 理学硕士 / 主修：计算机科学

在职培训

- 有关微软网络系统的技术培训课程。
- 有关信息系统的产品销售 / 营销培训。
- 高级英语读写和批判性思维培训。
- 专业英语演说 / 展示技能培训。

---

establish [ɪˈstæblɪʃ]
v 建立，创建

development [dɪˈveləpmənt]
n 发展

proposition [ˌprɑːpəˈzɪʃn]
n 定位

conference [ˈkɑːnfərəns]
n 会议，研讨会

advanced [ədˈvænst]
a 进阶的

critical [ˈkrɪtɪkl]
a 关键的，批判的

客服代表

Lorrie Ford
1 Central Street, New City, CA 57379
Tel: 473-5737-5838   Email: lf@mail.com

Summary

Experienced Call Center Representative who consistently meets and exceeds goals. Maintain a high-level of patience to maximize customer satisfaction and increase customer loyalty.

Highlights

* Problem solver
* Excellent interpersonal skills
* High standards
* Critical thinker
* Articulate
* Goal oriented

Experience

Call Center Representative   5/2012 to Present
Vision Customer Support Inc. Chicago, IL

* Understood customer demands and resolved complains in a timely manner
* Provided accurate and appropriate information to answer questions
* Achieved customer satisfaction rate of 90% within 8 months

Call Center Representative   9/2010 to 4/2012
Stars Software Inc. New York, NY

* Collected customer feedback and improved service process to exceed customer satisfaction goals
* Built relationships with other departments through clear communication
* Facilitated information flow between customer service, sales and marketing, account operation, and technical support to ensure objectives were met

Education

The University of Cityland, New City, CA 9/2006 to 7/2010
Bachelor of Business Administration

Courses included: Consumer Behaviors, Communication Theory, Psychology

Unit 1 高品质简历

客服代表 ▶ 中译

罗瑞·福特
中心街 1 号，新城，加州 57379
电话：473-5737-5838　电邮：lf@mail.com

摘要
经验丰富的客服中心代表，持续地达成并超越目标。运用耐心对待客户，使客户满意度提升到最高，并增加客户忠诚度。

主要人格特质

* 问题解决者
* 良好的人际关系处理技巧
* 高标准

* 批判性思考者
* 能言善道（清楚地表达）
* 目标导向

工作经验

客服中心代表　　　　　　　　　　　　　　**2012 年 5 月迄今**
愿景客服中心，芝加哥，伊利诺伊州
* 了解客户需求并即时解决其抱怨
* 针对客户问题提供正确恰当的信息
* 八个月内达成百分之九十的客户满意度

客服中心代表　　　　　　　　　　　　　　**2010 年 9 月至 2012 年 4 月**
星星软件公司，纽约，纽约
* 收集客户意见反馈，并改善服务程序，以超越客户满意的目标
* 通过清楚的沟通与其他部门建立良好关系
* 加速客服部、营销业务部、营业部和技术支援部的信息流通，以确保达成目标

教育

西蒂兰大学，新城，加州　　　　　　　　　　**2006 年 9 月至 2010 年 7 月**
商管学士学位
所修科目：消费者行为、沟通理论、心理学

---

consistently [kən'sɪstəntli]
ad 持续地

loyalty [ˈlɔɪəlti]
n 忠诚度

articulate [ɑː'tɪkjuleɪt]
a 能言善道的

satisfaction [ˌsætɪsˈfækʃn]
n 满意度

facilitate [fəˈsɪlɪteɪt]
v 加速

objective [əbˈdʒektɪv]
n 目标

难以置信的实用职场英语

实用句型 例句 搭配简历范本学习句型。

1 Work closely with [someone].

Work closely with assistant store managers.	与店面经理助理密切合作。
Work closely with specialists from Marketing Department.	与营销部门专员密切合作。
Work closely with customers to come up with solutions.	与客户密切合作以想出解决方案。

2 I am able to [do something].

I am able to plan, organize and supervise complex programs and special projects.	我有能力规划、安排并监督复杂的活动和特殊项目。
I am able to deal with difficult customers.	我有能力应付难相处的客户。
I am able to work effectively under pressure.	我有能力在高压下有效率地工作。

3 Responsible for [something].

Responsible for Partners conference, Partner Kick-Off, and major events.	负责伙伴研讨会、誓师大会和大型活动。
Responsible for generating new sales leads.	负责产生出更多有效潜在客户名单。
Responsible for tracking product inventory.	负责追踪产品库存量。

Unit 2 求职信
Cover Letter

别寄简历表

准备求职的人往往急着准备好简历（或简历的电子文档），然后在求职网站搜寻到有职缺的企业后，就不管三七二十一便急急忙忙地把模式化的简历发送出了。大家也许会想，这种求职步骤有什么问题吗？一般不都是这样做吗？请仔细地想一下，招聘企业每天收到海量的简历，每个都千篇一律地写着"我愿意认真学习，并对公司做出贡献"之类的老掉牙的句子。面试官看每篇都过目即忘，看不出有哪份是跟其他简历表有所区别，他们要如何决定谁才是最适当的人选呢？这也难怪求职者最常抱怨："我已投出数百封简历，可是都石沉大海呀！"要解决这样困境，就要跳脱"模式化"的思维，并朝向"个性化简历"的方向进行。

我在书店看过一本外文求职书，书名是《别寄简历》（*Don't Send a Resume*）。乍看之下会觉得疑惑，找工作不就是要寄出简历吗？怎么会让人不要寄呢？仔细阅读内容之后，了解到作者的意思是"不要在不了解公司与职位的情况下就贸然地将简历寄出去"。而是要"先对求职公司做彻底的研究，并对职缺的要求、工作内容有全盘的了解之后，再针对此企业做一份针对职缺内容的独一无二的简历表"。连简历表都要针对企业的要求来个性化制作了，求职信的"独特性"更不在话下。试想，一封连要寄给谁都不知道，写着"Dear Sir"的求职信，和一封很明确要寄给"Mr. Mark Smith, Head of Research Development"的求职信，哪一份才能引起注意呢？答案很明显，当然是后者。

因此，在写求职信之前，不要想抄些英语句子，拼拼凑凑地写出一封求职信。重要的是，先选定想求职的公司，通过公司网站了解其愿景、产品与发展，向业界的前辈或友人打听公司的状况，深入地研究职缺的要求、任务内容、评估标准等。然后，再针对此职缺所需的条件与内容，设计自己的求职信的内容、用字与语气，也就是要"事先做足功课"的意思。做好"了解公司与职缺内容"的功课之后，针对其设计的求职信内容才会言之有物！因此，请务必在针对心仪的企业与职缺做足"全盘了解"的功课之后，再套用以下所介绍的求职信格式！以下列出几个针对不同产业与情境所写的求职信，但重要的是读者还是要针对自己的求职产业个性化制作个人简历！

教学格式

```
                                      [Your Address / Contact Information]
                                      [Date]


[Employer Contact Information]
[Name, Title, Company, Address]


Dear Mr. / Ms. Last Name,


[Opening]
    说明欲申请的职位，和在何处看到职位的信息。


[Middle Paragraph #1]
    说明您的背景、专业技能、工作经验等。


[Middle Paragraph #2]
    说明您期望为公司带来的利益或帮助等。


[Final Paragraph]
    说明您想得到面谈机会的企图心，并说明方便联络的方式与时间。


Sincerely,
[Your Name]
```

下面整理出所需要填写的各项内容及注意事项：

[Your Address / Contact Information]

此为寄件人的详细地址与联络信息。

[Date]

信件应标明书写日期，以便日后追踪。

[Employer Contact Information]
[Name, Title, Company, Address]

此处应写收件人的姓名、职称、部门、公司等内容。

Dear Mr. / Ms. Last Name

信件署名之处应明确地写出要寄给谁,而非仅写 Dear Sir 这样不明确的信息。

[Opening]

说明欲申请的职位和在何处看到职位的信息。大企业招募很少仅招聘一两位员工的,更可能是每个部门都有六七个职位。如同先前讨论到的,若信息不明确,仅写"我想应征项目经理"这样的内容的话,看信的人可能会有"哪个部门?"或"负责什么产品的项目经理?"的疑惑,这会浪费大家的时间。为求精准有效率,最佳的方式是明确地表示"我想申请贵公司在新加坡分部的大型企业 ERP 项目经理一职。",若有编号更可以写出"职位编号 SG#769"以增加精确度。如此,看求职信的人会觉得申请者是一位细心且思维清楚的人。

[Middle Paragraph #1]

说明你的背景、专业技能、工作经验等。通常简历表内所列出的专业技能与工作经验是以条的形式列出的。为了再次强调与更详尽地说明,可以在求职信内对自身的技能与经验多加阐述。相同的,最好可以通过举出明确的数据,或可量化的信息来说明自己的成就。

[Middle Paragraph #2]

说明你期望为公司带来的利益或帮助等。如同之前讨论过的,申请工作不单是为了求职者本身的好处。重要的是求职者可以为公司带来什么好处呢?这是老板所关心的事。此段落就是要求职者就期望如何协助到公司的愿景加以说明。当然,要提出可行的方案,而非好高骛远的理想。

[Final Paragraph]

说明你想得到面谈机会的期望,并说明方便联络的方式与时间。最后,可以再度写出自己渴望得到面谈机会的决心,并将联络电话、电子信箱、方便联络的时间都详细列出。或者更主动的话,可以在此说明在几天时间内会亲自去电询问进度。

难以置信的实用职场英语

营销经理

777 Spring Ave.
New York, NY 88888
November 15, 2017

Mr. William Smith
Director of HR, Morgan Marketing Inc.
666 Summer Road
Chicago, IL 99999

Dear Mr. Smith,

    I am writing to express my interest in pursuing marketing opportunities at Morgan Marketing Inc. After reviewing your web page, I am very excited about the possibility of working as a marketing manager for Morgan Marketing Inc. The emphasis on developing a world-class team and providing excellent client services is especially attractive to me. I believe that my abilities match your values, as demonstrated in my CV.

    Through my relevant professional experience and my MBA work in marketing management, I have obtained the knowledge, experience, and skills to help empower companies to plan effective marketing strategies. I am confident that my prior experience in leading marketing projects has provided me with the skills needed to become a successful marketing manager at Morgan Marketing Inc.

    I have enclosed a copy of my CV for you to review. I would greatly appreciate the opportunity to learn more about Morgan Marketing. I will call you within this week to check if there may be a convenient time to meet with you. Thank you for your consideration.

Sincerely,
Mary Chen

 营销经理 ▶ 中译

春日路 777 号
纽约，纽约 88888
2017 年 11 月 15 日

威廉·史密斯先生
人资经理，摩根营销公司
夏日路 666 号
芝加哥，伊利诺伊州 99999

亲爱的史密斯先生，

  本人特此致信，表达对摩根营销公司的销售工作机会有浓厚的兴趣。在浏览贵公司的网页后，得知摩根营销公司正在招募营销经理，我可能符合应聘条件，因此对此感到十分兴奋。发展一个世界级团队，提供优质服务，对我而言也十分有吸引力。我认为个人的能力符合贵公司的标准，可参见简历了解我的能力。

  通过相关的专业经验和在营销管理方面的 MBA 研究工作，我拥有可以帮助公司制定有效营销策略的知识、经验和技能。先前领导营销项目的经历已经使我具备了成为一名成功的摩根营销公司营销经理所需的技能，我对此有着充分的自信。

  随信附上个人简历副本供贵公司审阅。若能获得进一步了解摩根营销经理职位的机会，本人深表感谢。我会在本周内致电贵公司，以便确定贵公司方便在某个时间与本人面谈。感谢贵公司考虑我的简历。

诚挚的，
玛丽·陈

---

emphasis ['emfəsɪs]
n 强调

attractive [ə'træktɪv]
a 有吸引力的

relevant ['reləvənt]
a 有关联性的

demonstrate ['demənstreɪt]
v 证明

strategy ['strætədʒɪ]
n 策略

appreciate [ə'priːʃɪeɪt]
v 感激

公关助理

778 ×× Road

A City, B Province 11111

March 8th, 2017

Ms. Grace Chang

Director of Public Relations

ABC Company

123 5th Blvd.

A City, B Province 11111

Dear Ms. Chang,

  I am writing to apply for the Public Relations Assistant position that appeared in the *Daily News* on May 15th. After reviewing the position description, I found every aspect of this professional opportunity appealing.

  Along with my class work at Roman College, I have been able to gain valuable, practical experience through my internships. A large portion of my internship involved assisting with the plan of marketing strategies. This assignment enabled me to gain a better understanding of how to use various media to reach the public.

  Enclosed you will find my latest resume. I will call next week to check the status of my application. Thank you in advance for your consideration.

Sincerely,

Sam Wilson

Unit 2 求职信

公关助理 ▶ 中译

××路 778 号

A 市，B 省 11111

2017 年 3 月 8 日

葛瑞丝·张小姐

公关经理

ABC 公司

第五大道 123 号

A 市，B 省 11111

张小姐，您好，

　　我写此信是为了要申请贵公司五月十五日在《每日新闻》上刊登的公关助理职位。在看职位描述后，我发现此职位的工作内容非常吸引我。

　　我在罗门大学学习期间，也通过实习得到了宝贵且实际的经验。我实习中很大一部分时间是参与协助规划营销策略。这样的任务让我更加深刻地认识到如何使用各种媒体工具接触到大众。

　　附件是我最新的简历。我下周会致电给您，以了解我的申请进度。先谢谢您！

诚挚的，
山姆·威尔森

---

appear [əˈpɪr]
v 出现，显示

description [dɪˈskrɪpʃn]
n 描述

aspect [ˈæspekt]
n 方面，角度

practical [ˈpræktɪkl]
a 实际的，务实的

involve [ɪnˈvɑːlv]
v 牵涉

assignment [əˈsaɪnmənt]
n 任务，工作

资料工程师

837 Good-Will Ave.
A City, B Province, 71717
March 15, 2017

Mr. Sherman Lee
HR Director
Crux Systems Inc.
454 1st Blvd.
C City, B Province 23622

Dear Mr. Lee,

    I was excited to see your opening for a Data Engineer and would like to gain an opportunity for an interview.

    My background includes serving as a Data Analyst within TDI Consulting Company. Most recently, I worked for Crux Systems, where my responsibilities included data mining and data analyzing. In these positions, I have demonstrated the ability to resolve a variety of data analysis issues, and integrate different data sources. I also bring to the table strong computer proficiencies in CRM database applications that support the management with clear and insightful analysis on the data at hand. Please refer to the enclosed resume for details of my experience and education.

    I am confident that I can offer the data analysis expertise and problem-solving skill you are seeking. Please feel free to call me at 373-4838-3938 to arrange an interview. Thank you for your consideration and I am looking forward to learning more about this opportunity.

Sincerely,
Lisa Lau

资料工程师 ▶ 中译

好善路 837 号
A 市，B 省 71717
2017 年 3 月 15 日

谢尔曼·李先生
人资经理
Crux 系统公司
第一大道 454 号
C 市，B 省 23622

李先生您好，

  本人看见贵公司招聘资料工程师后十分兴奋，也非常想得到一次面试机会。

  本人的工作背景包括担任 TDI 咨询公司的资料分析师。最近，在 Crux 系统公司工作期间，工作职责包括资料收集和资料分析。在任职过程中，本人已经证明了具备解决若干资料分析以及将不同资料来源整合的能力。同时具备坚实的 CRM 资料库应用程序方面的计算机专业能力，可以将资料用清晰和富有洞见的现有分析方式支援给管理层。请参阅本人的简历，了解工作经验和学历细节。

  本人自信可以提供贵公司正在寻求的资料分析专业知识和解决问题的技能。感谢贵公司考虑我的简历并期待进一步了解是否有获得面试的机会，欢迎以电话通知面试时间（373-4838-3938）。

诚挚的，
莉莎·罗

---

analyze ['ænəlaɪz]
v 分析

resolve [rɪ'zɑːlv]
v 解决

integrate ['ɪntɪɡreɪt]
v 整合

proficiency [prə'fɪʃnsi]
n 精通，熟练

insightful ['ɪnsaɪtfʊl]
a 有独特见解的

expertise [ˌekspɜː'tiːz]
n 专门能力

技术支持经理

558 Cedar Lane
Teaneck, NJ 58372
July 4th, 2018

Ms. Vivian Smith
Recruiting Manager
VB Technology Inc.
463 Grand Street
Chicago, IL 47362

Dear Ms. Smith,

  As an experienced technical support engineer, I believe I am well qualified for the position of Technical Support Manager that you advertised in Tech Today. Enclosed you will find my updated resume and find that I have sufficient experience in providing technical support to enterprise clients. In each case I was able to raise the standards of the troubleshooting procedure and increase customer satisfaction levels.

  Having exceeded my goals in my previous position, I would like to challenge myself further with a more demanding position. The position of Technical Support Manager in VB Technology Inc. appeals to me very much as this type of challenge.

  After you've had a chance to read my resume, please feel free to reach me at 353-5737-5837 to schedule an interview. Thank you very much for considering my application.

Sincerely,
Mark Hsieh

求职信范本 范例四：技术支持经理 ▶ 中译

西堤街 558 号
蒂内克市，新泽西州 58372
2018 年 7 月 4 日

薇薇安·史密斯小姐
招募经理
VB 科技公司
格兰大街 463 号
芝加哥，伊利诺伊州 47362

史密斯小姐，您好，

  作为一名经验丰富的技术支持工程师，本人认为有资格应聘贵公司在《科技日报》上刊登的技术支持经理职位。随信附上最新简历，你可以从中了解到我有充分的向企业客户提供技术支持的工作经验。在每个工作案例中，本人均能够提升故障排解程序的标准，并提高客户的满意度。

  由于已经超越了先前职位的工作目标，本人想进一步挑战自我，尝试应聘要求更高的职位。VB 技术公司的技术支持经理职位，对我而言，正属于这种类型的自我挑战。

  贵公司参考简历后，请随时拨打电话 353-5737-5837 联系我，以便安排一个面试时间。非常感谢贵公司考虑我的应聘。

诚挚的，
马克·谢

---

advertise [ˈædvərtaɪz]
v 登广告

sufficient [səˈfɪʃnt]
a 充足的

enterprise [ˈentərpraɪz]
n 企业

troubleshoot [ˈtrʌblʃuːt]
v 除错，解决问题

demanding [dɪˈmændɪŋ]
a 要求高的

challenge [ˈtʃælɪndʒ]
n 挑战

国际销售代表

To: Mr. Luke Gibson luke-G@core-data.com
From: Linda Heart lindaheart@mail600.com
Date: March 3rd, 2018
Subject: International sales rep application

Dear Mr. Gibson,

 Recently I have been researching the leading companies in international sales that are respected in the field. The name of Optima International keeps coming up as a top company.

 As an experienced international sales representative, I have an international trading background and a reliable analytical approach to international changes. Furthermore, I am a competitive person professionally. In my previous working experience, I collaborated with coworkers to gather, analyze, and process data to enable effective, fact-based decision making. I am a self-starter and eager to grow in a fast-paced international environment.

 My resume is enclosed. I would appreciate your consideration for an interview where I could demonstrate a keen business acumen in all practices, and discuss my international sales capabilities in more details. Please let me know if there is additional information I can provide to lead you to schedule an interview.

Sincerely,
Lisa Lau

Enclosure

Unit 2 求职信

求职信范本 范例五 — 国际销售代表 ▶ 中译

致：路克·吉伯森先生 luke-G@core-data.com
自：琳达·哈特 lindaheart@mail600.com
日期：2018年3月3日
主旨：国际销售代表职位申请

吉伯森先生，您好，

　　近来本人在研究国际销售行业中受业界敬重的领先公司。而奥提玛国际公司始终是业界中的佼佼者。

　　身为一名经验丰富的国际销售代表，本人有国际贸易背景，并对充满变化的国际销售采用可靠的分析方法。另外，我也是一名具有竞争力的专业人员。在以往的工作经验中，我与若干同事合作收集、分析和处理资料，以便基于事实进行有效的决策。本人是一个主动的人，并渴望在快节奏的国际环境中成长。

　　随信附上简历。若贵公司考虑进行面试，本人将十分感谢，而且只有在面试中我方能展示善于处理对各种商业事务的能力，并更详细讨论我的国际销售才能。若贵公司还需要进一步的信息，欢迎随时与我联络。

诚挚的，
莉莎·罗

内附文件

---

representative [ˌreprɪˈzentətɪv]
n 代表

approach [əˈproʊtʃ]
n 方式

competitive [kəmˈpetətɪv]
a 好竞争力的

collaborate [kəˈlæbəreɪt]
v 协同合作

acumen [ˈækjəmən]
n 才智，专业

capability [ˌkeɪpəˈbɪləti]
n 能力

搭配求职信范本学习句型。

 I am confident that my prior experience in [something] has provided me with the skills needed to become a successful [someone] at [some company].

I am confident that my prior experience in leading marketing projects has provided me with the skills needed to become a successful marketing manager at Morgan Marketing Inc.	我过去领导大型营销项目的经验，让我具备了在摩根营销公司成为成功的营销经理的能力。对此我深具信心。
I am confident that my prior experience in handling customer complaints has provided me with the skills needed to become a successful customer service representative at ABC Call Center.	我过去处理客户抱怨的经验，让我具备了在ABC电话客服中心成为出色的客服经理的能力，对此我深具信心。
I am confident that my prior experience in providing professional software training has provided me with skills needed to become a successful computer instructor at TDI Learning School.	我过去提供专业软件训练的经验，让我具备了在TDI训练学校成为成功的计算机讲师的能力。对此我深具信心。

 I am a [someone] and eager to grow in a fast-paced [something] environment.

I am a self-starter and eager to grow in a fast-paced international environment.	我是个自动自发的人，也渴望在快节奏的国际环境中不断成长。
I am a proactive person and eager to grow in a fast-paced sales environment.	我是个主动的人，也渴望在快节奏的销售环境中不断成长。
I am a competition lover and eager to grow in the fast-paced manufacturing industry.	我是个喜欢竞争的人，也渴望在快节奏的制造产业中不断成长。

Unit 2 求职信

3 **As an experienced** [someone]**, I believe I am well qualified for the position of** [position] **that you advertised in** [somewhere]**.**

As an experienced technical support engineer, I believe I am well qualified for the position of Technical Support Manager that you advertised in *Tech Today*.

身为有经验的技术支持工程师，我相信我能胜任您在《科技日报》所刊登的"技术支持经理"的职位。

As an experienced sales person, I believe I am well qualified for the position of Senior Account Manager that you advertised in *Daily News*.

身为有经验的销售人员，我相信我能胜任您在《每日新闻》所刊登的"资深销售经理"的职位。

As an experience accountant, I believe I am well qualified for the position of Accounting Manager that you advertised in *Money Magazine*.

身为有经验的会计师，我相信我能胜任您在《金钱杂志》所刊登的"会计经理"职位。

MEMO

031

Unit 3 感谢信
Follow-up Letter

保持追踪

很多工作申请人共同的经历：面谈时还相谈甚欢，面谈之后时间一天天过去，若十天半个月过去没联系自己，工作机会就很渺茫了。招聘企业面对众多申请者固然需要时间筛选考虑，但是也不代表申请者就应被动地等待结果。

此节要讨论的是面谈后"感谢信"的撰写，照中文字表面看起来好像就纯粹是出自礼貌，要"感谢"企业花时间面谈而已，但事实上，英语所称的**"follow-up letter"**的最重要的意义其实是让申请者"再度积极地表达对职位真的有兴趣，且想为公司效力的企图心"。因此，一份面谈后的感谢信（follow-up letter）通常会包括三个主要元素：

1. 再度归纳并强调自己的专业和能力
2. 阐述申请者是如何对职位有兴趣，并对达成公司目标有信心
3. 补充说明在面谈时遗漏的问题

通常 follow-up letter 寄出的时间可以是在面谈后的三天内，若没收到回复，可以在两周内再寄一次（有些人会直接打电话询问进度）。格式方面除了传统信件（以下的范例书写格式都是传统信件的格式）之外，也有人使用传真，或更多时候有人是直接写电子邮件。

有些人会认为，潜在雇主对申请者印象好坏，在面谈时就大致决定了，觉得面谈后再写份感谢信的作用似乎不大。事实并非如此，之前讨论过，申请者可以通过感谢信再次展现对工作的企图心，同时雇主在接到申请者所寄的感谢信时，更会生出"此人真的很积极主动呢！既然他／她对这份工作这么有热情，那就给他／她一个机会吧"的想法。由此可见感谢信的重要性了。

Unit 3 感谢信

凡事有始有终,面谈也不例外,写份感谢信让雇主感受到申请者的诚意,就算一次没有被录取,也会因为保持联络,可能日后带来其他的工作机会。下面就列出几个感谢信的范本给大家参考吧!

教学格式

```
                                    [Your Address / Contact Information]
                                    [Date]


[Employer Contact Information]
[Name, Title, Company, Address]


Dear Mr. / Ms. Last Name,


[Opening]
  说明是在何时,与哪位经理的面谈。


[Middle Paragraph #1]
  再度归纳并强调自己的专业和能力。


[Middle Paragraph #2]
  阐述申请者是如何对职位有兴趣,并对达成公司目标有信心。并补充说明在面谈时遗漏的问题。


[Final Paragraph]
  再次说明您想得到此工作机会的心情。


Sincerely,
[Your Name]
```

图像设计师

777 ×××. Road,
A City, B Province, 11037

September 18, 2017

Ms. Lily Chang
Human Resources Director
Creative Design Co.
3829 1st Ave.
C City, B Province 12345

Dear Ms. Chang,

    I truly enjoyed our discussion last Friday of the graphic designer position you would like to fill. I trust that you have recognized my interest and ambition in the "graphic designer" position, and my experience and competencies fit well with your requirements. I am eager to contribute my expertise to the position and believe that the extensive experience I've already developed makes me a very suitable candidate.

    Enclosed please find three references that you requested. I look forward to hearing from you regarding your hiring decision soon. Thank you once again for your time and for the congenial interview.

Sincerely,
Amy Liang

图像设计师 ▶ 中译

×××路777号
A市，B省11037

2017年9月18日

莉莉·常小姐
人资经理
创意设计公司
第一街3829号
C市，B省12345

常小姐您好，

　　上周五我们就贵公司正在招聘的图像设计师职位进行了讨论，本人对此次讨论感到十分高兴。相信贵公司已经认可了我对"图像设计师"职位的兴趣和热情，而且我的经验和能力均符合贵公司的要求。本人渴望将自己的专业知识投入此职位中，并认为大量的工作经验，使我成为适当的候选人。

　　随附贵公司要求的三封推荐信。期待贵公司尽快回复做出聘请的决定。对于贵公司抽出宝贵时间安排此次融洽的面试，再次表示感谢。

诚挚的，
艾米·梁

---

truly ['truːli]
ad 非常地

discussion [dɪ'skʌʃn]
n 讨论

recognize ['rekəgnaɪz]
v 识别，认出

ambition [æm'bɪʃn]
n 野心

competency ['kɑːmpɪtənsi]
n 能力，专才

requirement [rɪ'kwaɪərmənt]
n 要求

contribute [kən'trɪbjuːt]
v 贡献

expertise [ˌekspɜːr'tiːz]
n 特长，专业能力

extensive [ɪk'stensɪv]
a 广泛的

candidate ['kændɪdət]
n 候选人

reference ['refrəns]
n 推荐人，参考

congenial [kən'dʒiːniəl]
a 友善的，投缘的

 销售经理

447 Spring Ave.
Springfield, IL, 11111

May 23, 2018

Mr. Steven Fu
Recruiting Manager
High-Tech Systems Inc.
883 Summer Blvd.
Apple Town, IL, 22222

Dear Mr. Fu,

    Thank you for considering me for the Pre-Sales Manager position we discussed on May 20th. I would like to take this opportunity to express my continued interest in this opening and also emphasize my previous achievements. I would insure my performance fully meeting your department's needs.

- Developed pre-sales plans for all Illinois region in past six years
- Handled hardware and software problems and faults and referred on to technical colleagues
- Networked with existing clients in order to maintain links and promote additional solutions and upgrades
- Made cold-calls to create interest in products and solutions, and generate new sales leads

    Again, thank you for your time, and efforts to arrange the interview. I am looking forward to hearing from you soon.

Sincerely,
Lily Swift

销售经理 ▶ 中译

春日街 447 号
春田市，伊利诺伊州 11111

2018 年 5 月 23 日

史帝文 · 傅先生
招募经理
高科技系统公司
夏日大道 883 号
苹果镇，伊利诺伊州 22222

傅先生您好，

  我们已于五月二十日就销售经理职位进行了面试会谈，感谢贵公司考虑本人的应聘。我想借此机会表达对此职位的兴趣，并同时强调下列的工作成就确保我的工作表现将完全符合贵公司部门的需求。

- 在过去六年内为整个伊利诺伊州地区开发售前计划。
- 处理软硬件问题和故障并转交给技术部同事。
- 与现有客户组织成客户网络以便保持联系，并促销其他的解决方案和升级。
- 进行电话销售以激发客户对产品和解决方案的兴趣，并找到潜在客户名单。

再次感谢贵公司对此次面试安排投入的时间和精力。期望很快收到贵公司的回复。

诚挚的，
莉莉 · 斯威夫特

---

emphasize ['emfəsaɪz]
v 强调

achievement [ə'tʃiːvmənt]
n 成就

performance [pər'fɔːrməns]
n 表现

handle ['hændl]
v 处理

existing [ɪg'zɪstɪŋ]
a 现存的，现有的

maintain [meɪn'teɪn]
v 维持，保有

promote [prə'moʊt]
v 宣传，促销

additional [ə'dɪʃənl]
a 额外的

solution [sə'luːʃn]
n 解决方案

cold call
ph 电话销售

generate ['dʒenəreɪt]
v 产生

arrange [ə'reɪndʒ]
v 安排

客户经理

222 Oak Tree Street
Chicago, IL 88888
March 23, 2017

Mr. Jones White
Sales Director
ABC Organization
456 East Queen Street
Chicago, IL 88888

Dear Mr. White,

　　Thank you for providing me the opportunity to interview for the Account Manager position last Wednesday. I appreciate the time you spent during the interview and the tour you provided of your facility.

　　Our discussion regarding your products and services was very appealing to me. I am excited about the possibility of working with your team. I am confident that the types of sales experiences I've had, combined with my communication skill and English ability, will prove to be assets for your organization. Last Wednesday's interview only reinforced my desire to join your sales team and work for ABC Organization.

　　Thank you once again for your time and consideration.

Sincerely,
Judy Wilson

感谢信范本 范例三

客户经理 ▶ 中译

橡树街 222 号
芝加哥，伊利诺伊州 88888
2017 年 3 月 23 日

琼斯·怀特先生
销售总监
ABC 企业
东后街 456 号
芝加哥，伊利诺伊州 88888

怀特先生您好，

  感谢贵公司上周三安排本人参与客户经理职位面试的机会。感谢贵公司在面试中所花费的时间，以及引导参观贵公司的设施、设备。

  我们就贵公司产品和服务的讨论，对我而言十分具有吸引力，并对与贵公司团队合作的可能性感到十分兴奋。我自信我拥有的销售经验，再搭配我的沟通技能和英语能力，事实将证明对贵公司而言将是十分有价值的资产。上周三的面试更加坚定了我加入贵公司销售团队并为 ABC 公司工作的渴望。

  再次感谢贵公司的宝贵时间。

诚挚的，
茱蒂·威尔森

---

appreciate [əˈpriːʃieɪt]
v 感谢，激赏

facility [fəˈsɪləti]
n 设备

appealing [əˈpiːlɪŋ]
a 具吸引力的

confident [ˈkɑːnfɪdənt]
a 有信心的

asset [ˈæset]
n 财产，资产

reinforce [ˌriːɪnˈfɔːrs]
v 加强，稳固

难以置信的实用职场英语

搭配感谢信范本学习句型。

 I truly enjoyed our discussion [when] of the [position] you would like to fill.

I truly enjoyed our discussion last Friday of the graphic designer position you would like to fill.

我真的非常高兴上周五能有机会与您讨论贵公司要找的"绘图设计师"职位的细节。

I truly enjoyed our discussion on March 2nd of the Assistant Manager position you would like to fill.

我很高兴有机会在三月二日与您讨论贵公司要找的"助理经理"职位的细节。

I truly enjoyed our discussion last week of the Technical Support Engineer position you would like to fill.

我很高兴上周能有机会与您讨论贵公司要找的"技术支持工程师"职位的细节。

 I am confident that the type of [something] I've had, combined with my [something] ability, will prove to be assets for your organization.

I am confident that the types of sales experiences I've had, combined with my communication skill and English ability, will prove to be assets for your organization.

我自信地说我所拥有的销售经验,再搭配我的沟通技巧和英语能力,确实是对贵公司有价值的资产。

I am confident that the types of customer service experiences I've had, combined with my interpersonal and problem-solving skills, will prove to be assets for your company.

我自信地说我所拥有的客户服务经验,再搭配我的人际技巧和解决问题的能力,确实是对贵公司有价值的资产。

I am confident that the types of technical support experiences I've had, combined with my computer and trouble-shooting skills, will prove to be assets for your firm.

我自信地说我所拥有的技术支持经验,再搭配我的电脑和故障排除能力,确实是对贵公司有价值的资产。

Unit 3 感谢信

3 I would like to take this opportunity to express [something].

I would like to take this opportunity to express my continued interest in this opening.

我想利用此机会表达我对此职位的高度兴趣。

I would like to take this opportunity to emphasize my past experience and achievements.

我想利用此机会再度强调我过去的经验和成就。

I would like to take this opportunity to affirm my ambition and confidence to meet your company goals.

我想利用此机会再度肯定我可以帮贵公司达成目标的志向和信心。

MEMO

Unit 4 面试技巧
Interview Skills

团队利益

说到面试,工作申请者通常会想是否有什么"秘诀""技巧"或"窍门"。除了对自身领域的专业技术要熟悉、基本的英语能力要具备之外,另一个可以给面试官留下良好印象并增加录取率的关键点便是"优先考量公司利益"的态度。

在时下"人不为己,天诛地灭"的社会氛围中,这听起来似乎很矫情。的确,每个求职者在筛选工作时都先顾好"自己"的考量"离家近不近""薪水高不高"或"福利好不好"等。但请想清楚,现实状况下公司放出工作机会,有需求的是谁?发薪水的是谁?是公司,是老板。那么,为什么我们会一直想"公司可以提供给我什么好处",而非"我可以对公司做出什么贡献"呢?百分之九十的人都是先考虑到自己,若你可以当那特殊的百分之十的人,也就是"将公司利益摆在自身利益之前"的人的话,自然更容易得到企业主青睐,在面试中胜出。

请看真实面试例子:

面试官:请问你为什么对这个工作有兴趣?

求职者:因为我刚退伍,我爸叫我要找个工作。至少要有收入,待在家也不是办法。

面试官:你对此职位工作内容了解多少?

求职者:不是很了解,所以我想请问若出去拜访完客户才四点,那我可以提前回家吗?

Unit 4 面试技巧

从回答就可以听出，这样的求职者想到的都是"自身的利益"和"公司对我的好处"。但事实上，老板开公司不是做"慈善事业"，退伍就要老板收留吗？老板发薪请人工作是要让他提前回家休息吗？显然上述求职者把主宾角色颠倒了。

相反地，真的了解"以公司利益为出发点"精神的求职者在面谈时，会将焦点由自身转移到"如何协助公司获利"上。请看以下例子：

> 面试官：请问你为什么对这个工作有兴趣？
>
> 求职者：我是做业务出身的，且手上有完整客户名单。让我来销售贵公司的软件产品，不仅对我是种磨炼，我也有信心帮公司提升业绩。
>
> 面试官：你对此职位要求了解多少？
>
> 求职者：我已研究过贵公司网站、产品和工作内容。产品销售这部分我有相关经验并有信心帮公司拿单，英语能力的要求部分，我会去考托业来证明。

由此例子可以看出差异点。要有一场成功的面谈的最主要也是最简单的技巧，其实就是"凡事不要只顾自己的好处，而要以团队的利益考量为出发点"。若时常把这种思维摆在心里，自然就跟多数"先想到自己利益"的人区分开来，并在竞争中胜出了。

问关于申请者的背景

Interviewer: Please tell us your educational background.

Jack: Sure. I just graduated from Roman College, and I've obtained my bachelor's degree in Computer Science.

Interviewer: Have you got any working experience?

Jack: Well, I don't have much working experience, but my passion for computer programming has motivated me to choose software design as my future career.

Interviewer: Okay, good. And what's your major strength?

Jack: Besides computer knowledge, I also have good interpersonal and communication skills.

问关于申请者的背景 ▶ 中译

面试官：请谈谈你的教育背景。

杰　克：好的。我刚从罗门大学毕业，我已取得计算机科学的学士学位。

面试官：你有任何工作经验吗？

杰　克：我还没有很多工作经验，但我对计算机编程技术的热情促使我今后想朝软件设计师方向发展。

面试官：好的，很好。那你的强项是什么？

杰　克：除了计算机知识之外，我还有良好的人际和沟通能力。

---

obtain [əbˈteɪn]
v 取得，获得

passion [ˈpæʃn]
n 热忱

motivate [ˈmoʊtɪveɪt]
v 激励

strength [streŋθ]
n 强项

interpersonal [ˌɪntərˈpɜːrsənl]
a 人际的

Unit 4 面试技巧

 问申请者的爱好

Interviewer: How many foreign languages do you speak?

Jack: Besides Chinese, I also speak English fluently. And as I stayed in Japan for 2 years before, I can communicate in Japanese as well.

Interviewer: What are your interests?

Jack: Doing yoga is my favorite pastime. Practicing yoga makes me feel relaxed and boosts my energy.

Interviewer: What's your working style?

Jack: Well, I like to do things in a steady pace, and ensure that all assigned tasks are done accurately.

 问申请者的爱好 ▶ 中译

面试官：你会讲几种外语？

杰　克：除了中文，我会讲流利的英语。因我在日本待过两年，我也可以用日文沟通。

面试官：你的兴趣是什么？

杰　克：我有空就做瑜伽。练习瑜伽让我感到放松，且增强了我的活力。

面试官：你的工作风格是什么？

杰　克：我喜欢以稳定的步调来完成工作，并确认所有交代的任务都准确无误地完成。

---

foreign [ˈfɔːrən]
a 国外的

fluently [ˈfluːəntli]
ad 流利地

pastime [ˈpæstaɪm]
n 休闲活动

boost [buːst]
v 增加

accurately [ˈækjərətli]
ad 精确地

问申请者对人格特质的看法

Interviewer: What do your friends say about you?

Jack: My friends always consider me as a reliable, optimistic, and creative person.

Interviewer: What kind of persons would you refuse to work with?

Jack: I don't like to work with selfish colleagues, and people who are too stubborn to accept new ideas.

Interviewer: What qualities do you look for in a leader?

Jack: I think a good leader should empower team members, and possess strategic thinking skills.

 问申请者对人格特质的看法 ▶ 中译

面试官：你朋友都如何描述你？
杰　克：我朋友都认为我是一个可靠、乐观和有创意的人。
面试官：你不喜欢跟哪种人共事？
杰　克：我不喜欢跟自私的同事共事，还有过于固执无法接受新想法的人。
面试官：你认为领导人要有何特质？
杰　克：我认为好的领导人要授权给团队成员，且要具备策略思考的能力。

---

optimistic [ˌɑːptɪˈmɪstɪk]
a 乐观的

stubborn [ˈstʌbərn]
a 固执的

strategic [strəˈtiːdʒɪk]
a 策略性的

refuse [rɪˈfjuːz]
v 拒绝

empower [ɪmˈpaʊər]
v 授权

Unit 4 面试技巧

问申请者过去的工作经验

Interviewer: Why did you leave your last job?

Jack: ABC Company is a rather small company and there was not much room for me to advance. I am eager to work in a more challenging environment.

Interviewer: What was your most significant accomplishment?

Jack: Well, completing the TCI project was my biggest achievement at ABC Company. Not only did I put a lot of efforts on that project, but I also learned to consolidate resources effectively.

Interviewer: How did you deal with difficult customers?

Jack: I only focus on providing practical solutions to their problems and show my willingness to assist them.

问申请者过去的工作经验 ▶ 中译

面试官：你为何要离开上一个公司？

杰　克：ABC 公司是个小公司，比较没有适合我的发展空间了。我想要在更具挑战性的环境工作。

面试官：你最大的成就是什么？

杰　克：完成 TCI 项目是我在 ABC 公司期间最大的成就。我不仅花了很多心力在那上面，我还学到如何有效地整合资源。

面试官：你如何处理难相处的客户？

杰　克：我只会专注在为他们的问题提供可行的解决办法，并显示我愿意协助他们解释的态度。

---

advance [əd'væns]
v 精进

challenging ['tʃælɪndʒɪŋ]
a 有挑战性的

significant [sɪg'nɪfɪkənt]
a 重大的

achievement [ə'tʃiːvmənt]
n 成就

consolidate [kən'sɑːlɪdeɪt]
v 整合，统筹

willingness ['wɪlɪŋnəs]
n 愿意

047

难以置信的实用职场英语

问申请者对未来的展望与发展

Interviewer: What do you see yourself doing in three years?

Jack: In three years, I see myself in a middle management position and lead a small team.

Interviewer: What do you plan to do in order to achieve this goal?

Jack: Well, I definitely need to sharpen my professional skills, and I would like to take more communication training.

Interviewer: Can you give us a reason to hire you?

Jack: I believe I am the best candidate because I have experience, excellent communication skills, and I am confident to help the company close more deals.

问申请者对未来的展望与发展 ▶ 中译

面试官：你三年后想做什么？

杰　克：三年后，我想当中层主管，并且带领小团队。

面试官：你计划做什么来达成此目标？

杰　克：我当然要继续加强我的专业技能，另外我也想要参加些沟通技巧的训练。

面试官：请你提出我们要聘任你的理由。

杰　克：我相信我是最佳的候选人，因为我有经验，有优良的沟通技巧，且我有信心帮公司完成更多的交易。

---

definitely [ˈdefɪnətli]
ad 确实，的确

sharpen [ˈʃɑːrpən]
v 加强

candidate [ˈkændɪdət]
n 候选人

confident [ˈkɑːnfɪdənt]
a 有信心的

Unit 4 面试技巧

实用句型
 搭配情境对话学习句型。

 简历及面试

1 **My passion for [something] has motivated me to choose [something] as my future career.**

My passion for computer programming has motivated me to choose software design as my future career.	我对计算机编程技术的热情促使我今后想朝软件设计师方向发展。
My passion for children has motivated me to choose elementary school teaching as my future career.	我对小孩的热情促使我今后想以教小学生当未来的职业。
My passion for writing has motivated me to choose author as my future career.	我对创作的热爱促使我今后想以写作为职业。

2 **I believe I am the best candidate because I have [something], [something], and I am confident to [do something]**

I believe I am the best candidate because I have experience, excellent communication skills, and I am confident to help the company close more deals.	我相信我是最佳的候选人，因为我有经验和优良的沟通技巧，且我有信心帮公司完成更多交易。
I believe I am the best candidate because I have English ability, professional computer skills, and I am confident to achieve company's goals.	我相信我是最佳的候选人，因为我有英语能力、专业的计算机技能，我有信心达成公司的目标。
I believe I am the best candidate because I am good at cold calls, know how to persuade people, and I am confident to meet company's sales targets.	我相信我是最佳的候选人，因为我擅长陌生电话销售，知道如何说服客户，并有信心达成公司的业绩目标。

049

3. My friends always consider me as a [adj.], [adj.], and [adj.] person.

My friends always consider me as a reliable, optimistic, and creative person.

我朋友都认为我是一个可靠、乐观和有创意的人。

My friends always consider me as a friendly, honest, and considerate person.

我朋友都认为我是一个友善、诚实，又会为他人着想的人。

My colleagues always consider me as a competent, articulate, and bold person.

我同事都认为我是一个能力强、能言会道且勇敢进取的人。

MEMO

Cross Culture and Socializing
跨文化社交技巧

前言

　　东方文化较为保守内敛，人们不擅长与人社交或主动与人攀谈。相较之下，西方人较为开放热情。在一般日常状况（如火车上）或正式社交场合（如商业接待会上），看到不认识的人也较愿意主动接近与其认识。

　　有前往美国／加拿大旅游经验的读者可能都会有这样的经验：在清晨的街道上，三两行人在路上走，即便是与不相识的人擦身而过，对方有可能对着你微笑点头，并道声 "Good morning. How are you?" 他不见得是真的要我们回答我们是否安好，但遇到人会点头致意并打声招呼，几乎已是他们日常生活中文化习惯的直觉反应了。在上述的情境下，我们也可以简单地说声 "Good morning." 回应即可，不必担心对方要进一步攀谈或是可能会有什么其他的要求。

　　日常生活中的情境便已是如此，在国际商务来往中，恰当的社交礼仪的重要性自然是更不在话下了。在中国，职场员工可能在各自的专业领域上表现亮眼，但在人际关系处理上的能力便略显薄弱。若有接待外宾或参加接待会等机会，很多人便以"自己不善交际"或"没社交经验"等理由推掉。

　　事实上，在正式的场合自然地与人认识、问候、攀谈等技巧，是可以学习，并通过一次又一次的练习来熟悉的。本章节的目的，就是通过以下几个主题：寒暄、活络气氛、社交技巧与禁忌等角度切入，帮助大家了解，在商务环境中，如何开口，可以聊什么话题，尽量避免讨论什么敏感议题等，让读者在英语学习中，体会到英语使用者的文化习惯。

Unit 1 寒暄
Small Talk

开口问候

"看到人要打招呼！"这句再熟悉不过的话正是我们自孩童时代，父母就开始灌输给我们的概念。的确是，与人初次见面自然是要开口问候，更别说在商务场合，与我们会面的人是我们的上司、客户、厂商，甚至是业务伙伴了。与这些在业务上甚为重要的人会面，好好地寒暄打招呼问候，是使对方对我们有良好第一印象的方式。讨论到寒暄的话语，我们自小就开始背过一句最常用的"How are you?"对吗？这句话的确是美国人常讲的问候语没错，但我们还有以下选择：

例 Hi, May. How have you been?
梅，近来可好？

例 Hi, Bob. What have you been up to?
鲍伯，最近忙些什么？

例 Hi, Andy. It's been a long time. How are you?
安迪，好久没见，还好吗？

例 Hi, Nancy. How's everything going?
南西，一切都还好吗？

例 Hey, Kevin. What's up?
嘿，凯文。怎样，还好吗？

没预期的状况下巧遇某朋友，也可以说：

例 Judy! It's good to see you. What're you doing here?
茱蒂！真高兴见到你。怎么会到这来呀？

例 Oh, Emily. What a surprise! How're you getting along at the new company?
哦，茱蒂。真令人吃惊！你去新公司工作还好吗？

例 Linda! What brings you here?
琳达！什么风把你吹来的？

由这些例子不难看出，即便是简单的一句问候，也可以有不同的说法。我们不必拘泥于课本上的某一句特定英语。回应方面也一样，除了课本中所教的"I am fine. Thank you."之外，也可以有另外一些回答：

例 I am doing pretty well.
我过得不错呀。

例 Same old same old.
就老样子呀。
Same same.
老样子。
The same as usual.
老样子。

例 Not too bad.
还可以。

例 I feel fantastic.
我感觉好极了。

例 Everything is great.
一切都好呀！

接着，我想到过去有同学提出这样的一个问题："人家问我'How are you'，那我是应该照实地跟他/她讲我真正过得如何吗？"这是个有趣的问题，请先想象一下以下情境：

Mary: How are you doing recently, Jack?
杰克，近来可好？

Jack: Well, terrible really. My dog was sick, and my girlfriend broke up with me. And worst of all, I was laid off last week.
嗯，还真的蛮糟的。我的狗生病了，女友要跟我分手。更惨的是，我上周被解雇了。

说真的，要是真的按照 Jack 这样充满负面的抱怨来说，还真的不是 Mary 原本预期会听到的答案呢。搞不好 Mary 心里还不禁会担心"说他失业？该不会跟我借钱吧？"事实上，问候者所提的"How are you doing recently?"只是一般的礼貌性寒暄问候语，并不是真的要听对方回答一些生活琐事或坏消息。

尤其是在商务场合或办公环境中，生意人在最初的基本问候之后，多数就会直接进入讨论商业议题了。因此，他们预期对话刚开始的寒暄问候只是个开头，而非真的要就"你好不好"这个问题本身再继续聊下去。就好像我们中国人见人喜欢问"吃了吗？"，也仅是一般问候的意思，并非代表"若你还没吃，我就要请你吃饭"之意，这两者间道理是一样的。因此，初步的寒暄问候，就简短应对即可，应将对话要点放在随后要讨论的业务正事上。接着，就一起来看一下针对不同情境可能的寒暄对话吧！

Unit 1 寒暄

情境对话 场景一 接待柜台

Receptionist: Good morning, Sir. How may I help you?

Jack: Hello. My name is Jack Sheehan. I am from High-Tech Systems in Canada.

Receptionist: Please take a seat.

Jack: I have an appointment with Ms. Kelly Smith at 10 please.

Receptionist: All right, I'll let her know you're here. Would you like water, coffee, or tea?

Jack: Oh, a glass of warm water is fine. Thank you.

接待人员：先生，早安。有什么可以效劳的吗？
杰　　克：你好，我是杰克·辛汉。我来自加拿大的"高科技系统公司"。
接待人员：请那边稍坐。
杰　　克：我跟凯莉小姐约十点会面，谢谢。
接待人员：好的，我会告知她您到了。您是喝水、喝咖啡还是喝茶？
杰　　克：一杯温水就可以了，谢谢你。

receptionist [rɪˈsepʃənɪst]
n 接待人员
take a seat
ph 请坐
appointment [əˈpɔɪntmənt]
n 约会，会议

情境对话 场景二 初次会面

Mary: Excuse me, are you Mr. Kevin Hart from New York?

Kevin: That's right.

Mary: How do you do, Mr. Hart. I am Mary Chen here at Good-Will Consulting.

Kevin: Oh, Ms. Chen. Pleased to meet you.

Mary: Welcome to Beijing. Is this your first visit to China?

Kevin: Well, actually this is my second visit.

玛丽：不好意思，您是纽约来的凯文·哈特先生吗？
凯文：是的。
玛丽：哈特先生，幸会了。我是"好意顾问公司"的玛丽·陈。
凯文：陈小姐你好。很高兴认识你。
玛丽：欢迎来到北京。您第一次到中国来吗？
凯文：嗯，这已经是我第二次来了。

excuse [ɪkˈskjuːs]
v 原谅
consulting [kənˈsʌltɪŋ]
a 专职顾问的
welcome [ˈwelkəm]
v 欢迎

055

机场接机

Mary: You must be Jack. Hi, I am Mary.

Jack: Yes, I am. Mary, it's wonderful to finally meet you in person after all our mail communications.

Mary: Exactly. So how was your journey?

Jack: Everything went pretty well. No problem at all.

Mary: I think I could drive you to the hotel first.

Jack: No, it's okay. I think we should go straight to the office.

玛丽：您一定是杰克吧？你好，我是玛丽。
杰克：是的，我是。玛丽，你好。平常都是信件沟通，很高兴终于见到你本人了。
玛丽：的确是。那么你此次旅程还好吗？
杰克：所有事都很好。完全没问题。
玛丽：我想说我可以先载你去饭店。
杰克：应该不用，没关系。我想我们可以直接前往办公室。

communication [kə,mju:nɪ'keɪʃn]
n 沟通

journey ['dʒɜ:rni]
n 旅程

straight [streɪt]
ad 直接地，立即地

 互相介绍并转介绍他人

Mary: Let me introduce myself. My name is Mary Ford.

Jack: Nice to meet you, Mary. I am Jack Wilson.

Mary: May I introduce you to our VP of Sales. This is Mr. Terry Good.

Jack: Hello, Mr. Good. How are you doing?

Terry: I am doing great, thank you. Please call me Terry.

Jack: It's my pleasure to meet you, Terry.

玛丽：让我先自我介绍一下。我是玛丽·福特。
杰克：很高兴认识你，玛丽。我是杰克·威尔森。
玛丽：让我帮您介绍我们的销售副总。这位是泰瑞·古德先生。
杰克：古德先生，您好吗？
泰瑞：我很好，谢谢。叫我泰瑞就可以了。
杰克：我很荣幸认识你，泰瑞。

introduce [ˌɪntrə'du:s]
v 介绍

pleasure ['pleʒər]
n 愉悦，高兴

meet [mi:t]
v 会面

Unit 1 寒暄

 确认对方

Mary: I don't think we've met. I am Mary Ford.

Jack: I am Jack Thomson. Nice to meet you.

Mary: Sorry, I didn't catch your name.

Jack: My name is Jack Thomson. It's t-h-o-m-s-o-n.

Mary: Thank you. So Mr. Thomson, are you here in Chicago for pleasure?

Jack: No, it's for business.

玛丽：我们没见过面吧。我是玛丽·福特。
杰克：我是杰克·汤马森。很高兴认识你。
玛丽：不好意思，我没听清楚你的名字。
杰克：我名字是杰克·汤马森。拼法是 t-h-o-m-s-o-n。
玛丽：谢谢。那你到芝加哥是度假吗，汤马森先生？
杰克：不是，是商务。

catch [kætʃ]
v 接住，抓到

pleasure ['pleʒər]
n 愉快，娱乐

business ['bɪznəs]
n 生意，商业

 表示关心

Mary: Hello, Jack. When did you arrive?

Jack: I arrived yesterday evening at around 10.

Mary: Did you have a good trip?

Jack: Well, my flight was delayed a bit. But besides that, everything was all right.

Mary: Where are you staying?

Jack: I am staying at the Grand Hotel downtown. It's very comfortable.

玛丽：你好，杰克。你什么时候抵达的呀？
杰克：我是昨晚大约十点到达的。
玛丽：那旅途还好吗？
杰克：航班有点儿延误。但除此之外，其他事都很顺利。
玛丽：你住哪呢？
杰克：我住市中心的格兰饭店。那饭店很舒适。

flight [flaɪt]
n 班机

delay [dɪ'leɪ]
v 延误

besides [bɪ'saɪdz]
prep 除此之外

057

难以置信的实用职场英语

 提供协助

Mary: Can I help you with your bags?

Jack: It's okay. I am fine.

Mary: Right. My car is parked over there.

Jack: Before we get going, I'd like to wash my hands first.

Mary: Sure. There is a restroom just this way please.

Jack: All right. Thank you.

玛丽:要我帮你提包吗?
杰克:没关系。我可以提。
玛丽:好的。我车就停在那儿。
杰克:我们离开之前,我想先洗个手。
玛丽:当然。这边刚好有个洗手间。
杰克:好的,谢谢。

park [pɑːrk]
v 停车
would like to
ph 想要
restroom ['restruːm]
n 洗手间

 相互介绍认识

Mary: The person I'd like you to meet is Ms. Lily Chen. She's our marketing manager.

Jack: It's great to finally meet you.

Lily: It's a pleasure to meet you too.

Mary: The two of you haven't met before, have you?

Jack: No, we haven't. We've exchanged a lot of emails.

Lily: It's nice to put a face to a name.

玛丽:我要介绍给你认识的人是陈莉莉小姐。她是我们的行销经理。
杰克:你好,终于见面了。
莉莉:我也很高兴与你见面。
玛丽:你们两位之前没见过面吧?
杰克:没有。我们仅通过电子邮件沟通过。
莉莉:终于可以把长相和名字结合起来了。

marketing ['mɑːrkɪtɪŋ]
n 营销
manager ['mænɪdʒər]
n 经理
exchange [ɪksˈtʃeɪndʒ]
v 交换

Unit 1 寒暄

实用句型 例句 搭配情境对话学习句型。

1

I have an appointment with [someone] at [time] please.

I have an appointment with Ms. Kelly Smith at 10 please.	我跟凯莉·史密斯小姐约十点会面，谢谢。
I have an appointment with Dr. Scott at 2pm please.	我下午两点跟斯科特医生有约，谢谢。
I have an appointment with your Marketing Director, Ms. Jason, please.	我跟你们营销经理杰森女士有约，谢谢。

2

It's wonderful to finally meet you in person after all our [something].

It's wonderful to finally meet you in person after all our mail communications.	在信件往来之后，真高兴有机会当面见到你本人。
It's pleasant to finally meet you in person after all our phone calls.	平时都是电话沟通，真荣幸终于可以见到你本人了。
It's my pleasure to finally meet you in person after all our emails.	在使用电邮沟通之后，终于可以见到您本人是我的荣幸。

3

The person I'd like you to meet is [someone]. She's our [position].

The person I'd like you to meet is Ms. Lily Chen. She's our marketing manager.	我要介绍给你认识的人是莉莉·陈女士。她是我们的营销经理。
The gentleman I'd like you to meet is Mr. Smith. He's our VP of Sales.	我要介绍给你认识的先生是史密斯先生。他是我们的销售副总裁。
The person I'd like you to meet is Mrs. Wilson. She's our General Manager.	我要介绍给你认识的人是威尔森夫人。她是我们的总经理。

Unit 2 活络气氛
Ambiance Exciting

> 拉近距离

打完招呼之后,就马上直接进入主题讨论策略、问业绩、讨论数字的机会也不是很大。通常,要讨论真正严肃的商业主题之前,还是需要讲些比较温和日常的话题来活络气氛,拉近彼此的距离。很多人觉得要找话题聊,那就讨论"时事"最保险了。"时事"就是每天新闻播放的,双方都知道的事,聊起来比较不费力。

但事实上,"时事"多数也都是颇为严肃的"重要新闻",不太适合在商务情境中当活络气氛的话题。比方说,要是你问对方"你对欧洲难民潮有何看法",或是"你觉得美国枪械泛滥该如何解决"。对方心中搞不好会想"这么大的问题,我要怎么回答呀",或是"这种问题真的要讨论,三天三夜也讨论不出个所以然呀"。因此,就算是双方都知道的"时事",讨论过于严肃的话题不但无法活络气氛,反而会使双方可能因一言不合吵了起来。这样的话题还是不适合提出讨论的。那么可以活络气氛、让彼此不显生疏的聊天话题可能会是什么呢?建议从几个比较不会有争议的小话题开始。如天气、喝饮料、运动等较为轻松的话题。

再者,以问对方"How's the weather in Beijing?"这句来当例子。这句话逐词念出来就没事了吗?事实上有研究显示,人在沟通时讲出某句话,这句话其实仅传达出我们真正意思的百分之三十(30%)而已。另外的百分之七十(70%)的意义呢?其实是靠说话时的语调(tone)、声音(voice)、面部表情(facial expression)、身体语言(body language)等方式来传达给听话者的。因此,在讲一句问候的话时,不要仅仅将文字说出,还要注意自己的声调是冷淡还是热情,面部表情是面无表情还是面带微笑,身体语言是僵硬不自然还是活跃有生气。这些外在的因素都会影响听话者对我们所说的话的感受。

Unit 2 活络气氛

比方说，若我们仅是将句子平淡地说出：

🅔 What do you usually do when you have free time?
你休闲的时候都在做什么？

对方一听就能感觉到我们是在说"课本英语"（Textbook English）了。

但若我们是按自己的话，并以自然的语调流畅地表达出：

🅔 What's your favorite pastime?
你有空都做什么？

🅔 Any plans for the weekend?
周末有计划吗？

并加上温和的语调、开心的表情和自然的手势，便可让对方感受到，我们不是在背课本英语，而是打从心底想跟他们寒暄，以拉近彼此距离并想成为他们的朋友或业务伙伴。如此，往后的关系建立也会更加容易。

难以置信的实用职场英语

 初次到访情境

Mary: Is this your first time to visit Beijing?

Jack: You're right. This is my first time here.

Mary: Have you had a chance to look around?

Jack: I haven't had time to see anything yet.

Mary: I suggest you visit the Fragrant Hills.

Jack: I'd love to. It seems to be a wonderful place.

玛丽：这是你第一次来北京吗？
杰克：是的。这是我第一次来这。
玛丽：你有机会四处走走了吗？
杰克：我都还找不到时间逛逛呢。
玛丽：我建议你去香山看看。
杰克：我很想去。那看起来是个很棒的地方。

chance [tʃæns]
n 机会
suggest [sə'dʒest]
v 建议
wonderful ['wʌndərfl]
a 很棒的

 轻松互动情境

Mary: Let's go out for coffee.

Jack: That sounds like a wonderful idea.

Mary: Would you mind walking a bit? Well, the best coffee shop here is two blocks away.

Jack: Not at all. It's absolutely fine with me.

Mary: Look at the rain. It's really pouring outside.

Jack: Don't worry. I keep extra umbrellas here.

玛丽：我们出去喝杯咖啡吧！
杰克：听起来是个好主意。
玛丽：要走一段路可以吗？本地最好的咖啡厅在两条街以外。
杰克：可以呀。我没问题。
玛丽：看呀，下雨了。还下得真大呀。
杰克：别担心。我这有额外准备的雨伞。

block [blɑːk]
n 街道
absolutely ['æbsəluːtli]
ad 的确，确实
pour [pɔːr]
v 倾泻，涌流
extra ['ekstrə]
a 额外的

Unit 2 活络气氛

见面关怀情境

Mary: Let me take your coat.

Jack: Thank you. It's very nice of you.

Mary: How was your weekend? Did you do anything special?

Jack: Well, I just stayed home and tried to relax.

Mary: All right, perhaps we should begin our meeting.

Jack: Yes, we've got a pretty full agenda.

玛丽：让我帮你拿外套吧。
杰克：谢谢，你真好。
玛丽：周末过得好吗？做了什么特殊活动吗？
杰克：嗯，就待在家放轻松。
玛丽：好的，那要不然我们开始说正事吧。
杰克：是的，我们今天议程很满。

coat [koʊt]
n 外套

relax [rɪ'læks]
v 放松

agenda [ə'dʒendə]
n 议程

闲聊天气情境

Mary: Hey, Jack. How have you been?

Jack: Actually, I just returned from a business trip to Chicago.

Mary: Oh, really? At this time of the year, it must be really cold in Chicago, right?

Jack: Exactly! The temperature in Chicago was 20 degrees below zero.

Mary: I personally prefer warmer climates.

Jack: Yeah, same here.

玛丽：嘿，杰克。近来可好？
杰克：事实上，我刚从芝加哥出差回来呢。
玛丽：真的呀？现在这种时候，芝加哥很冷吧？
杰克：的确是。芝加哥的气温大约零下二十度。
玛丽：我自己喜欢温暖的气候。
杰克：是呀，我也是。

temperature ['temprətʃər]
n 温度

personally ['pɜːrsənəli]
ad 个人地

climate ['klaɪmət]
n 气候

063

难以置信的实用职场英语

 职务内容情境

Mary: You must be Jack, right? Linda told me that you joined the company recently.

Jack: That's correct. I started working here only two weeks ago.

Mary: Well, what did you do previously?

Jack: I worked as a marketing specialist at ABC Company. I was in charge of promoting software products.

Mary: Sounds wonderful.

Jack: Well, I've also found the tasks I am involved in now are very exciting.

玛丽：你一定就是杰克吧？琳达跟我说你才刚进公司不久。
杰克：是呀。我两周前才开始在这上班呢。
玛丽：那你之前是做什么的呀？
杰克：我在 ABC 公司担任营销专员。我负责推销软件产品。
玛丽：听起来不错。
杰克：嗯，我发现我在这负责的任务也挺有趣的。

previously [ˈpriːviəsli]
ad 之前地
in charge of
ph 负责
promote [prəˈmoʊt]
v 推销
involve [ɪnˈvɑːlv]
v 涉及，卷入

 礼貌协助情境

Mary: Do you need some help with that report?

Jack: Thanks, but I think I can handle it.

Mary: How about taking a short break?

Jack: Okay, let's do so. Maybe just ten minutes.

Mary: I am going to get a cup of coffee. Would you like one?

Jack: Yeah, sure. Black with some cream, please.

玛丽：你做那份报告需要帮助吗？
杰克：我可以搞定，谢谢。
玛丽：那要不要先休息一下？
杰克：好的，我们先休息吧。就十分钟就好。
玛丽：我要去买杯咖啡。你要一杯吗？
杰克：好呀。黑咖啡加点奶精，谢谢。

handle [ˈhændl]
v 处理
break [breɪk]
n 休息
black [blæk]
n 黑咖啡

Unit 2 活络气氛

介绍景点情境

Mary: Have you had a chance to visit other tourist attractions in China?

Jack: No, but I'd like to go to Beijing and visit the Fragrant Hills, so what should I do?

Mary: Well, I think you can purchase a train ticket to Beijing first.

Jack: That's a good idea. Thanks. What else?

Mary: And you could also read some guides about the Fragrant Hills.

Jack: That sounds good too. Thank you.

玛丽：你有机会四处看看中国的旅游景点吗？
杰克：没有，但我想去北京爬香山。我该做些什么？
玛丽：那你要先买张前往北京的火车票。
杰克：好主意，谢谢。然后呢？
玛丽：然后就买本介绍香山的旅游指南来看。
杰克：听起来也不错，谢谢你。

attraction [əˈtrækʃn]
n 吸引物，旅游景点

purchase [ˈpɜːrtʃəs]
v 购买，采购

guide [gaɪd]
n 指南

未来规划情境

Mary: What's something you'd really like to do, Jack?

Jack: I really want to go to the US next summer and take some business courses.

Mary: Wow, that sounds wonderful.

Jack: I haven't decided which city to in. Do you have any suggestions?

Mary: Well, New York, perhaps. I think it's a fantastic city.

Jack: Good idea. Thanks.

玛丽：杰克，你有什么想完成的事？
杰克：我真的很想明年夏天前往美国去上些商业课程。
玛丽：哇，听起来真棒。
杰克：我还没决定要去哪个城市。你有何建议？
玛丽：可能就纽约吧。我觉得那是个很棒的都市。
杰克：好主意，谢谢。

course [kɔːrs]
n 课程

suggestion [səˈdʒestʃən]
n 建议

fantastic [fænˈtæstɪk]
a 极好的

难以置信的实用职场英语

实用句型 例句 搭配情境对话学习句型。

1. I worked as a [position] at [company]. I was in charge of [tasks].

I worked as a marketing specialist at ABC Company. I was in charge of promoting software products.
我在ABC公司担任营销专员。我负责推销软件产品。

I worked as an Engineer at BBB Company. I was in charge of equipment maintenance.
我之前在BBB公司担任工程师。我负责设备维修。

I worked as a sales representative at CCC Company. I was in charge of making cold calls.
我之前在CCC公司当销售代表。我负责做陌生电话销售。

2. Do you need some help with that [something]?

Do you need some help with that report?
你做那份报告需要帮助吗?

Do you need some help with that heavy bag?
你需要我帮你提那个很重的袋子吗?

Do you need some help with that marketing project?
你进行的营销项目需要帮忙吗?

3. I really want to go to [somewhere] [sometime] and [do something].

I really want to go to the US next summer and take some business courses.
我真的很想明年夏天前往美国去上些商业课程。

I really want to go to Japan next year and visit my relatives.
我明年真的想去日本去拜访一些亲戚。

I really want to go to Germany next quarter and explore some new business opportunities.
我下一季想去德国开拓一些新的业务机会。

社交技巧
Social Skills

轻松的话题

除了在讨论商业正事之前要先有寒暄、聊点轻松话题之外，开会中间休息时间、在茶水间遇到同事、下班后请外宾晚餐、利用周末带外宾逛逛，或甚至参加正式的会议晚宴等，都要与人社交攀谈。最常听到人们提出的困扰就是："我就不知道要跟不熟的人聊些什么呀。"事实上，"商务环境"本来就不是充满自己家人与好朋友的"舒适圈"，否则怎么会称做生意呢？这种场合自然是不会有我们已熟识的交心朋友了。但在职场上，就算不熟也要勉强自己主动亲近他人，想些话题攀谈，关心他人的近况等。

跟他人可以轻松聊开的话题种类很多。以下列出几个主要的话题种类：

- **各自的兴趣**：运动、健身、瑜伽、球类、音乐、美术、收集等。
- **各式的天气**：南美的阳光、北美的雪景、欧洲的浓雾、亚洲的雨季等。
- **各国的美食**：日式生食、意大利餐、美式起司、中国菜等。
- **各地的文化**：西方的热情开放、东方的保守含蓄等。
- **近期的活动**：电影、音乐会、乐团演唱、舞蹈表演、美术展览等。
- **有趣的假期**：旅游景点、游轮航行、海滩潜水、登山挑战等。

这些话题一旦先起了个头，彼此可能会发现共通之处，例如，你喜欢听音乐会，交谈之后发现对方也有相同的兴趣，下一步便有可能建立更深厚的联结感了。比方说，邀请对方在周末时来家里烤肉，顺便欣赏音乐；交谈之后，发现外宾想尝试地道中国小吃，便可主动提出下班带他去夜市逛逛。

这些都是对认识彼此、建立关系（relationship building）有实质效果的。除了敏感、尖锐、对立或过于私人的话题应避免之外，其他温和、软性的话题都可以自由地发挥。重点是要"真心诚意"地对他人有兴趣，而不是对他人问东问西，只为了要捞到对自己有利的信息。如果是有目的的接近，人是有敏感意识的，自然会觉察出来，因此，抱持着"开放真诚"的态度比思忖"应该聊什么话题"重要得多了。在社交上关系建立得稳固，自然对日后商业的交流也有莫大的助益。

EXERCISE

1. 以下哪种情况是在商务场合中有可能会需要社交攀谈的时机？

　　A. 大型商业会议中与厂商照面

　　B. 开会到一半

　　C. 上司在跟部属讨论项目时

　　D. 同事讨论产品开发遇到瓶颈时

答案：A

2. 在商务场合中，社交攀谈最主要的目的是什么？

　　A. 寻找打高尔夫的球友

　　B. 与共事伙伴建立实质关系

　　C. 方便学习各国语言

　　D. 探听竞争对手的商业策略

答案：B

Unit 3 社交技巧

聊个人兴趣

Mary: What do you usually do in your spare time?

Jack: I go fishing with my son. How about you?

Mary: Well, I am pretty interested in music, so I play the piano.

Jack: Do you play any sports?

Mary: My husband and I both enjoy tennis. Sometimes we play at the tennis courts by our house.

Jack: Oh, really? I am also a tennis fan!

玛丽：你空闲时都做些什么？
杰克：我都跟我儿子去钓鱼。那你呢？
玛丽：嗯，我对音乐很有兴趣，所以我练钢琴。
杰克：你玩球类活动吗？
玛丽：我和我先生都喜欢网球。有时候我们会在家附近的网球场打球。
杰克：真的呀？ 我也爱打网球。

spare [spɛr]
a 空暇的
fish [fɪʃ]
v 钓鱼
tennis court
ph 网球场

聊电影表演

Mary: What's your favorite movie?

Jack: Oh, it's got to be *Titanic*.

Mary: Cool. That was an excellent production, wasn't it?

Jack: Exactly. DeCaprio played the lead in that movie, and he is still one of my favorite actors.

Mary: Yeah, tell me about it.

Jack: Oh, and the critics gave the movie rave reviews.

玛丽：你最喜欢哪部电影呢？
杰克：哦，那就非《泰坦尼克号》莫属啦！
玛丽：好酷。那部片拍得很棒，对吧？
杰克：的确是。迪卡普里奥在那部片里是主角，他还是我最喜欢的演员之一。
玛丽：那还用说吗？
杰克：还有，影评人都给那部片很高的评价呢！

excellent ['ɛksələnt]
a 美好的，极佳的
production [prə'dʌkʃn]
n 生产，产品
critic ['krɪtɪk]
n 评论
rave review
ph 好评，褒扬

069

聊度假活动

Mary: Where do you plan to go for a vacation this winter?

Jack: Well, I am thinking to take my family to go skiing.

Mary: That sounds marvelous.

Jack: Yeah. We will stay in a ski resort in Springfield. So how about you?

Mary: Well, my husband and I will go hiking and camp in a tent.

Jack: Wonderful. I am sure you will enjoy the peace and quiet in the mountains.

玛丽：今年冬天你打算去什么地方度假呢？
杰克：我在想和家人去滑雪。
玛丽：听起来好棒呀！
杰克：是呀。我们会住在春田市的滑雪旅馆。那你呢？
玛丽：嗯，我和我先生会去爬山和搭帐篷露营。
杰克：真好！我相信你们会享受山上的平和和宁静的。

vacation [vəˈkeɪʃn]
n 度假，假期
marvelous [ˈmɑːrvələs]
a 令人惊叹的
resort [rɪˈzɔːrt]
n 度假村，饭店
tent [tent]
n 帐篷

聊家人才艺

Mary: That's an interesting painting you've got on the wall.

Jack: Yeah, my daughter painted it.

Mary: Really? It's very colorful.

Jack: That's her specialty.

Mary: Your daughter is really talented.

Jack: To be an artist is one of her dreams.

玛丽：你挂在墙上那幅画真有趣。
杰克：是呀。我女儿画的。
玛丽：真的吗？色彩缤纷。
杰克：那是她的专长。
玛丽：你女儿真有天赋。
杰克：成为画家是她的梦想之一。

colorful [ˈkʌlərfl]
a 五彩缤纷的
specialty [ˈspeʃəlti]
n 专长，长才
talented [ˈtæləntɪd]
a 有天分的
artist [ˈɑːrtɪst]
n 艺术家

聊差旅经验

Mary: So, Jack, is this your first time in Shanghai?

Jack: Actually, no. I've been here a few times already.

Mary: For business?

Jack: Well, for both business and pleasure actually. I did a lot of business with a software company in Shanghai, so I came here a few times. And I was here to the World Expo in 2010.

Mary: That's interesting. And did you like it?

Jack: Yes, I loved it. I think the expo was fantastic.

玛丽：杰克，这是你第一次到上海吗？
杰克：其实不是。我已来过几次了。
玛丽：是出差吗？
杰克：事实上，出差和旅游都有。我跟上海的软件厂商有生意往来，所以我来过几次。还有我在2010年来参观过"世博会"。
玛丽：真有趣。那你喜欢吗？
杰克：我很喜欢呀。我觉得"世博会"超赞的。

for business
ph 出差
pleasure ['pleʒər]
n 娱乐
expo (= exposition)
abbr 展览会

 聊工作心得

Mary: Do you enjoy what you do for work?

Jack: Yes, I certainly do. I especially like that I get to interact with customers regularly.

Mary: That sounds really nice.

Jack: Besides I get along really well with my colleagues. We exchange creative ideas from time to time.

Mary: I am sure. Do you also get along well with your boss?

Jack: Certainly. She's a good manager, and she always encourages me and gives me a lot of freedom.

玛丽：你喜欢你的工作吗？
杰克：很喜欢呀。我特别喜欢可以时常跟客户互动。
玛丽：不错呀！
杰克：另外，我也跟同事相处融洽。我们时常交换好点子。
玛丽：当然。那你和老板处得好吗？
杰克：很好。她是个不错的管理者，她常常鼓励我，也给我很大的自由。

creative [kri'eɪtɪv]
a 有创意的
interact [ˌɪntər'ækt]
v 互动
encourage [ɪn'kɜːrɪdʒ]
v 鼓励

难以置信的实用职场英语

 聊阅读偏好

Mary: You mentioned that you spend a lot of time reading, right?

Jack: Exactly, at least 3 hours a day.

Mary: That's cool. What do you read?

Jack: Well, my favorite books are mystery novels.

Mary: You mean, like Sherlock Holmes's stories?

Jack: Yeah, I am crazy about that kind of stories. They really set my brain ticking.

玛丽：你说你花很多时间阅读吗？
杰克：的确，每天至少三小时。
玛丽：好酷。你都读些什么？
杰克：我最喜欢看悬疑小说。
玛丽：你是说，像是福尔摩斯故事吗？
杰克：是呀，我超爱那类故事的。它们会让我脑筋动起来。

mention ['menʃn]
v 提及

mystery ['mɪstri]
n 神秘，推理

novel ['nɑ:vl]
n 小说

set my brain ticking
ph 动脑

 聊休闲计划

Mary: Where are you going for your vacation this summer?

Jack: Well, my family will go to Japan. But we haven't decided what we want to do yet.

Mary: Perhaps you can go shopping.

Jack: Yeah, that's a choice. What about you? What are you going to do?

Mary: I wish I knew. My kids want to go camping, but I'd rather just stay home.

Jack: I understand what you mean. Just relax and not think about traveling. That's a real vacation.

玛丽：你夏天要去哪里度假？
杰克：我们一家会去日本，但还没决定要做些什么。
玛丽：或许可以去购物吧。
杰克：是呀，那是个选项。那你呢？你要做什么？
玛丽：我还不知道。我小孩想去露营，但我反而想待在家。
杰克：我了解你的意思。就放松也不要烦恼旅游的事。那才是真正的度假呀。

yet [jet]
ad 尚未，还（没）

perhaps [pər'hæps]
ad 也许，可能

camp [kæmp]
v 露营

Unit 3 社交技巧

实用句型 例句 搭配情境对话学习句型。

Chapter 2 跨文化社交技巧

1 My [someone] and I both enjoy [something].

My husband and I both enjoy tennis.　　我先生和我都喜欢网球。

My daughter and I both enjoy playing the piano.　　我女儿和我都喜欢弹钢琴。

My supervisor and I both enjoy golf.　　我老板和我都喜欢高尔夫球。

2 That's an interesting [something] you've [do something].

That's an interesting painting you've got on the wall.　　你挂在墙上那幅画真有趣。

That's an interesting remark you've put on the report.　　你写在报告上的评语真有趣。

That's an interesting idea you've raised during the meeting.　　你在会议中提及的点子真有趣。

3 I get along really well with my [someone]. We [do something] from time to time.

I get along really well with my colleagues. We exchange creative ideas from time to time.　　我也跟同事相处融洽。我们时常交换好点子。

I get along really well with my friends. We share innermost secrets from time to time.　　我跟朋友相处融洽。我们时常分享内心的秘密。

I get along really well with my business partners. We discuss market trends from time to time.　　我跟商务伙伴相处融洽。我们时常讨论市场趋势。

Unit 4 社交禁忌
Social Taboo

不乱问问题

一位朋友与加拿大籍老师聊到各国文化问题，朋友提到"美国人讲话都很直接"，加拿大籍老师回答，"我觉得中国人也很直接。见人劈头就问年纪、薪水等私人问题，这样难道不直接吗？"的确，由于传统文化的关系，我们倾向很快地跟对方建立交心、亲近的友谊关系，所以会急于跟对方切入私人话题。但是，这种行为在老外的眼中看来是窥探他们的隐私。

套句川普（Donald Trump）在电视节目《谁是接班人》（*The Apprentice*）中常说的一句话"Nothing personal. It's just business."。的确，商场上生意就是生意，没必要将私人的事情或情感牵扯进来。社交圈内也不例外，当问别人"你为何不结婚"这种和生意成交一点关系也没有的问题时，别人就会反感，这甚至影响后续的生意进展。因此，要讨论"社交禁忌"的话，唯一原则就是：勿窥探他人的隐私。

即便在如此清楚的原则之下，还是有人会说："但我还是想多深入地了解对方，想问一点交心的问题啊！"如果情况迫使你一定要问及他人私事的话，也应该以"让对方有心理准备"的礼貌性用语来开头，比方说：

例 Do you mind if I ask you a personal question?
你介意我问个私人的问题吗？

也不要直接地问：

例 Tell me what you think.
跟我讲你的想法。

而是和缓礼貌性地询问：

例 May I know what your opinion is of this issue?
我可以知道你对此议题的看法吗？

Unit 4 社交禁忌

　　到目前为止，我们了解到，为避免踩到"社交地雷"，坚守"不要问及隐私"和"保持礼貌"两大原则是最安全的做法了。那么，到底讨论些什么话题是安全的，又不会涉及他人隐私招人反感呢？最好是讨论"不具争议性的话题"。比方说，聊天气、旅游景点、运动、文化、美食、兴趣等，都是可以消除紧张关系，让彼此心情放松，并拉近彼此距离的话题。除了聊天主题的选择之外，态度与诚意也很重要。如同之前一再提及的，在练习这些社交对话时不是"将句子内的字词念出来"就好，这样在对方听起来也只是在背"课本英语"呀！而是要将"诚心"融入讲话的语调之中。从对话中，对方真的是可以感觉到你是打从心底里对他的国家、文化或喜好等感兴趣。如此，对方也才会愿意和我们多分享一些信息。

EXERCISE

1. 以下何种话题〔不是〕社交禁忌的话题？
　　A. 赚多少钱？
　　B. 生几个小孩？
　　C. 总统大选要投谁？
　　D. 您喜欢听哪一类的音乐？

答案：D

2. 什么样的话题是"较具争议性的话题"？
　　A. 政治
　　B. 运动
　　C. 文化
　　D. 美食

答案：A

难以置信的实用职场英语

 不要问人家年纪

Mary: How old are you?

Jack: Hm... I believe I am younger than you are.

玛丽：你几岁？
杰克：嗯……我应该是比你年轻。

believe [bɪˈliːv]
v 相信
younger [ˈjʌŋɡər]
a 较年轻的

 可以讨论对方的国家

Mary: Are you from the US originally?

Jack: No, I am actually from Canada.

Mary: Oh, really? I've been to Vancouver twice.

Jack: That's nice. I am actually from a little village just outside Vancouver.

玛丽：你来自美国吗？
杰克：不是，我来自加拿大。
玛丽：真的吗？我去过温哥华两次。
杰克：很棒呀。我就住在温哥华旁边的一个小镇上。

originally [əˈrɪdʒənəli]
ad 最初的，原始的
twice [twaɪs]
ad 两次
village [ˈvɪlɪdʒ]
n 小村庄

Unit 4 社交禁忌

 不要问婚姻状况 （X）

Mary: Are you married?

Jack: Yes. Why?

玛丽：你结婚了吗？
杰克：结婚了。为什么问这个？

marry ['mæri]
v 娶，嫁

why [waɪ]
ad 为什么

 可以聊聊对方的兴趣

Mary: So, what do you enjoy doing in your free time?

Jack: I love cooking. How about you?

Mary: I am not a good cook, really. I often do yoga after work.

Jack: That sounds very interesting.

玛丽：你有空都做些什么活动？
杰克：我爱烹饪。你呢？
玛丽：我其实厨艺不佳。我下班后都做瑜伽。
杰克：听起来很有趣。

free time
ph 空闲时间

cook [kʊk]
v 烹饪

interesting ['ɪntrəstɪŋ]
a 有趣的

难以置信的实用职场英语

 不要问人薪水

Mary: How much money do you earn every month?

Jack: Not much.

玛丽：你每个月赚多少钱？
杰克：没多少。

earn [ɜːrn]
v 赚

 可以讨论公司状况

Mary: What company are you with?

Jack: I am the head of sales at Hi-Tech Company.

Mary: What does your company do exactly?

Jack: We make software for data analysis.

玛丽：你在哪家公司上班？
杰克：我在"高科技公司"当销售经理。
玛丽：那你们公司是做什么的呢？
杰克：我们是做资料分析软件的。

exactly [ɪgˈzæktli]
ad 精确地，完全地
software [ˈsɔːftwer]
n 软件
analysis [əˈnæləsɪs]
n 分析

Unit 4 社交禁忌

 切勿讨论政治 (X)

Mary: Do you vote GOP or D.N.C.?

Jack: Uh... Neither.

玛丽：你要投"共和党"还是"民主党"？
杰克：呃……两个都不投。

neither ['naɪðər]
a 两者都不

 聊聊办公环境无妨

Mary: This is a lovely office you have here.

Jack: Thank you. This office is very bright and airy.

Mary: Have you been in this office complex long?

Jack: Actually, we just moved into this office complex three months ago.

玛丽：你办公室真漂亮。
杰克：谢谢。这间办公室很明亮，空气也流通。
玛丽：你们搬到这个办公大楼很久了吗？
杰克：事实上，我们三个月前才搬到此办公大楼来的呢。

lovely ['lʌvli]
a 可爱的，美好的
bright [braɪt]
a 明亮的
airy ['eri]
a 通风良好的
complex [kəm'pleks]
n 建筑群

难以置信的实用职场英语

 避免聊及严肃却无解的时事

Mary: The European migrant crisis is a big problem. What do you think?

Jack: I prefer to talk about something more interesting.

玛丽：欧洲难民潮是个大问题。你怎么看？
杰克：我宁愿聊些有趣点的话题。

migrant ['maɪgrənt]
n 移居者

crisis ['kraɪsɪs]
n 危机

 聊点轻松的旅游景点吧

Mary: Have you got a chance to go around the city yet?

Jack: Actually, I've got the evening free tomorrow.

Mary: If I have time, I can show you one of the fantastic art galleries nearby. Let me check my schedule first.

Jack: That would be nice. Thank you.

玛丽：你有机会在市内逛逛了吗？
杰克：其实我明天傍晚有空。
玛丽：若我有空，我可以带你去逛逛附近一个很赞的美术馆。让我先看看日程表。
杰克：那真是太棒了。谢谢你。

fantastic [fæn'tæstɪk]
a 很赞的

gallery ['gæləri]
n 美术馆

schedule ['skedʒuːl]
n 行程表

Unit 4 社交禁忌

 勿聊财务状况或借钱

Mary: I am in the red this month. Can I borrow $5,000 from you?

Jack: I wish I could help you out, but loaning $5,000 is not in my budget.

玛丽：我这个月入不敷出了。可以跟你借五千美元吗？
杰克：我还真希望我可以帮你，但我没这个预算可以借出五千美元。

borrow [ˈbɑːroʊ]
v 借入
loan [loʊn]
v 借出

 聊天气是最安全的话题

Mary: What's the weather like in India?

Jack: Well, during summer we usually get hot days, and sometimes it rains a lot.

Mary: I imagine the winters in India must be pretty cold, right?

Jack: Well, they're not as cold as you might think.

玛丽：印度的天气如何？
杰克：夏天真的很热，有时也会下大雨。
玛丽：我想在印度冬天也是很冷吧？
杰克：也没你想象中的冷。

weather [ˈweðər]
n 天气
India [ˈɪndɪə]
n 印度
imagine [ɪˈmædʒɪn]
v 想象

勿探他人隐私

Mary: Why are you still single?

Jack: Simply because I am.

玛丽：你为何还单身？
杰克：没为什么。

single ['sɪŋgl]
a 单身的
simply ['sɪmpli]
ad 仅仅，只不过

 ## 在餐厅用餐就讨论餐点吧

Mary: This is a very typical Chinese restaurant here.

Jack: This looks like a really lovely place.

Mary: Have you decided what to order yet?

Jack: It all looks so tasty. I might need a couple more minutes please.

玛丽：这是家典型的中餐馆。
杰克：看起来是个温馨的地方。
玛丽：你决定要点什么了吗？
杰克：看起来都很好吃。我还要几分钟再决定，谢谢。

typical ['tɪpɪkl]
a 典型的
tasty ['teɪsti]
a 美味的

Unit 4 社交禁忌

 勿论及宗教

Mary: Are you religious?

Jack: Uh... do I have to answer?

玛丽：你信教吗？
杰克：呃……一定要回答吗？

religious [rɪ'lɪdʒəs]
a 宗教的，虔诚的

 真心邀请外宾到家作客吧

Mary: I was wondering if you would like to join us for dinner this Friday?

Jack: That sounds really great. Thank you very much.

Mary: My husband is a great cook, and he's going to cook some Chinese dishes. I am sure you will love it.

Jack: Oh, Chinese food is my favorite.

玛丽：本周五你想来与我们共进晚餐吗？
杰克：听起来很棒。谢谢。
玛丽：我老公很会做饭，他要做些中国菜。我想你一定会喜欢的。
杰克：中餐是我的最爱了！

wonder ['wʌndər]
v 想知道

favorite ['feɪvərɪt]
a 最喜欢的

083

难以置信的实用职场英语

实用句型

 搭配情境对话学习句型。

1 I often do [something] [sometime].

I often do yoga after work.	我下班后都做瑜伽。
I often go shopping on the weekend.	我周末都去购物。
I often go skiing during the winter.	我冬天都会去滑雪。

2 We just moved into this [somewhere] [sometime] ago.

We just moved into this office complex three months ago.	我们三个月前才刚搬到这栋办公大楼。
We just moved to this apartment complex a year ago.	我们去年才刚搬到这栋公寓大楼。
We just moved to this neighborhood last month.	我们上个月才刚搬到这个地区。

3 I was wondering if you would like to join us for [something] this [sometime]?

I was wondering if you would like to join us for dinner this Friday?	本周五你想来与我们共进晚餐吗?
I was wondering if you would like to join our party this weekend?	周末你想来参加我们办的派对吗?
I was wondering if you would like to go to Japan with us this summer?	今年夏天你想和我们一起去日本玩吗?

Telephoning & E-mail
商务电话与电邮

前言

随着互联网的盛行,商务上的沟通更加便利了。以往出国开会还要专程搭飞机过去,现在只要通过电话、视频会议或线上研讨会等工具就可以开会沟通。传统邮件三天才会寄达的信件,现在通过电子邮件只要几秒的时间就可送达。因此,办公环境中工作者使用电话英语和电子邮件英语沟通的次数大增,也可以说是必备的技能了。

可惜的是,在业界存在的状况通常是:某秘书或助理接到讲英语的电话时,不是脑筋一片空白愣在那儿,结结巴巴地回答单词,就是急着要将电话转给别人。或是要写个电子邮件询问外国厂商产品规格或报价时,所写的英语句子不是语法错误百出、拼写乱七八糟,就是再怎么写句子看起来就是不漂亮也不地道,还一直停留在儿童英语句子的水平。这导致外国人也看不懂邮件要表达的意思,从而延误回信的内容与时机。殊不知这些状况是可以通过练习改善的。比方说,接电话的人英语口语能力还不到可以回答询问产品问题的程度,但也可通过一句简单的 "Hold on, please. I'll transfer your call to the person in charge."(请稍候,我将您转接给负责的人。)来顺利地将电话转接给可负责的人。

此章节就让我们来对"电话英语""邮件英语"做个全面性讨论,让有上述状况的上班族有机会熟悉电话英语的用词用句,今后再接到外国人的电话时就不会手足无措了。

写电话备忘
Telephone Message

> 备忘 memo

讨论到写电话备忘时，我们可能会马上想到"那是接电话的接待人员的事"。但事实上，除了接待人员会接听电话，还有秘书也会帮老板接听电话和记留言，一般职员也可能要帮同事接听电话和记留言。因此，接到外宾电话要回应，帮人接听或转接还要写电话备忘录，这些其实是每个职场人员都必备的技能。

首先，要有效地记录电话备忘录内容，要确认记下以下的信息：

1. 人：Who is calling?

包括 first name（名）和 last name（姓）都要问清楚。若不知拼法，也可说"Could you spell that, please?"来加以询问和确认。

2. 人：Who does he / she want to speak to?

除了询问对方要找的人是谁之外，最好也要确认一下部门。

3. 时：When is the call received / message taken?

接到电话或信息的日期、时间为何。

4. 事：What's it about?

有些老板除了要求秘书过滤电话之外，还会要求要询问对方来电的"目的"是什么，如此也会知道大概是关于什么事。这时，接电话者可以询问"Can I just ask what it's about?"来确认一下对方的目的。

5. 回电号码：What is his / her phone number?

既然是稍后要回复对方，对方的电话号码自然是不可或缺的。

Unit 1 写电话备忘

有了这些元素之后，综合起来就会形成一张表格，如以下的电话留言记录：

```
                Telephone Message
    Date: _____    Time: _____
    To: _____
    From: _____
    Telephone #: _____
    Message: _____
    _____
    Message taken by: _____
```

接着，来讨论如果我们的角色是接电话的人，有什么实用的语句可以使用呢？请看以下的整理：

1. 接起电话的问候语

例 ABC Company. This is Mary speaking.
ABC 公司，我是玛丽。

例 How can I help you?
有什么可以为您效劳吗？

例 What can I do for you, sir?
先生，有什么我可以协助的吗？

2. 帮人转接的用语

例 Can you hold on a moment, please?
请稍后，谢谢。

例 Can you hold the line, please?
请在线上稍等，谢谢。

> I'll put you through.
> 我帮您转过去。

> I am connecting you now.
> 我帮您转接。

> His line is busy. Would you like to wait?
> 他电话忙线中。您想稍等吗?

3. 说明对方要找的人不在时的用语

> I am afraid Mr. Chen is unavailable at the moment.
> 很抱歉,陈先生不在座位上。

> Ms. Smith is on a business trip this week.
> 史密斯女士本周出差。

> I am sorry, but Mr. Ding is not in the office today.
> 很抱歉,丁先生今天不在办公室。

> Ms. Lee is on another line.
> 李女士在电话中。

> Mr. Lin is out for lunch and won't be back until 2 p.m.
> 林先生外出午餐,两点才会回来。

4. 记留言用语

> Can I take a message?
> 要我帮您留言吗?

> Would you like to leave a message?
> 您要留言吗?

> Would you like to call back later?
> 您想等会再打来吗?

> Shall I ask him to call you back?
> 我请他回电给您好吗?

Unit 1 写电话备忘

5. 确认留言用语

例 Let me just read that back to you.
我重述一下您的留言。

例 You'd like to schedule a meeting on Wednesday, right?
您想要约个周三的会议，没错吧？

例 I'll make sure Mr. Kim gets your message.
我会将留言转交给金先生的。

接着，我们就来将这些实用语句应用在实际情境中吧！

EXERCISE

1. 以下何者〔不是〕有效记录电话备忘录所需的信息？
A. 来电者
B. 时间
C. 地点
D. 缘由

答案：C

2. 如果来电者要找的人不在位置上时，怎么回答比较恰当？
A. I don't know where Mr. Chen is.
（我不知陈先生在哪。）
B. Sorry, but Mr. Chen is not in at the moment.
（很抱歉，陈先生目前不在座位上。）
C. Please do not bother him.
（请不要打扰他。）
D. Mr. Chen is an experienced manager.
（陈先生是很有经验的经理人。）

答案：B

Mary: Best Software Systems. Mary speaking.

Jack: Hello. This is Jack Thomson from High Tech. Could I speak to Ms. Sandra Anderson, please?

Mary: I am afraid Ms. Anderson is in a meeting now. Can I take a message?

Jack: Sure, please. Please ask her to call me back. This is Jack Thomson from High Tech. I need to discuss some details of the PDI Project.

Mary: All right. Let me write them down... Does Ms. Anderson have your number?

Jack: I think she does. Well, it's 778-8787-8989, just in case.

MEMO:

Telephone Message

Date: March 12, 2017   Time: 3:25 p.m.

To: Ms. Sandra Anderson

From: Mr. Jack Thomson, High Tech.

Telephone #: 778-8787-8989

Message: Jack wanted to discuss details of the PDI Project. Please call him back.

Message taken by: Mary C.

Unit 1 写电话备忘

 会议中 ▶ 中译

玛丽：最佳软件公司。你好，我是玛丽。

杰克：你好。我是高科技公司的杰克·汤玛森。麻烦找一下珊卓·安德森女士，谢谢。

玛丽：安德森女士现在会议中。我帮您留言好吗？

杰克：好的，谢谢。请告知她回电话给我。我是高科技公司的杰克·汤玛森。我要跟她讨论 PDI 项目的细节。

玛丽：好的。让我记一下。安德森女士有您的电话吧？

杰克：我想她应该有。你再记一下好了，我电话是 778-8787-8989。

备忘录：

电话留言

日期：<u>2017 年 3 月 12 日</u>　　　　时间：<u>下午 3 点 25 分</u>

致：<u>珊卓·安德森女士</u>

来自：<u>高科技公司，杰克·汤玛森先生</u>

电话号码：<u>778-8787-8989</u>

讯息：<u>杰克想讨论 PDI 项目的细节。请回电给他。</u>

留言记录者：<u>玛丽 C</u>

---

afraid [əˈfreɪd]
a 害怕，恐怕

meeting [ˈmiːtɪŋ]
n 会议，见面

message [ˈmesɪdʒ]
n 信息

discuss [dɪˈskʌs]
v 讨论

detail [ˈdiːteɪl]
n 细节

project [ˈprɑːdʒekt]
n 项目

 占线中

Mary: Good Insurance. This is Mary Ford speaking.

Jack: Hi Mary. This is Jack Wilson here. How are you?

Mary: Oh, hi Jack. Not so bad. So what can I do for you, Jack?

Jack: Well, listen, Mary. Actually I wanted to speak to Mr. Morgan and ask him about the project meeting next week. Is he there at the moment?

Mary: All right. Just hang on a moment please while I make the connection... Well, sorry Jack. Mr. Morgan's line is engaged.

Jack: It's okay. I'll try calling later.

MEMO:

Telephone Message

Date: March 12, 2017   Time: 3:25 p.m.

To: Mr. Morgan

From: Jack Wilson

Telephone #:

Message: Jack wanted to ask about the project meeting next week. He'll call back later.

Message taken by: Mary Ford

Unit 1 写电话备忘

占线中 ▶ 中译

玛丽：好保险公司。我是玛丽·福特。
杰克：嗨，玛丽。我是杰克·威尔森。你好吗？
玛丽：嗨，杰克。还可以。我可以帮你什么吗？
杰克：嗯，听着，玛丽。我其实是要找摩根先生，要问他下周项目会议的事。他现在在吗？
玛丽：好的，不要挂断，我帮你接过去……啊，不好意思，杰克，摩根先生电话占线中。
杰克：没关系。我等会再打过来。

备忘录：

电话留言

日期：<u>2017 年 3 月 12 日</u>　　　时间：<u>下午 3 点 25 分</u>

致：<u>摩根先生</u>

来自：<u>杰克·威尔森</u>

电话号码：<u>　　　　　</u>

讯息：<u>杰克想问您下周专案会议的事，他稍后会再打来。</u>

留言记录者：<u>玛丽·福特</u>

---

insurance [ɪnˈʃʊrəns]
n 保险

moment [ˈmoʊmənt]
n 时刻

hang on
ph （电话）不挂断

connection [kəˈnekʃn]
n 连线

engage [ɪnˈgeɪdʒ]
v 占用，从事

Mary: LTC Company. This is Mary Miller speaking. How can I help you?

Jack: Hello. I am calling about your product. I purchased your A400 vacuum cleaner online last week and have a question about the switches. Are you the right person to ask?

Mary: Well, I am sorry, but all our customer service representatives are on the phone with other clients at the moment. Would you like to wait?

Jack: Well, I can leave my contact information so one of your reps could return my call.

Mary: Sure, sir. Could I have your name and phone number, please?

Jack: Okay. My name is Jack Chen. It's J-A-C-K and C-H-E-N. My phone number is 123-456-789.

MEMO:

Telephone Message

Date: March 12, 2017   Time: 3:25 p.m.

To: customer service representative

From: Jack Chen

Telephone #: 123-456-789

Message: Mr. Jack Chen purchased A400 vacuum cleaner last week and encountered some problems with the switches. Please return his call.

Message taken by: Mary Miller

忙碌中 ▶ 中译

玛丽：LTC 公司。我是玛丽·米勒。有什么可以效劳的吗？

杰克：你好。我是要询问产品问题。我上周在网上购买了你们的 A400 型号的吸尘器，但开关有点问题。这类问题是问你吗？

玛丽：很不好意思，其他客服人员目前都在电话中协助其他客户。您要等待吗？

杰克：嗯，我可将联络方式留下，客服人员稍后再回电给我也可以。

玛丽：当然，先生。那请告知我您的姓名和电话。

杰克：好的。我的名字是杰克·陈。拼法是 J-A-C-K 和 C-H-E-N。我的电话是 123-456-789。

备忘录：

电话留言	
日期：_2017 年 3 月 12 日_	时间：_下午 3 点 25 分_
致：_客户服务代表_	
来自：_杰克·陈先生_	
电话号码：_123-456-789_	
讯息：_杰克·陈先生购买 A400 型号的吸尘器，遇到开关方面的问题。请回电给他。_	
留言记录者：_玛丽·米勒_	

---

purchase ['pɜːrtʃəs]
v 购买

vacuum cleaner
ph 吸尘器

product ['prɑːdʌkt]
n 产品

question ['kwestʃən]
n 问题

switch [swɪtʃ]
n 开关

representative [ˌreprɪ'zentətɪv]
n 代表

client ['klaɪənt]
n 客户

contact ['kɑːntækt]
n 联络

contact ['kɑːntækt]
v 与……联络

return [rɪ'tɜːrn]
v 返回，回归

难以置信的实用职场英语

实用句型 **例句** 搭配备忘范本学习句型。

 [解释接听者无法接听之原因,并要求留言] 的句型。

I am afraid Ms. Anderson is in a meeting now. Can I take a message?	安德森小姐现在正在开会。我帮您留言好吗?
I am afraid Ms. Anderson is on the phone now. Would you like to leave a message?	安德森小姐现在电话中。您想要留言吗?
I am afraid Ms. Anderson is with a client now. Would you like her to call you back?	安德森小姐现在有客户。您想要她稍后回电给您吗?

 [协助转接] 的句型。

Just hang on a moment please, while I make the connection.	我帮您转接,请不要挂断。
Just a moment, please. I'll put you through.	请稍候。我替您转过去。
One moment, please. I am connecting you now.	请稍等。我帮你转接。

 [说明来电原因] 的句型。

I am calling about your product.	我打电话是要询问你们产品的问题。
I would like to discuss the payment schedule for your order.	我想要讨论您订单的付款方式。
We need to organize a marketing event. Do you have time right now?	我们要规划一场营销活动。你现在有空讨论吗?

电话技巧
Telephoning Skills

电话小贴士

除了上述电话留言的情境之外,电话技巧更可能让人顺利找到想找的人。在说明打电话来意之前,有可能会先有寒暄的话语。比方说:

例 How are you doing? 你好吗?
Not bad at all. 还可以。

例 How's business? 生意如何?
A bit busy, as usual. 一样,有点忙。

例 How are things in Beijing? 北京那边的事还好吗?
Things are good here. 这里都好。

例 How's the weather over there? 那边天气如何?
It's getting a bit cold. 有点变冷了。

例 What have you been up to? 你最近如何?
Same old same old. 就老样子。

稍微寒暄一下之后,就可以进入主题说明打电话的来意了。复杂的商务问题较难以在电话上说清楚。因此,打电话目的多半是想约个会议时间(making arrangements)以便深谈,或有可能是客户打电话给企业询问(enquiry)产品信息,或是要跟客服中心(customer complain)抱怨产品信息。这些电话情境稍后会有各种范例介绍。

除了打电话的开场和主要内容的讨论之外,我们此处来讨论一下打电话当中可能会出现的"小状况",比方说,打手机时信号不良、电池没电、太吵听不清楚、打错电话等。若有这些小状况发生时,可以说什么话来应对呢?请看以下实用语句的整理:

难以置信的实用职场英语

1. 没听清楚信息时

例 Sorry, I didn't catch that.
不好意思，我刚没听到。

例 Sorry, could you repeat that, please?
不好意思，再讲一次，好吗？

例 Could you say that a bit more slowly, please?
麻烦您讲慢一点，好吗？

例 Sorry, can you speak up a bit, please?
不好意思，请大声一点？

例 Could you spell that for me, please?
可以麻烦您拼出来吗？

2. 告知打错电话时

例 I think you have the wrong number.
我想您是打错电话了。

例 This number is no longer in service.
此电话号码已不能使用。

例 You need to talk to marketing, but I am afraid you've reached sales.
你要跟营销部谈，但恐怕你打到销售部了。

3. 手机信号不良

例 My battery is nearly out.
我电池快没电了。

例 I am losing you. I am going into an elevator.
我快听不清楚了，我要进电梯了。

例 There are some problems with the connection.
连线有点问题。

098

4. 听不清楚对方时

例 I can barely hear you.
我听不太清楚。

例 It's very noisy here.
这儿很吵。

例 Can you hear me?
听得清楚吗？

例 It's a terrible connection.
信号不良。

例 Hang up and I'll try again.
先挂掉，我再打一次。

例 The line is terrible. Let me call you right back.
信号很差。我再打给你一次。

电话情况不外乎就是"开场""找人""留言""讨论正事""结束"，再外加上述在电话讨论中可能会发生的小状况。如果这些情境下的用语都得心应手的话，在办公室场合接到电话就可马上应用了。接着，就来看一下可能的电话情境吧！

难以置信的实用职场英语

企业客户打电话给客服中心回报系统问题

Mary: Collins Systems. Technical Support Hotline. Mary speaking. How may I help you?

Jack: Hello. This is Jack Lee calling from CTX Company. There appears to be a problem with the ERP system. Are you the right person to talk to?

Mary: Yes, I am. Sir, could you explain the problem in more detail?

Jack: Well, when we tried to key in new customer data, the system just hanged.

Mary: I see. In order to solve the problem, I am going to need some more details, like when and how this problem started. So what I am going to do is to fax you a problem-report-form. Please fax it back to me after you complete it. Can I have your fax number please?

Jack: Sure. It's 666-888-9999. Thank you and I'll be waiting for the form.

企业客户打电话给客服中心回报系统问题 ▶ 中译

玛丽：科林斯系统公司，技术支持热线。我是玛丽。有什么可以帮助您的？

杰克：你好。我是CTX公司的李·杰克。我们ERP系统似乎出现了点问题。你是可以帮助解决问题的人吗？

玛丽：我可以帮助您。先生，您可以解释一下问题的细节吗？

杰克：就是当我要输入新客户资料时，系统就会死机。

玛丽：了解。为了解决问题，我需要更多些细节，比如说什么时候开始有这问题的，此情况是如何发生的。所以，我会将问题提报单传真给您。请填好之后再传真回来给我。可以告知我您的传真号码吗？

杰克：当然。号码是666-888-9999。谢谢，我会等表格传过来。

---

technical [ˈteknɪkl]
a 技术的

appear [əˈpɪr]
v 显示，显现

explain [ɪkˈspleɪn]
v 解释

customer [ˈkʌstəmər]
n 客户

hang [hæŋ]
v （电脑）死机

solve [sɑːlv]
v 解决

complete [kəmˈpliːt]
v 完成

Unit 2 电话技巧

厂商打电话讨论出差细节

Mary: Hello, Top Fashion New York. This is Mary. How can I help you?

Jack: Hello, Mary. This is Jack Marco speaking, from R&M Retail in Italy. I am just calling about the upcoming fashion show in New York. Are you in the middle of anything?

Mary: Not at all. This is perfect timing. Go ahead. We'll meet at the fashion show in New York in two weeks, right?

Jack: Yeah, and that's why I am calling. I have already booked my flight. It's TA954 from Milan to New York on Sunday, July 8th. And it would be great if you could help me book a hotel.

Mary: Wait a second. I'd better write that down. TA954... on Sunday... All right, got that. I'll arrange for someone to pick you up. And I'll reserve a hotel for you. No problem.

Jack: Wonderful! I am looking forward to seeing you in New York.

厂商打电话讨论出差细节 ▶ 中译

玛丽：你好，这是纽约顶级流行。我是玛丽。很高兴为您服务。

杰克：你好，玛丽。我是意大利 R&M 零售的杰克·马可。我打电话是要和你讨论接下来的纽约时装展。你在忙其他事吗？

玛丽：没有。这时间我可以讨论。说吧。我们两周后就会在纽约时装展上见了，没错吧？

杰克：是的，那也是我打电话的原因。我班机已经订好了。是七月八日，周日由米兰飞往纽约的 TA954 号班机。若你可以帮我订家酒店，那是再好不过了。

玛丽：等一下，让我先记一下。TA954 号班机……周日……。好的，我记下了。我会派人去接你。我也可以帮你订酒店。没问题。

杰克：太棒了。我期待在纽约与你见面。

---

upcoming [ˈʌpkʌmɪŋ]
a 接下来的，即将来的

middle [ˈmɪdl]
n 中间

perfect [ˈpɜːrfɪkt]
a 完美的

flight [flaɪt]
n 班机

arrange [əˈreɪndʒ]
v 安排

reserve [rɪˈzɜːrv]
v 预留

look forward to
ph 期望

难以置信的实用职场英语

 公司内部不同部门预约会议时间

Mary: Good morning, Jack. This is Mary calling from the Sales Department.

Jack: Oh, Good morning. What can I do for you, Mary?

Mary: Well, I am calling with regard to the annual company briefing next month. It would be great if we could review some of the details and go through the agenda this week.

Jack: It's a good idea, Mary. Let's arrange a meeting this week to discuss it. Is 2 p.m. on Wednesday okay with you?

Mary: Yes, I am available on Wednesday at 2 p.m. I'll prepare the necessary documents before our meeting.

Jack: All right. And I'll also invite Terry and Lisa to attend. They always contribute creative ideas.

 公司内部不同部门预约会议时间 ▶ 中译

玛丽：早安，杰克。我是销售部的玛丽。

杰克：早安，我可以帮你什么吗？玛丽。

玛丽：我打电话来是要讨论下个月举办一年一度公司简报会议的事。本周我们最好碰个面，讨论一下细节和检视一下议程。

杰克：好主意，玛丽。就让我们安排本周开会讨论吧。周三下午两点你方便吗？

玛丽：周三下午两点我可以的。我会在会议之前将所需文件先准备好。

杰克：好的。我也会邀请泰瑞和莉莎来参加。他们总是会贡献一些创新的点子。

---

regard [rɪˈgɑːrd]
n 关心，考虑

annual [ˈænjuəl]
a 年度的

briefing [ˈbriːfɪŋ]
n 简报

review [rɪˈvjuː]
v 检视，回顾

agenda [əˈdʒendə]
n 议程

available [əˈveɪləbl]
a 可获得的

prepare [prɪˈper]
v 准备

necessary [ˈnesəseri]
a 需要的

document [ˈdɑːkjumənt]
n 文件

invite [ɪnˈvaɪt]
v 邀请

contribute [kənˈtrɪbjuːt]
v 贡献

Unit 2 电话技巧

实用句型 例句

搭配情境对话学习句型。

1 [说明打电话目的，询问问题] 的句型。

This is Jack Lee calling from CTX Company. There appears to be a problem with the ERP system. Are you the right person to talk to?

我是 CTX 公司的李·杰克。我们 ERP 系统似乎出现了点问题。您是负责这方面的人吗？

This is Ann Chen calling from III Company. I'd like to request some samples of your products. Could you help?

我是 III 公司的安·陈。我想要索取你们产品的样本。你可以帮忙吗？

This is Tom Hsu. I need to check the status of an order. Could you put me through to your sales department please?

我是汤姆·徐。我要检查订单的状况。你可以帮我转接到销售部吗，谢谢。

2 询问 [对方是否有空讲电话] 的句型。

Are you in the middle of anything?

你有在忙其他的事吗？

Is this the right time for you to talk?

现在你有空讲话吗？

Would you want me to call back in 10 minutes?

还是你想要我十分钟后再打给你吗？

3 [约会议时间] 的句型。

Let's arrange a meeting this week. Is 2 p.m. on Wednesday okay with you?

我们本周安排个会议吧。周三下午两点你方便吗？

Let's make an appointment this week. Will 4 p.m. on Friday suit you?

我们本周安排个会议吧。周五下午四点方便吗？

Let's schedule an interview this week. Are you available this Thursday at 10 a.m.?

我们本周安排个面谈吧。你周四早上十点有空吗？

103

E-mail 对应状况
E-mail Response

文字介绍

随着互联网的发展，职场上交流也渐由传统的需二到三天才会送达的书信变为只需几秒就会送达的电子邮件了。虽说两者似乎都是文字、段落等的书写，但在格式上与书写风格上还是有些许差异的。比如说，传统书信就不太可能出现"表情符号"的内容，但在电子邮件内可能就常会看到☺（I am happy. / smiley face）等以表情来代替文字的内容。因此，在书写风格上，传统信件更加正式，电子邮件则较为轻松自由。以下我们列出几个正式和非正式的写法进行比较：

Informal 非正式	Formal 正式
I am writing to ask... 我写信是为了要问……	This is to enquire... 此信是为询问……
Please answer me asap. 请尽早回答我。	I look forward to your prompt reply. 我期待您的即时回复。
You can get in touch with me... 你可以跟我联络……	Please feel free to contact me... 欢迎随时与我联络……
I want to tell you that... 我想告知你……	I am writing to inform you that... 我写信是为了通知你……
Please help me, thank you. 请帮我，谢谢。	Your assistance will be highly appreciated. 您能提供帮助，我们很是感激。
Let's set up a meeting. 我们来安排个会议。	Let's arrange an appointment. 我们来安排个会议。

由以上的句子对照可以看出非正式语气用词，和正式语气用词之间的不同了吧。事实上，并非写电子邮件时仅能使用非正式的写法。若您写电子邮件给重要客户或厂商，还是使用正式写法比较保险。

设定好电子邮件的书写对象和语气正式度之后，接着要注意的便是内容了。电子邮件被大众广泛使用，不就是因为其方便、快捷的特性吗？那么，电子邮件的内容为了让人可以快速地了解，更应该明确又简洁有力。请比较以下两个句子：

模糊：

例 Jerry, don't forget about the meeting next week.
杰瑞，别忘了下周的会议。

明确：

例 Jerry. I just want to remind you about the meeting scheduled for Tuesday, March 3rd at 10 a.m. We can meet in meeting room 203 and we need to discuss the details of the PBI project.
杰瑞，我是要提醒你我们有个会议在三月三日，周二早上十点。我们在二〇三会议室见，要讨论 PBI 项目的细节。

我们可以看出上述两句的明显差异。第一句只有说：有个会议，但万一收信人同时有好几个会议要参加呢？这会让人混淆，到底是在说哪个会议呢？第二句就明确得多了，句中把明确的 Who（人）、What（事）、When（时）、Where（地）、Why（原因）都列得清清楚楚的，这样的提醒才会有效，否则电子邮件写了没达到效果也是枉然。由此我们可以学到，写一封让人一目了然的电子邮件，最重要的就是要有明确的信息与内容。接着，就来看一下电子邮件运用在各种情境中的书写范例吧。

 询问

From: mary.lin@abc-company.com
To: david.Chen@laptop-company.com
Date: 8/5/2018
Subject: T109 Laptops

Dear Mr. Chen,

  I am writing to enquire about the T109 model laptops you informed us of last month (July). As we're planning to expand our department, we need 10 more latest-model laptops. Could you please send us a brochure and price list?

  We would also appreciate a visit from your sales representative in order to get more information about your laptop products. Would you please ask one of your reps to contact us next week?

  I am looking forward to your reply.

Yours sincerely,
Mary Lin
Purchasing Specialist

Unit 3 E-mail 对应状况

  询问 ▶ 中译

寄自：mary.lin@abc-company.com
致：david.Chen@laptop-company.com
日期：2018 年 8 月 5 日
主旨：T109 笔记本电脑

陈先生，您好，

  想询问关于您上个月（七月）跟我们提到的 T109 型笔记本电脑的信息。我们正规划要扩大部门，因此需要十台最新型的笔记本电脑。您可以寄目录和价格表来给我们参考吗？

  若您可以派位销售代表来跟我们介绍一下笔记本电脑产品，那是最好不过了。您下周可以派位销售代表跟我们联络吗？

  我期待您的回复。

诚挚的，
玛丽·林
采购专员

---

enquire [ɪnˈkwaɪər]
v 询问，打听

expand [ɪkˈspænd]
v 扩大，扩展

brochure [broʊˈʃʊr]
n 目录

appreciate [əˈpriːʃieɪt]
v 欣赏，感谢

representative [ˌreprɪˈzentətɪv]
n 代表

contact [ˈkɑːntækt]
v 与……接触

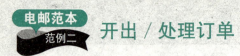

开出 / 处理订单

From: linda.kim@laptop-company.com
To: mark.smith@abc-company.com
CC: lily.white@laptop-company.com
Date: 4/2/2017
Subject: PO#12345

Dear Mr. Smith,

    Thank you for your purchase order #12345, which we received on March 15, for the T109 Laptop. Your order has been processed and your Purchasing Department will be advised directly as to the confirmation of terms and shipping dates.

    Lily White, Manager of the Sales Department, will advise you of confirmed delivery dates and can provide you with answers to questions on order processing. Ms. White can be reached directly by calling 123-456-789.

    We appreciate your order and the confidence you have shown in our laptop products. We look forward to hearing from you in the future if there is any way in which we may be of assistance to you.

Sincerely yours,
Linda Kim

开出／处理订单 ▶ 中译

寄自：linda.kim@laptop-company.com
致：mark.smith@abc-company.com
复本：lily.white@laptop-company.com
日期：2017年4月2日
主旨：PO#12345

史密斯先生，您好，

　　谢谢您下的订单 #12345 购买 T109 笔记本电脑，此订单我们已在三月十五日收到。您的订单已在处理当中。贵公司的采购部门会收到条款与交货日期的确认书。

　　我们的销售部经理，莉莉·怀特，她会通知您确认的交货日期，且也可以回答您关于此订单的所有问题。怀特小姐的电话是 123-456-789。

　　我们非常感谢您的订单，也感谢您对我们笔记本电脑产品的信心。我们期待在未来有为您服务的机会，欢迎您随时与我们联络。

诚挚的，
琳达·金

---

purchase ['pɜːrtʃəs]
n 购买

receive [rɪ'siːv]
v 接收

process ['prɑːses]
v 处理

advise [əd'vaɪz]
v 建议

directly [də'rektli]
ad 直接地

confirmation [,kɑːnfər'meɪʃn]
n 确认书

term [tɜːrm]
n 条款

shipping ['ʃɪpɪŋ]
n 寄送

delivery [dɪ'lɪvəri]
n 递送

confidence ['kɑːnfɪdəns]
n 信心

 消息告知

From: ann.liu@event-company.com
To: jack.sheen@abc-company.com
CC: rosa.heart@event-company.com
Date: 2/4/2017
Subject: 2nd Annual Marketing Society Conference Invitation

Dear Mr. Sheen,

    This email is to inform you that the 2nd Annual Marketing Society Conference will be held at The City Hotel in downtown Springfield on March 3rd.

    This year's conference will feature speakers who are recognized experts in sales, marketing, and public relations fields, and topics with many implications for the future (please refer to the attached pdf). Ample time is also scheduled for discussion periods.

    We have obtained special rates from the management of The City Hotel. Information on accommodations, transportation, and registration is also attached. If you have any further questions, please call the event coordinator, Ms. Rosa Heart, at 123-456-789.

Sincerely yours,
Ann Liu

消息告知 ▶ 中译

寄自：ann.liu@event-company.com
致：jack.sheen@abc-company.com
复本：rosa.heart@event-company.com
日期：2017年2月4日
主旨：第二届年度营销学会会议邀请

信先生，您好，

　　此邮件是要通知您，第二届年度营销学会会议将于三月三日在春田市市中心的"都市饭店"举办。

　　今年的会议特点是，我们邀请到销售、营销和公关领域的知名人士来当演讲嘉宾，还会讨论到与未来相关的主题（请看附件 pdf 档案）。我们也安排充分的时间给大家做讨论。

　　参加者可享有"都市饭店"的优惠价格。关于住房、交通、登记等信息也都附在电邮之内了。若您还有任何问题，请打电话给活动协调员，罗莎·哈特小姐，电话是 123-456-789。

诚挚的，
安·刘

---

conference [ˈkɑːnfərəns]
n 会议

downtown [ˌdaʊnˈtaʊn]
n 市中心

recognized [ˈrekəɡnaɪzd]
a 认可的

expert [ˈekspɜːrt]
n 专家

implication [ˌɪmplɪˈkeɪʃn]
n 牵连

obtain [əbˈteɪn]
v 取得

accommodation [əˌkɑːməˈdeɪʃn]
n （饭店）住房

transportation [ˌtrænspɔːrˈteɪʃn]
n 交通

registration [ˌredʒɪˈstreɪʃn]
n 注册

further [ˈfɜːrðər]
a 更进一步的

 处理抱怨

From: tim.line@mail100.com
To: grace.yeh@fax-company.com
Date: 5/25/2018
Subject: Customer Complain

Ms. Yeh,

    I would like to file a complaint about the fax machine I purchased. The Smooth Fax Machine T1000 that I bought from you on May 5th receives documents but does not transmit them. I made several phone calls to your customer service hotline about this serious problem and asked whether I could either exchange or return the defective machine, but no one was able to provide me proper solutions. The only information I was given was that I couldn't return the fax machine without prior approval. If you could issue such an approval, please do so immediately.

    Please let me know what I should do next.

Yours,
Tim Lin

处理抱怨 ▶ 中译

寄自：tim.line@mail100.com
致：grace.yeh@fax-company.com
日期：2018 年 5 月 25 日
主旨：客户抱怨

叶女士，

  我要投诉关于我从贵公司买的传真机。本人在五月五日跟贵公司买的流畅传真机 T1000 可以接收传真，但无法传文件出去。我针对此严重问题打过好几次电话给客户服务热线，并询问我是否可以换货或是退货？但没有人可以直接告诉我该怎么解决。我所得到的信息只有：没事先批准就不能退货。若您可以批准这样的退货事宜，那么请马上帮我办理。

  请告知我接下来我该怎么做。

提姆·林
敬上

---

complaint [kəm'pleɪnt]
n 抱怨

transmit [træns'mɪt]
v 传送

exchange [ɪks'tʃeɪndʒ]
v 交换

defective [dɪ'fektɪv]
a 有缺陷的

solution [sə'luːʃn]
n 解决方案

approval [ə'pruːvl]
n 认可，批准

immediately [ɪ'miːdiətli]
ad 立即地

信息沟通

From: lisa.wu@abc-company.com
To: bob.hsu@xyz-company.com
CC: mary.lee@xyz-company.com
Date: 10/12/2017
Subject: Meeting Schedule

Dear Mr. Hsu,

 Last week when we spoke on the phone, you expressed interest in a tour of our plant. I am writing to arrange a meeting with you and Ms. Lee to visit our manufacturing factory in New City.

 I would like to propose Wednesday, October 21st at either 10 a.m. or 2 p.m. The tour should last approximately 1.5 hours. Please let me know which time will suit you and Ms. Lee better.

 I am looking forward to seeing you both soon.

Sincerely yours,
Lisa Wu

信息沟通 ▶ 中译

寄自：lisa.wu@abc-company.com
致：bob.hsu@xyz-company.com
复本：mary.lee@xyz-company.com
日期：2017年10月12日
主旨：会议时间

徐先生，您好，

　　上周我们通电话时，您曾提到对参观我们工厂有兴趣。我写此邮件的目的是想与您和李小姐会面去参观位于新市的工厂。

　　我提议十月二十一（周三）早上十点或下午两点的时间。参观一趟约需一个半小时。请再通知我哪个时段对您和李小姐较为方便。

　　我期待很快能再与你们会面。

诚挚的，
莉莎·吴

---

express [ɪkˈspres]
v 陈述

arrange [əˈreɪndʒ]
v 安排

manufacturing [ˌmænjuˈfæktʃərɪŋ]
n 制造业

propose [prəˈpouz]
v 提议

approximately [əˈprɑːksɪmətli]
ad 约略地

搭配电邮范本学习句型。

 We would appreciate a visit from your [someone] in order to [do something].

We would appreciate a visit from your sales representative in order to get more information about your laptop products.	若您可请业务代表来一趟那是最好不过了，我们想要多了解贵公司的笔记本电脑产品。
We would appreciate a visit from your support engineer in order to get this technical problem resolved.	请派支持工程师来解决这个技术问题。
I would appreciate a visit from your insurance agent in order to learn more about your insurance policies.	请派保险业务员来一趟，我想要了解贵公司的保险政策。

 This email is to [purpose].

This email is to inform you that the Conference will be held at The City Hotel in downtown Springfield on March 3rd.	此邮件是要通知您，会议将于三月三日在春田市中心的"都市饭店"举办。
This email is to remind you of the weekly sales meeting this afternoon at 2.	此邮件是要提醒您，每周的销售会议会在下午两点开始。
This email is to notify all managers that the review meeting has been cancelled.	此邮件是要通知所有的经理人，检讨会议已取消。

 The [something] should last approximately [some time].

The tour should last approximately 1.5 hours.	参观行程大约需一个半小时。
The meeting is expected to last around 3 hours.	会议预期会持续三小时。
The speech will last approximately 2 hours.	此演讲会持续约两小时。

电子邮件技巧
E-mail Skills

主旨及内文

电子邮件的书写，除了上一章节所讨论到的书写风格正式度、主要内容的明确度和各种情境的应用之外，还有其他要点，让电子邮件整体变得更有效。其中一个要点便是电子邮件的 "subject"（主旨）了。让我们先来比较一下以下的两个主旨范例：

[主旨 A]　Subject: Meeting
　　　　　主旨：会议

[主旨 B]　Subject: Fri. 10/5, 2 p.m. Meeting w / Sales Dept.
　　　　　主旨：周五，十月五日下午两点，与销售部开会

[主旨 A] 在主题处仅写出会议，看电子邮件的人脑中会浮现"哪个会议呀？"的疑虑。尤其是现在职场上每个人手上都有好几个项目，要参加数个会议，这样的主题让人看不出是在指哪一个特定的会议，只会增加收件人的困扰。反观 [主旨 B] 将日期、时间和目的都很明确地指明了，让人一目了然，不用再花精力去猜测，这样写标题的方式自然是首选。

接着再看第二个范例：

[主旨 A]　Subject: Invoice
　　　　　主旨：付款通知

[主旨 B]　Subject: Invoice#354 / Amount: $799
　　　　　主旨：付款通知#354 / 金额：$799

很明显地，[主旨 A] 仅标出一个"Invoice"字，接收电子邮件的人完全看不出是在指哪一张 invoice 里。反观 [主旨 B] 就显得非常明确，不仅将发票号码标出，金额也连带列出了。这样的好处是，收电子邮件的人今后若需靠标题来储存或查找信件，也更加便利了。

我们来讨论一下书写的"语气"问题。此处的"语气"有别于上一章讨论的"正式不正式"的书写风格，而是"通过书写所展现出来的对对方的口吻"的语气。请看以下的例子：

[激动的语气]

例 Jack, I am still waiting for a reply!! Didn't you promise that you'd give me the report on MONDAY? What's wrong with you?
杰克，我还在等你的回应！！你不是答应过周一要给报告吗？你有什么问题吗？

[和缓的语气]

例 Hello, Jack. I'd like to check the progress of the annual sales report you're working on. You were supposed to hand it in on *Monday* and it's now Wednesday. Can we meet and discuss?
杰克，你好。我想确认一下你的年度业务报告的进度。报告应该〔周一〕就要交出，现在已经是周三了。我们见面讨论一下可以吗？

可以看出来吗？上述两个句子在讲同一件事，但"语气"却完全不同！哪一个句子会让人紧张？哪一个句子让人可以接受呢？非常明显，[和缓的语气]的句子才是在职场上跟人互动时所应使用的句子！由此例子我们可以学到的是，书写电子邮件请避免使用"全部大写"的字体，夸张地使用数个惊叹号、负面的词和句子。

以下，我们来看在商务邮件中实用的书写例句整理。

1. 邀请讨论

例 Did you see the article about the "Big Data" trend in today's Tech Times? Let's find sometime this week to discuss it.
你看到今天"今日科技"上有关"大数据"趋势的文章了吗？本周我们找个时间讨论一下吧。

2. 欢迎转发

> Please feel free to forward the following reference information to other members who might be interested.
> 欢迎将以下参考信息转发给有兴趣的员工看看。

3. 预先交代

> I'll be traveling to Japan the next two weeks, so if anything comes up, please email me. I'll check my E-mail regularly.
> 我未来两周会去日本出差，所以有任何事情请发邮件给我。我会定期收信。

4. 提醒会议

> Just a kind reminder about the conference call with MAK Company tomorrow at 10 a.m.
> 仅是要提醒你明天早上十点要跟 MAK 公司开线上会议。

5. 回复客户

> This is to inform you that your order #445 was received and processed. Your products will be shipped tomorrow.
> 我是要通知您订单 #445 已收到并处理了。您的产品会于明天寄出。

6. 要求资料

> When you've got a minute, will you E-mail me the minutes from yesterday's sales meeting please?
> 如果你有空，请你将昨天销售会议的记录通过邮件给我一份。

尚未收到款项，改写前

Dear Mr. Chen,

    I asked you to send me the payment of $599 long time ago, but I still have NOT received ANYTHING. What's going on?! This is NOT a good situation. Please call Sherry Wu at extension 123 to get this issue resolved. PLEASE TAKE CARE OF THIS ISSUE IMMEDIATELY.

Linda Hsu

 尚未收到款项，改写前 ▶ 中译

陈先生你好，

    很久之前我就请你寄五百九十九美元款项过来，但我到现在**还是没**收到任何东西。怎么回事呀？！这种情况**很不好**。请打电话给分机 123 的吴雪莉，将此事解决一下。**请马上处理此事**。

琳达·徐

---

payment ['peɪmənt]
n 付款，款项

receive [rɪ'siːv]
v 接收

situation [ˌsɪtʃu'eɪʃn]
n 情况

issue ['ɪʃuː]
n 事件，议题

immediately [ɪ'miːdiətli]
ad 立即，马上

Unit 4 电子邮件技巧

 尚未收到款项，改写后

Dear Mr. Chen,

  We would like to remind you again that we have not received any payment on your account balance of $599. If you need extra time or would like to arrange a special payment schedule, please call Ms. Sherry Wu of the credit department at extension 123 within this week. Otherwise, we will expect to receive a check via mail by June 25th, please.

  We appreciate your prompt attention to this issue.

Linda Hsu

 尚未收到款项，改写后 ▶ 中译

陈先生你好，

  我们想再次提醒您，您五百九十九美元的款项我们一直没有收到。若您需要多点时间或安排特殊的分期偿还方式，请本周内跟我们信用部门的雪莉·吴小姐联络，她的分机是 123。要是您没找她的话，我们便认为您会在六月二十五日之前将款项的支票寄过来。

  很感激您立即处理此事。

琳达·徐

---

remind [rɪˈmaɪnd]
v 提醒

balance [ˈbæləns]
n 余额

extra [ˈekstrə]
a 额外的

arrange [əˈreɪndʒ]
v 安排

credit [ˈkredɪt]
n 信用

extension [ɪkˈstenʃn]
n 分机

expect [ɪkˈspekt]
v 预期，期望

check [tʃek]
n 支票

appreciate [əˈpriːʃieɪt]
v 感激

prompt [prɑːmpt]
a 迅速的

attention [əˈtenʃn]
n 注意

退回业务策略报告，改写前

Hello Mary,

  You sent me the sales strategy report last week, but I was NOT satisfied with that. You didn't include specific sales numbers at all. And the tone is way TOO informal. You know that our Executive Officers will read this, right? Do you want them to think you are not professional enough?

  Please revise it right away.

Jack Liu

退回业务策略报告，改写前 ▶ 中译

玛丽你好，

  上周你交给我销售策略报告，但我觉得**不**是很满意。你完全没加入明确的销售数字。而且口吻**太**不正式。你知道执行官会看这份报告，对吧？你想让他们认为你不够专业吗？

  请马上修改。

杰克·刘

---

strategy [ˈstrætədʒi]
n 策略

satisfy [ˈsætɪsfaɪ]
v 满意

include [ɪnˈkluːd]
v 包括

specific [spəˈsɪfɪk]
a 特定的

tone [toʊn]
n 口气，口吻

informal [ɪnˈfɔːrml]
a 不正式的

executive officer
ph 执行长

professional [prəˈfeʃnl]
a 专业的

revise [rɪˈvaɪz]
v 修改

Unit 4 电子邮件技巧

退回业务策略报告，改写后

Hello Mary,

　　Thank you for handing in the sales strategy report last Thursday. I read through it and feel that you should include more specific information regarding our sales figures in Unit#3. I also feel that the tone could be a bit more formal since this report is prepared for our Executive Officers, and needs to reflect our professionalism.

　　Thank you for your efforts on this.

Jack Liu

退回业务策略报告，改写后 ▶ 中译

玛丽你好，

　　谢谢你上周四交了销售策略报告。我看过一次了，认为你应该在第三节加些明确的业务数据。另外，我认为书写语气应再正式一点，毕竟这份报告是要准备给执行官看的，也需要显示出我们的专业度。

　　谢谢你，辛苦了。

杰克·刘

---

hand in
ph 送交

figure ['fɪɡjər]
n 数字

prepare [prɪ'per]
v 准备

reflect [rɪ'flekt]
v 反映出

effort ['efərt]
n 心力，精神

搭配电邮范本学习句型。

We would like to remind you again that [some issue].

We would like to remind you again that I have not received any payment on your account balance of $599.

我们想再次提醒您,我们尚未收到您五百九十九美元的款项。

I would like to remind you again that I have not received the report which was due two days ago.

我想再次提醒你,我尚未收到两天前就应该交出的报告。

I would like to remind you again that I have not received the quotation you said you were going to send last week.

我想再次提醒你,我尚未收到你上周就说会寄出的产品报价单。

Thank you for [doing something].

Thank you for handing in the sales strategy report last Thursday.

谢谢你上周四所交出的销售策略报告。

Thank you for dispatching the product sample by courier this morning.

谢谢你早上快递产品样本过来。

Thank you for sharing with me the customer feedback results last week.

谢谢你上周跟我分享客户意见调查结果。

Presentations and Speeches
简报及演说技巧

前言

在现今的商业环境中，公司老板要跟员工沟通愿景与方向，内部主管要跟属下开会讨论业绩与策略，业务人员要跟客户介绍产品与服务等，这些活动都需要商务人士具备良好的简报能力。但"简报能力"不单单是做PPT，然后人站到台上将简报念一次就算的。"优良的简报能力"要考虑的条件包括简报主题是否吸引人，内容是否一目了然，简报者口头表达是否顺畅，其遣词造句是否清楚易懂，肢体语言是否配合，声音语调是否明显，心态表情是否有热忱，与听众的互动是否自然等。这么多的因素要考虑，再外加上要使用"英语"来做简报，这对商务人士来说可是个不小的挑战。

所幸，要养成杰出的"英语简报能力"也并非天马行空毫无头绪可循。通常，在一场英语简报中，还是有固定的内容、格式、语句、用词可以遵循的。比方说，简报的开场白（Opening）部分，不是想到什么就讲什么。而是固定地包括"欢迎词""自我介绍""引入讲题""说明大纲""时间"和"邀请问题"等几个基本要素。一般来说，演讲者在上台前五分钟会感到最为紧张，但随着进入状态之后，越讲越顺，焦虑感便会降低。因此，演讲者特别要将开场五分钟的内容准备妥当，甚至背得滚瓜烂熟，接续到后来讨论自己熟悉的专业内容时，其实就更加得心应手了。

此章节的目的就是将简报内容的成分、架构与实用的语句和用词整理出来，让商务人士可以事先了解并准备，以期在实际做简报时可以更顺畅自然。

Unit 1 将数据做成简报
Presenting the Data

上升下滑

在做简报介绍公司背景或产品功能时,制作者对于属于自己领域的"专业术语"或"技术行话"通常是已经了若指掌了。就算使用英语描述时不是讲完整句子,仅提到该领域的几个关键术语,老外听了还是可以稍微了解意思的。但如果是在描述数据的变化与趋势时,仅会讲"The sales go up and then go down. After that, the sales go up again and then go down again."这样的描述句,数据描述得不精确,会让听者会错意,还很容易显示出制作者的水平。

因此,此章节要讨论的便是任何产业的上班族,要描述业绩、市场占有率等数字时,都必定会遇到的状况:这些"数据升降"的英语,该怎么讲呢?一般来说,演讲者应朝四个主要方向来学习这类"上升"与"下滑"的字词,也就是:"一般上升"的说法、"一般下滑"的说法、"大幅上扬"的说法与"大幅下跌"的说法。朝着这四个方向准备,做数据简报时会使用到的句子应都能包括进去了。管理层在听关于数据的变化简报时,对"大幅度地飙升"或"大幅度地骤降"部分会更特别注意。因此,在图表内若有特殊"飙高"或"骤降"的数字变化,可以做特别说明。另外,除了"上扬"或"下滑"的情况之外,数据也有可能是呈现"波动、摆荡"或"持平、没变化"等状况。描述这些变化的字词也会在后续加以补充。

在使用"上升"与"下滑"的说法之外,通常也会加上形容程度的"副词"来显示数字变化的程度。比方说可能有以下组合:

动词+副词	形容词+名词	中译
[something] + plunge sharply	sharp plunge	大幅坠落
[something] + increase slowly	slow increase	缓慢成长
[something] + decline dramatically	dramatic decline	明显降低
[something] + slump significantly	significant slump	大量衰退
[something] + rise modestly	modest rise	稳定成长

Unit 1 将数据做成简报

当然，这些动词与副词可以依照实际的简报状况做不同的组合。而这些组合也应符合数据本身的变化。比方说：失业率仅上升百分之零点一，若这时候将之描述为"The unemployment rate rose significantly."（失业率明显地大幅上升。）似乎便不太符合实际的状况。但若表达成"The unemployment rate rose slightly."（失业率微幅上升。）则可以跟数字搭配。又或是把"业绩翻倍"描述成"The sales increased gradually."（业绩逐步增加。）也无法显示出"翻倍成长"的意义。但若是描述成"The sales soared dramatically."（业绩明显地攀升。）便跟实际的状况较为接近了。在了解这些要点之后，以下便让我们一起来学习写简报时描述数据趋势的用词与说法吧。

图表	表示法	中译
	go up	上升
	rise	上扬，增加
	increase	增加
	advance	前进，上涨
	climb	攀升，增加
	grow	成长，上升
	improve	进展，进步

图表	表示法	中译
	take off	飙升
	soar	高涨
	boost	促进，提高
	skyrocket	飙高，猛涨
	roar	高升
	shoot up	飙飞
	reach a peak / peak	达到高峰

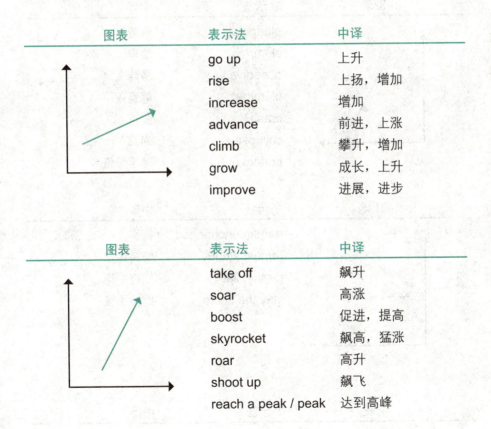

127

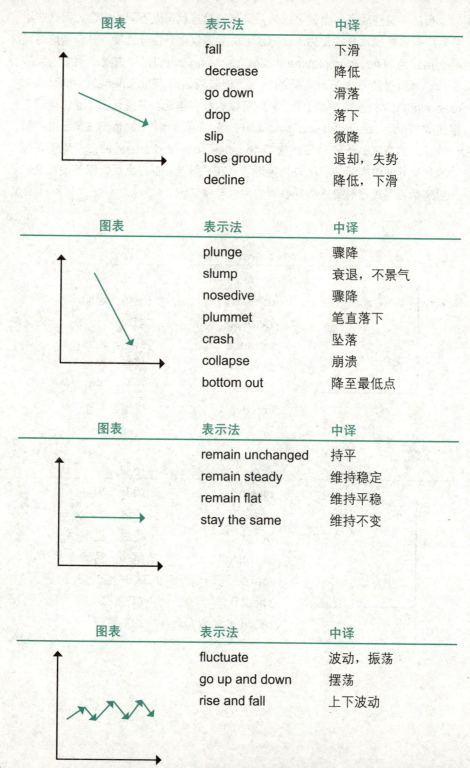

图表	表示法	中译
	fall	下滑
	decrease	降低
	go down	滑落
	drop	落下
	slip	微降
	lose ground	退却，失势
	decline	降低，下滑

图表	表示法	中译
	plunge	骤降
	slump	衰退，不景气
	nosedive	骤降
	plummet	笔直落下
	crash	坠落
	collapse	崩溃
	bottom out	降至最低点

图表	表示法	中译
	remain unchanged	持平
	remain steady	维持稳定
	remain flat	维持平稳
	stay the same	维持不变

图表	表示法	中译
	fluctuate	波动，振荡
	go up and down	摆荡
	rise and fall	上下波动

Unit 1 将数据做成简报

单词补充

（使用副词形容其程度）

弱

- **slowly** — The price of rice rose slowly.
  米价缓慢上涨。

- **slightly** — Sales increased slightly in July.
  七月业绩稍有增加。

中

- **steadily** — Turnover has increased steadily since May.
  业绩自五月以来稳定增长。

- **gradually** — The number of customers increased gradually.
  客户数逐渐增加。

- **modestly** — Order volume declined modestly.
  订单量稍微减少。

- **moderately** — Energy consumption rose moderately.
  能源消耗量温和地增加。

强

- **significantly** — Interest rates dropped significantly.
  利率骤降。

- **suddenly** — Tourist numbers increased suddenly.
  旅客人数突然增多。

- **sharply** — Hotel rates dropped sharply in China.
  在中国，酒店价格大幅下降。

- **considerably** — Income fell considerably last year.
  去年收入大幅下滑。

- **quickly** — The number of online stores climbed quickly.
  网上商店数量快速攀升。

- **rapidly** — The oil price plunged rapidly.
  油价急速下跌。

- **dramatically** — Medical costs have grown dramatically.
  医疗费用大幅上升。

- **surprisingly** — The unemployment rate decreased surprisingly.
  失业率以惊人的速度下降。

129

曲线图

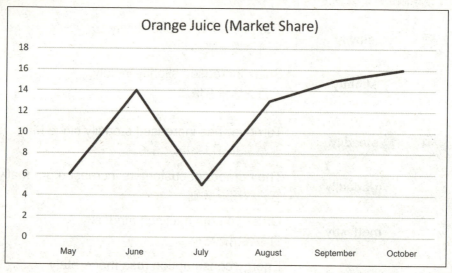

Description

All right, so the graph I'd like to show you is the market share of our "Orange Juice" for the first six months after it was launched in May 2015. As you can see from this graph, we started off with a rather low market share of approximately 6%. After a month, the share improved sharply, climbing to 14% in June. In July, however, the market share plunged to 5% due to more competition from other beverage companies. Fortunately, this was only a temporary setback, since customers still found our beverage products high quality. And over the next three months, the figures continued to hike steadily and reached record levels each month: 13%, 15%, and 16% in August, September, and October, respectively.

Unit 1 将数据做成简报

描述练习 范例一 曲线图 ▶ 中译

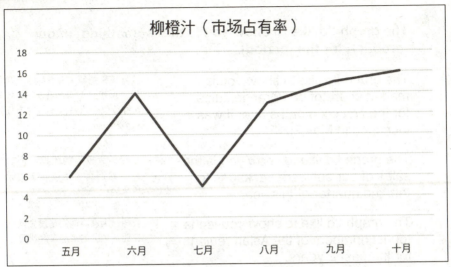

口语描述

好的，我接下来想给大家看的图是我们"柳橙汁"产品在 2015 年 5 月首度上市后的六个月的市场占有率。如同各位可看到的图表显示，刚开始的市占率仅约百分之六。一个月之后，市场占有率就大幅攀升到六月的百分之十四了。然而，到了七月，因其他饮料公司的竞争的原因，市场占有率便骤降到百分之五。所幸这只是暂时性的，客户还是认为我们的饮料产品品质优良。接下来的三个月，数据持续上扬并且每个月皆创新高：八月、九月和十月的数据分别是百分之十三、百分之十五和百分之十六。

graph [græf]
n 图表

launch [lɔ:ntʃ]
v 上市，推出

approximately [əˈprɑːksɪmətli]
ad 大约，约略

competition [ˌkɑːmpəˈtɪʃn]
n 竞争

beverage [ˈbevərɪdʒ]
n 饮料

fortunately [ˈfɔːrtʃənətli]
ad 幸运地

temporary [ˈtempəreri]
a 暂时的

setback [ˈsetbæk]
n 挫折，挫败

respectively [rɪˈspektɪvli]
ad 个别地，对应地

plunge [plʌndʒ]
v 骤降

搭配描述练习学习句型。

1 **The graph I'd like to show you is the [something] of our [product] for the [period].**

The graph I'd like to show you is the market share of our Orange Juice for the first six months after it was launched in May 2015.

我接下来想给大家看的图是我们"柳橙汁"产品在 2015 年 5 月首度上市后六个月的市场占有率。

The graph I'd like to show you is the sales of our software packages for the 2nd quarter of this year.

我想给大家看的图是我们的套装软件在今年第二季的销售业绩。

The graph I'd like to show you is the tourist numbers of the Asian region for the past 2 years.

我想给大家看的图是过去两年在亚洲地区的旅游人数状况。

2 **In [time], however, the [something] plunged / skyrocketed to [number] because of / owing to [reasons].**

In July, however, the market share plunged to 5% owing to more competition from other beverage companies.

然而,到了七月,因其他饮料公司竞争的原因,市场占有率便骤降到百分之五。

In 2015, however, the unemployment rate increased to 4.5% owing to company closure of some SMB companies.

然而,在 2015 年,因中小企业公司倒闭的原因,失业率上升到百分之四点五。

In January, however, the number of tourists dropped dramatically because of the bad weather conditions.

然而,在一月,因气候不佳的原因,旅游人数骤减。

Unit 1 将数据做成简报

3 Over the [time], [something] continued / will continue to increase / decrease steadily.

Over the next 2 months, sales continued to increase steadily.

接下来两个月，业绩持续稳定增长。

Over the past 5 years, the oil price continued to decline steadily.

过去五年来，油价持续稳定下降。

Over the next 3 years, income will continue to rise gradually.

在未来三年，收入会持续稳定上升。

MEMO

简报图文配置
Layout of Texts and Graphics

图文整合

在制作简报 PPT 时，有些演讲者喜欢多放些文字，有些则喜欢以图表的方式来呈现——毕竟 "A picture is worth a thousand words." 一张图胜过千言万语！但实际上，文字过多却没有图片，或仅有图片却不搭配文字描述，两种状况都不理想。当然，最佳的状况是文字和图片两者的数量要平均，在 PPT 版面上的呈现以让听众感到容易接受为目的。一般来说，一张幻灯片内的字数呈现，最佳的组合是 "6×6"。意思是说，一页幻灯片内，最多列出六个要点，而每个要点内的文字最多六个字。比方说：

讨论项目

1. Set up achievable goals
   设定可达成的目标

2. Marketing strategies for international markets
   国际市场的营销策略

3. Review budget plans for Q2
   审查第二季的预算规划

4. Check R&D progress
   检查研发进度

5. Maintain customer satisfaction
   维持顾客满意度

6. Q/A session
   问题与讨论

Unit 2 简报图文配置

这样的排版是最易于听众阅读的。另外，在"6×6"的文字组合之外，若幻灯片页面还有充分的空间，则可以加入与该页幻灯片主题相关的图片。比方说，讨论到"产品在北美市场分布"时，便可穿插"北美"的地图，以便听众更容易了解并融入该主题。但切勿仅为了将空间塞满，勉强地使用和该幻灯片主题无关的照片。

另外，在增加相关图表方面，除了地图，还可能使用多种其他的图表呈现。比方说：长条图、圆饼图、折线图、组织图、表格、流程图，或用以呈现特定产品专业规格的技术图等。以下便呈现各式图表的不同之处，并通过"圆饼图"搭配案例情境来做描述图表内容的练习。

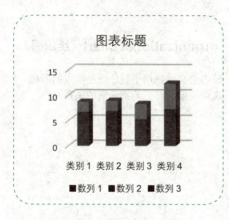

bar chart（长条图）

通常用于比较时间序列资料时，比方说一年十二个月的业绩数据变化。

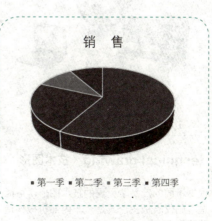

pie chart（圆饼图）

用于描述量、频率或百分比之间的相对关系，如产品的市场占有率的百分比等。

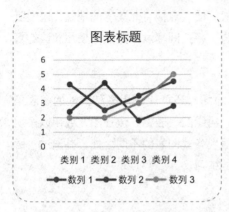

line graph（折线图）

通常用于显示相同时间间隔或某特定时间内的趋势。

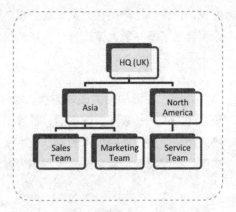

organizational chart（组织图）

顾名思义就是用于显示企业组织的架构，说明阶层、部门与责任间的关系。

technical drawing（技术图形）

根据不同的产品所呈现的技术图形，可能是电脑仪表板图，或是汽车内部机械构造等图形。

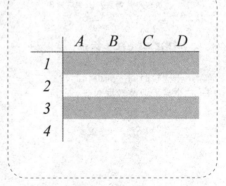

table（表格）

在将所有数据转换成图形前，都会将资料输入表格内，方便整理数据，以便做出有效的图形。

Unit 2 简报图文配置

flow chart（流程图）

目的在清楚地呈现每一项作业流程，让相关作业人员对整体的流程与步骤一目了然。

map（地图）

针对某特定地区做数据分析时，可在地图内显示资料。比方说想了解美国各州的人口分布资料，便可通过美国版图来呈现，这会比仅显示数字清楚。

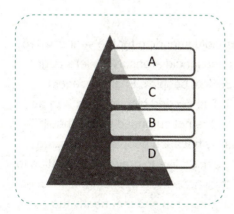

pyramid chart（金字塔图）

显示比例或阶层式的信息。

 圆饼图

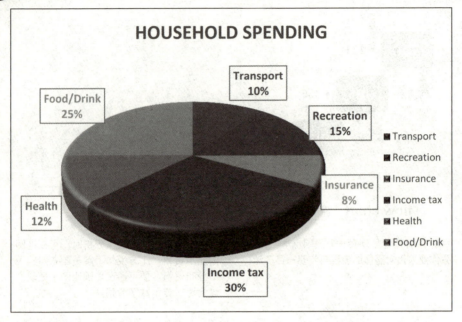

Description

This pie chart shows people's total household spending for the year of 2015 and how it is divided among the various household areas. Now, let's begin with the biggest area. We can see that 30% of people's total household spending went into "Income tax" in 2015. The second biggest area with a total of 25% is "Food / Drink". I guess you are not surprised to see that 15% was spent on "Recreation". This was mainly because people emphasized the importance of work-life balance last year. I'd like to draw your attention to the "Health" which accounts for 12% of total household spending. It includes dental services and health care. And lastly, you can see that nearly the same amount — that's 10% and 8%, was spent on "Transport" and "Insurance", respectively.

圆饼图 ▶ 中译

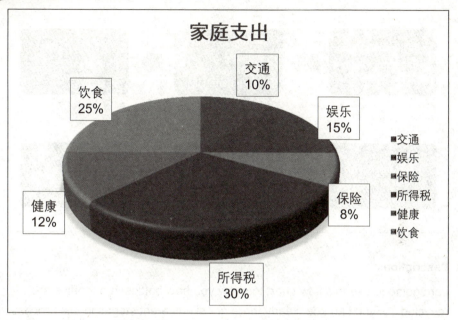

口语描述

这个图显示在 2015 年人们的家庭支出和在各个领域的分配。现在，让我们开始看最大的部分。由此我们可以看到，在 2015 年，人们的家庭支出的百分之三十是花在"所得税"上。另外有百分之二十五的支出是花在第二大领域，也就是"饮食"部分。我想您也不会惊讶于百分之十五的支出花费在"娱乐"上。这主要是因为去年人们就一直强调工作与生活平衡的重要性。我想请大家注意，"健康"这部分占了总家庭支出的百分之十二。这部分包括牙科服务和医疗保健。最后，大家可以看到相差不多的数字，分别是百分之十花在"交通费"上和百分之八花在"保险"上。

---

household ['haʊshoʊld]
n 家庭

divide [dɪ'vaɪd]
v 划分，区隔

various ['veriəs]
a 各式各样的

spending ['spendɪŋ]
n 花费

income ['ɪnkʌm]
n 收入

recreation [ˌriːkri'eɪʃn]
n 娱乐

emphasize ['emfəsaɪz]
v 强调

balance ['bæləns]
n 平衡

dental ['dentl]
a 牙齿的

transport ['trænspɔːrt]
n 交通

insurance [ɪn'ʃʊərəns]
n 保险

流程图

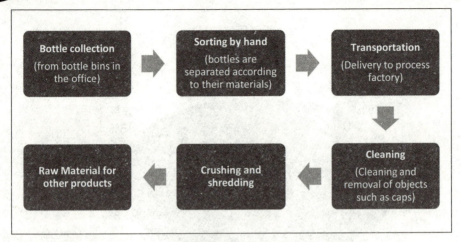

Description

I am going to use this flow chart to show you how bottles in our office are recycled. As you can see clearly there are six different stages in this process, from the initial collection of bottles to the eventual production of other various useable products. All right, so at the first stage in the bottle recycling process, waste bottles are collected from bottle bins, where all colleagues in the office leave their used bottles. All bottles are then sorted by hand and separated according to material, such as metal, objects made out of rigid plastics, flexible plastics, or drink cartons, with any material that is not suitable for recycling being removed. Next, the categorized bottles are transported to a bottle process factory. Stage four of the process involves cleaning. All bottles are cleaned, and foreign objects such as caps are taken out. Following this, all bottles are crushed and shredded into small fragments. Finally, all pure PET fragments can be processed further and used as the raw material for a range of products such as carpets or back into PET bottles.

Unit 2 简报图文配置

描述练习 范例二 流程图 ▶ 中译

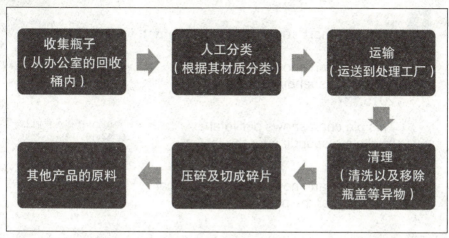

口语描述

我会利用这个流程图向大家说明在办公室回收的瓶子是如何再生利用的。大家可以清楚地看到，空瓶回收再利用过程有六个不同的阶段，包括从最初的空瓶收集到最后的生产其他有用产品。好的，在空瓶回收过程中的第一阶段是，将公司员工丢入回收桶内的瓶子收集起来。接着将所有瓶子根据材质人工分类，如金属、硬质塑料所制的瓶子，柔性塑料的瓶子或饮料纸盒等，并将不适合回收利用的材质移除。接着，将分类好的空瓶运送到空瓶处理工厂。过程四是将空瓶清洗干净。所有的瓶子清洗之后，如果有瓶盖等异物便将之取出。接着，所有瓶子都被压碎与切成碎片。最后，所有 PET 碎片可以做进一步加工并作为其他产品的原料，如地毯或再度制成 PET 瓶。

---

stage [steɪdʒ]
n 阶段

eventual [ɪˈventʃuəl]
a 最终的，最后的

separate [ˈseprət]
v 分离，分开

material [məˈtɪriəl]
n 材料，物质

rigid [ˈrɪdʒɪd]
a 坚硬的

flexible [ˈfleksəbl]
a 有弹性的

categorize [ˈkætəgəraɪz]
v 分类

transport [ˈtrænspɔːrt]
v 运送

involve [ɪnˈvɑːlv]
v 涉及，关联

crush [krʌʃ]
v 压碎

shred [ʃred]
v 切碎，撕成碎片

fragment [ˈfrægmənt]
n 碎片，破片

搭配描述练习学习句型。

1

This pie chart shows our total [something] for [time].

This pie chart shows people's total household spending for the year of 2015.	这张圆饼图显示人们在 2015 年的家庭支出。
This pie chart shows our total marketing spending for the last quarter.	这张圆饼图显示我们上一季的营销费用。
This pie chart shows our total medical spending for the past two years.	这张圆饼图显示我们过去两年的医疗费用。

2

We can see that [amount] of [something] went into [something] in [time].

We can see that 30% of people's total household spending went into income tax in 2015.	我们可以看到，在 2015 年百分之三十的家庭支出是花在所得税上了。
We can see that 40% of our total marketing spending went into customer campaigns in Q2.	我们可以看到在第二季，百分之四十的营销支出是花在办客户活动上了。
We can see that 28% of our total medical spending went into seeing doctors care last year.	我们可以看到在去年，百分之二十八的医疗支出是花在医院就诊上了。

3

I'd like to draw your attention to [something] which account for [amount] of [something].

I'd like to draw your attention to the health which accounts for 12% of total household spending.	我想请各位注意看健康部分，那占了总家庭支出的百分之十二。
I'd like to draw your attention to the promotion which accounts for 20% of total marketing spending.	我想请各位注意看促销部分，那占了总营销支出的百分之二十。
I'd like to draw your attention to the prescription drugs which account for 11% of our total expenditure.	我想请各位注意看处方药部分，那占了总支出的百分之十一。

Unit 3 拟演说稿
Draft for Speech

演说诀窍

在准备简报演说之前，除了准备幻灯片之外，演讲者可能还会想搭配着幻灯片上的要点信息，将演讲稿逐字地写下（或打印出来），当成备忘稿，在台上忘记讲词时还可以瞄一下稿件。甚至于 PowerPoint 软件也有给演讲者写"备忘稿"的功能，让人可以在 PPT 幻灯片下方书写内容。

的确，将演讲内容写／印出来会让演讲者有心理较安定的感觉。但请特别注意，讲稿仅是当提示用途，讲者万万不可拿着讲稿就直接照着念。如此，像机器人一般硬生生地逐字念稿，不生动也不自然，听众听不到重点不说，还极有可能听了三五分钟就失去兴趣了。有些已有工作经验的人可能会认为，所介绍的产品都已是自己可以掌握的内容，就当场看着幻灯片内容，想到什么讲什么就好。这样的做法可能对以母语演讲时有用，但若是以英语做简报，在英语非母语的情况之下，要当场构思句子并顺畅地表达，可能会有些难度。

那么，在做英语简报前最佳的做法，不仅是将要讲的英语句子／内容写下就好，最好是可以念到滚瓜烂熟，几乎可以背出来为止。届时在简报当中，仅要靠幻灯片内的关键词提示即可，其他的完整句子与内容，要以自然生动的方式呈现出来，最好还要搭配声音、语调，甚至肢体动作，才能让听众更加融入情境并对简报内容产生共鸣。再者，为了吸引听众的注意，在简报演说时要注意以下三个自然英语的声音规则：

1. Chunking (Pause) 词组中间要加以停顿

在简报演说之时，绝对不可能是将句子按一个词一个词的方式念出来。而是将句子分成好几组"词群"，然后将句子依一组一组的方式呈现。这意味着要将句子正确地依一组一组的方式呈现出来，就必须先知道要将句子中的哪些词归在一组。在念词组时中间要停顿，若在不正确的位置停顿，可能导致听者会错意。因此，即便事先准备好简报内容稿件了，也应在"断开词组"方面多加练习。

2. Adding Stress 在要点上加强重音

知道在何处断开句子之后，接下来要在特定的要点上加强重音。另外，要是将重音放在不同的地方，整句话的意思也有可能随之改变，因此，在准备时应先将要强调的要点标出，以便简报演说时知道要在哪里加强重音。

3. Changing Pace 速度改变

简报演说中讲句子时，有些词可以连在一起很快带过去，重要的词要刻意放慢速度加以强调。如此语调便形成抑扬顿挫之势。

接下来，我们便通过以下的简报稿件，请读者加入上述三个"自然语调"的要素来加以练习。

> **EXERCISE**

1. 以英语搭配幻灯片演讲，如何准备演说稿的方式较佳？
   A. 将稿子逐字印出并照着念
   B. 将文字全数放到幻灯片，让观众自行阅读
   C. 将内容摘要列出，并练习到滚瓜烂熟
   D. 看到幻灯片的当下即兴演讲

答案：C

2. 在简报演讲时，为了让听众了解重点，要注意什么规则？
   A. 照稿平铺直叙即可
   B. 在要点上加强重音
   C. 在讲台表演，夸大肢体语言
   D. 什么都不必准备，放大量影片给观众看

答案：B

Unit 3 拟演说稿

软件研讨会开场介绍

Good morning, ladies and gentlemen. First of all, I'd like to thank all of you for attending this product launch event today. Let me just kick off the event by introducing myself. My name is Sandra Anderson, and I am responsible for product marketing at Best Software Company. As you may already know, Best Software Company is the market leader in developing and selling network software packages and we also focus on providing enterprise clients excellent after-sales services. I am here today to present our newly released version of Link-All system. I've split my presentation into three major sections. First, I'll talk about some exciting new features of this updated software solution. Second, I'll move on to demonstrate how enterprise clients can benefit from deploying this system. And finally, I'll speak about how our comprehensive customer services works. The presentation will last approximately 25 minutes. I'll also allocate 5 minutes for the Q&A session. I'd be glad to take any questions at the end of my presentation. Once again, I am truly grateful that you could come today and learn more about our unique software product. All right. Let's begin by looking at this network chart.

软件研讨会开场介绍 ▶ 中译

各位女士先生，大家早安。首先，我要感谢大家来参加今天的这场产品上市活动。我先自我介绍一下。我是珊卓·安德森，我在最佳软件公司是负责产品营销的。您可能已经知道，最佳软件公司是市场的领军企业，主要开发并销售网络软件套装，我们也非常注重给企业客户提供优良的售后服务。我今天要给大家介绍的是"全连接"系统的最新版本。我会将简报分成三大部分。首先，我会先讨论此改良版本的最新特点与功能。其次，我会操作给大家看，企业导入我们这套系统会得到的优势。最后，我会告诉大家我们全面性的客户服务是如何运作的。我的简报演说大约历时二十五分钟。另会有五分钟的问题讨论时间。简报演说之后欢迎大家提问。我想再度感谢大家今天可以来，并多加了解我们独特的软件产品。好的。我们就先开始看一下这张网络架构图。

---

launch [lɔːntʃ]
n 上市，发表

kick off
ph 开始

responsible [rɪˈspɑːnsəbl]
a 负责的

develop [dɪˈveləp]
v 开发，发展

enterprise [ˈentərpraɪz]
n 企业，事业

version [ˈvɜːrʒn]
n 版本

feature [ˈfiːtʃər]
n 特性，特点

demonstrate [ˈdemənstreɪt]
v 示范，操作

comprehensive [ˌkɑːmprɪˈhensɪv]
a 全面性的

approximately [əˈprɑːksɪmətli]
ad 大约，约略

grateful [ˈɡreɪtfl]
a 感激的，愉快的

unique [juˈniːk]
a 独一无二的，特别的

产品之设计与功能介绍

All right, so as you can see from the photo on the slide, this is our latest model of UTX laundry machine. This new line of laundry machines is environmentally friendly. Now let's turn to another important point, which is their unique design. I'd like all of you to pay extra attention to three new design features. First of all, the laundry machines are more colorful. We think that customers, especially mothers, would appreciate more colors in their homes, and our laundry machines provide just that. Customers have 5 colors to choose from, including yellow, red, white, mauve, and green. The second design feature is the automatic temperature control. Rather than simply mixing hot and cold water, this temperature control function adjusts the water to the optimal temperature automatically. And last but not least, the new laundry machine has a compact design, which means it takes up less space. I'd like to emphasize that this new UTX laundry machine is by far the most powerful model on the market, and I am sure that our customers would be very satisfied with all these new features. Now I'll be happy to answer any questions you may have.

 产品之设计与功能介绍 ▶ 中译

好的，大家可以从幻灯片上的照片看到，这是我们最新型号的 UTX 洗衣机。这种新的洗衣机是环保机型。现在，让我们讨论此型号的另一要点，也就是其独特的设计。我请大家特别注意此型号三个新的设计特点。首先，此型号洗衣机色彩丰富。我们认为客户，尤其是妈妈们，会喜欢在自己家中增添更多的色彩，因此我们的洗衣机便提供了这一点。客户有五种颜色可供选择，包括黄色、红色、白色、淡紫色和绿色。其第二个特点就是自动温度控制。不仅是单纯地混合冷热水，这种温度控制功能可以自动调整，以达到最佳洗衣温度。最后，此款新的洗衣机具有精巧的设计，这意味着它占用更少的空间。我想强调的是，此款新的 UTX 洗衣机是目前市场上功能最强大的机型，我肯定客户会对这些新的功能感到非常满意。现在，有任何问题欢迎提出，我很乐意为您解说。

---

latest ['leɪtɪst]
a 最新的

laundry machine
ph 洗衣机

environmentally friendly
ph 对环境友善的

unique [juˈniːk]
a 独特的

feature [ˈfiːtʃər]
n 特性

mauve [moʊv]
n 淡紫色

automatic [ˌɔːtəˈmætɪk]
a 自动化的

mix [mɪks]
v 混合

adjust [əˈdʒʌst]
v 调整

optimal [ˈɑːptɪməl]
a 最佳的

compact [ˈkɑːmpækt]
a 精巧的

powerful [ˈpaʊərfl]
a 强大有力的

实用句型

例句 搭配演说范本学习句型。

1 **As you may already know, [Company] is the market leader in [making some products] and we focus on [doing something].**

As you may already know, Best Software Company is the market leader in developing and selling network software packages and we also focus on providing enterprise clients excellent after-sales services.	您可能已经知道，最佳软件公司是市场领军企业，主要开发销售网络套装软件，我们也注重给企业客户提供完善的售后服务。
As you may already know, Beauti-Face is the market leader in selling skin care creams and we focus on making beauty products with safe and natural ingredients.	您可能已经知道，美肤公司是市场领军企业，主要销售护肤乳液，我们的产品均使用安全与天然的成分。
As you may already know, Fast-Vehicle is the market leader in designing and selling sedans and we focus on offering customers complete vehicle maintenance.	您可能已经知道，快捷交通公司是市场领军企业，主要设计和销售家庭房车，我们也注重提供给客户完整的汽车保养。

2 **All right, as you can see from the [something] on the slide, this is our latest [something].**

All right, so as you can see from the photo on the slide, this is our latest model of UTX laundry machine.	好的，大家可以看到幻灯片上的照片，这是我们最新型的 UTX 洗衣机。
All right, as you can see from the pie chart on the slide, this is our updated market share information.	好的，大家可以看到幻灯片上的圆饼图，这是我们近期市场占有率的信息。
All right, as you can see from the figures in this table, these are the units of cars we produce in the second quarter of this year.	好的，大家可以看到这表格内的数字，这些是今年第二季我们车辆产出的数量。

I'd like to emphasize that this new [product name] is by far the most [adj.] model on the market.

I'd like to emphasize that this new UTX laundry machine is by far the most powerful model on the market.

我想强调这台新的 UTX 洗衣机是目前市面上功能最强大的机型。

I'd like to stress that this new Orange Smartphone is by far the most popular model on the market.

我想强调这只"橘子"智能手机是市面上最受欢迎的机种。

I'd like to affirm that this new Max Software system is by far the most widely-deployed solution on the market.

我想强调的是这套新的"极大"软件系统是目前市面上最多人采用的解决方案。

MEMO

演说技巧
Speech Skills

> 简报架构

　　一场成功并吸引人的英语简报，除了演讲者对简报的专业内容（公司产品、产业服务、专业术语等）的熟悉之外，整体的架构的重要性也是不可忽略的。若简报没有架构的话，则演讲者可能会想到什么讲什么，听众也听得一头雾水。那么，一般来说英语简报的架构会包含什么元素在内呢？此节我们便对英语简报的"开场介绍""要点强调""与听众互动""演讲风格设定""做出结论"与"问题讨论"六大部分来做详细解释。

1. 开场介绍

　　人的注意集中力通常持续时间不会太长，也就是说演讲者必须在简报演说的前三五分钟，就抓住听众的注意力，并引起听众对简报主题的兴趣。开场介绍部分通常包括固定的几个要素，也就是：自我介绍、简报主题说明、大纲细节说明和所需时间规划等。为了吸引听众的注意，暂且不要一下就讨论生硬的主题，可试着以丢出问题给听众思考，或将讲题与日常生活的状况连接等方式带入主题。但最好别讲笑话，尤其是较为正式的简报会，开场白就讲笑话（也并非每人都觉得好笑）会让听众有"这演讲者／研讨会似乎不是很专业"的感觉。

2. 要点强调

　　在一段二十分钟的简报演说中，演讲者针对讲题可能会讨论三个或四个要点。而这几个要点的重要性应该不会都是相同的。演讲者可利用强调性语句、声调、表情、手势等来传达"某个要点很重要，值得注意"的信息。例如：It is very obvious that...（很显然的……）、The critical point is...（关键点是……）、Most importantly...（最重要的是……），或 We must pay extra attention to...（我们必须将注意力放在……）等语句，来吸引听众的注意力。

3. 与听众互动

　　若一场简报演说仅是演讲者自顾讲着 PPT 的内容，听众仅是接收信息，不用多久听众就感到疲乏并失去兴趣了。为了让听众一直保持兴趣，演讲者最好设计与听众互动的时间。比方说，提问题给听众思考，请听众发表意见，或让听众分小组讨论等。根据以往的经验，在座的听众会提问讨论，发表意见的可能就那一两位特定的人。为了让每个听众都有机会，演讲者也可运用直接点名发言的方式。

4. 演讲风格设定

每个演讲者可能因个性不同，或因会议性质不同，而展现出不同的简报演说风格。比如说演讲者个性较为拘谨，那么做简报时可能也会是正经八百的态度。如果演讲者个性外向风趣，那么演讲时便较可能带动活泼轻松的气氛。又或是会议场合本属于正式的研讨会，那演讲者的言语自然也应庄重谨慎些。若仅是在公司内部开会，语言用词上自然也会较口语随性。简报风格的设定并无标准答案，根据不同状况与场合，演讲者应有"要将简报会塑造成何种风格"的判断能力。

5. 做出结论

简报内容都讲完了之后，在尾声应将要点归纳一次，并提醒听众后续所应采取的行动（action items）。比如说，一场介绍新产品的简报会，演讲者不会要听众只是来听听产品功能之后，什么行动都没有就直接离开吧？应该在简报之后，让听众有后续可采取的行动，可能是要听听完产品介绍后，现场下订单可以享有九折优惠；或是听完业绩简报后，要想出提升业绩的策略等。演讲者应在简报尾声帮听众归纳要点结论，并提出"后续行动"让听众遵循。

6. 问题讨论

简报之后一定都会有问题讨论时间让听众提问或交换意见。演讲者的责任是控制每人提问或发言的时间，避免仅特定一两位一直提问或占用时间发言。演讲者回答问题也应言简意赅，以简答为主。如果需后续讨论，可邀请提问者在会后进行深入讨论。

了解这六大部分在简报内扮演的重要性之后，我们就带入情境当中来看看可以使用的实用英语语句吧！

Unit 4 演说技巧

 开场白介绍

- **Good morning, ladies and gentlemen. Let me start by introducing myself. I am Jerry Smith. I am in charge of Sales and Marketing.**
  各位女士先生,早上好。让我先自我介绍。我是杰瑞·史密斯。我负责营销与销售的工作。

- **The topic of today's presentation is what strategies we could adopt to increase market awareness and sales revenue of our products.**
  今天简报的主题是,我们为了提高产品在市场的能见度与销售业绩所可以采取的策略。

- **I've divided my presentation into three major sections.**
  我将简报分成三个主要部分。

- **In my presentation, I'll focus on three main points. Point one deals with product innovations, point two will be about promotions, and point three is the ways to drive revenues.**
  在我的简报中,我会将焦点放在三个要点上。第一点是跟产品创新有关,第二点是跟促销有关,第三点是要讨论增加业绩的方式。

- **It will take about 30 minutes to cover these important issues.**
  我会花三十分钟的时间来讨论这些议题。

- **Please interrupt me as we go along should you have any questions. All right, now let's begin by looking at this chart here.**
  如果简报中您有任何问题,欢迎随时提出讨论。好的,现在让我们开始看这张图表。

---

adopt [ə'dɑ:pt]
v. 采取,采用

awareness [ə'wernəs]
n. 意识,能见度

section ['sekʃn]
n. 部分

innovation [ˌɪnə'veɪʃn]
n. 创新

interrupt [ˌɪntə'rʌpt]
v. 打断

要点强调

- **I'd like to emphasize the importance of customer feedback.**
  我要强调客户反馈意见的重要性。

- **The essential point is that we have to adjust product specifications in order to fulfill clients' demands.**
  重点是我们必须调整产品规格以满足客户的需求。

- **One point you will immediately notice is the sharp drop in customer satisfaction reported in Asia.**
  您马上会注意到的要点是，在亚洲的客户满意度骤降。

- **If we don't solve this pricing problem now, I am afraid we'll run into serious trouble pretty soon.**
  若我们现在不解决此定价问题，恐怕很快我们会有大麻烦。

- **I'd particularly like to draw your attention to the dramatic increase in the number of customer complaints in Q2 of this year.**
  我特别要请大家注意的是，今年第二季客户抱怨数大幅上升了。

- **Let me reiterate, it is absolutely critical to be open to hearing customers' feedback.**
  我要重申，听取客户反馈意见是非常重要的。

---

emphasize ['emfəsaɪz]
v 强调

specification [ˌspesɪfɪ'keɪʃn]
n 规格

immediately [ɪ'miːdiətli]
ad 立即，马上

dramatic [drə'mætɪk]
a 大量的，显而易见的

reiterate [ri'ɪtəreɪt]
v 重申

Unit 4 演说技巧

与听众互动

- I'd also like to hear from you guys. Are you really all satisfied with our products?
  我想听听大伙的意见。大家真的满意我们的产品吗？

- Linda, I know you've been working with R&D technicians. Can you comment on this, please?
  琳达，我知道你一直跟研发工程师合作。你可以对此发表你的看法吗？

- I'd like to see a show of hands. How many of you have ever lost your temper when dealing with complaints?
  我想做个调查。在座的有多少人曾经在处理抱怨时失去耐性？

- Jerry is an expert in this field, so I'd like to invite Jerry to come up here and share his experience with us. Jerry, please?
  杰瑞是这方面的专家，所以我想邀请杰瑞到台上，并跟我们分享他的经验。杰瑞，请吧。

- Please take 2 minutes to discuss this competition issue with your neighbors.
  请利用两分钟的时间，跟你隔壁的人讨论你对竞争的看法。

- So Liz, imagine you receive a phone call from an angry customer. What would you do first?
  好的，莉兹，请想象你接到一个暴怒的客户所打来的电话。你会先怎么做？

---

satisfy ['sætɪsfaɪ]
v 满意

technician [tek'nɪʃn]
n 工程师，技术员

temper ['tempər]
n 脾气

competition [ˌkɑːmpə'tɪʃn]
n 竞争

imagine [ɪ'mædʒɪn]
v 想象

难以置信的实用职场英语

讲演风格

- [自然] **How are you guys doing? Thank you for coming.**
  大家好吗？谢谢出席。

- [正式] **Good morning ladies and gentlemen. Welcome to today's seminar.**
  各位女士先生，大家早上好。欢迎参加今天的研讨会。

- [温和] **Would you agree that we should adjust prices a bit?**
  大家同意我们应该稍微调整价格吗？

- [强烈] **It is very clear that we must raise product prices.**
  很显然，我们的产品必须涨价了。

- [轻松] **This might cause a little problem.**
  这可能会引起一点问题。

- [紧张] **This will definitely be a disaster for us.**
  这对我们来说完全是场灾难。

---

seminar ['semɪnɑːr]
n 研讨会

adjust [ə'dʒʌst]
v 调整

cause [kɔːz]
v 引发

definitely ['defɪnətli]
ad 确实地，的确

disaster [dɪ'zæstər]
n 灾难

尾声 / 结论

- **All right. That covers about everything I wanted to say about marketing strategies. Let me summarize the key issues again.**
  好的。关于营销策略的议题我都讨论过了。让我将要点再归纳一下。

- **Okay, that ends the last part of my presentation. Before I stop, I'd like to run through my main points.**
  好的,这就是我简报的最终部分。在我结束之前,我很快地再提一下要点。

- **In conclusion, my suggestions are to collect customer feedback first and design products that better suit customers' needs.**
  最终结论,我的建议是先收集客户反馈意见,再设计符合客户需求的产品。

- **To sum up, I think we have to do some market research in order to understand the market trends.**
  总之,我认为我们要先做些市场调查,以便可以了解市场趋势。

- **I really appreciate your attention. And now I am interested in hearing your comments.**
  很感谢大家的聆听。现在我想听听你们的意见。

- **Thank you for listening attentively. Now, I welcome any questions you might have.**
  谢谢大家仔细地聆听。现在欢迎大家提出问题。

---

summarize [ˈsʌməraɪz]
v 归纳,总结

conclusion [kənˈkluːʒn]
n 结论

trend [trend]
n 趋势

comment [ˈkɑːment]
n 意见

attentively [əˈtentɪvli]
ad 仔细地,周到地

问题讨论

- **That's an interesting question. Thank you for bringing it up.**
  那是个有趣的问题。谢谢提出。

- **Thank you for raising the point, but could you be a bit more specific please?**
  谢谢您提出这个要点,但您可以说得更明确一点吗?

- **I am sorry, but I am afraid the question is outside the scope of my presentation.**
  不好意思,恐怕这个问题跟我简报主题无直接关系。

- **I think I covered that issue earlier, but we could discuss this further after my presentation if you'd like.**
  我想我先前已讨论过那个要点,但若您想要的话,会后我们可以再讨论一下。

- **That's a wonderful question. Let's go around the table and get different perspectives on this.**
  那是个很棒的问题。我们轮流听听看每个人不同的意见吧。

- **All right, we're short of time. I'll end my presentation here and thank you very much for your attention.**
  好的,我们没剩多少时间了。我的简报到此结束,谢谢大家的参与。

---

bring up
ph 提出,提起

specific [spə'sɪfɪk]
a 明确的,特定的

scope [skoʊp]
n 范围

perspective [pər'spɛktɪv]
n 角度,洞察力,切入点

attention [ə'tɛnʃn]
n 注意力

Unit 4 演说技巧

 搭配实用句子学习句型。

1 I'd particularly like to draw your attention to the [something].

I'd particularly like to draw your attention to the dramatic increase in the number of customer complaints in Q2 of this year.

我特别要请大家注意的是，今年第二季客户抱怨数大幅上升了。

I'd particularly like to draw your attention to the sharp fall in our laptop sales.

我特别想请大家注意的是，我们笔记本电脑的销售大幅下滑。

I'd particularly like to draw your attention to the rapid climb in the number of competitors.

我特别想请大家注意的是，竞争厂商的数量大幅增加。

2 All right. That covers about everything I wanted to say about [something]. Let me summarize [something] again.

All right. That covers about everything I wanted to say about marketing strategies. Let me summarize the key issues again.

好的。关于营销策略的议题我都讨论过了。让我将要点再归纳一下。

All right. That covers about everything I wanted to say about customer services. Let me summarize my main points again.

好的。关于客户服务的议题我都讨论完了。让我将要点再归纳一下。

All right. That covers about everything I wanted to say about product innovation. Let me summarize the major concepts again.

好的。关于产品创新的议题我都讨论完了。让我再将主要概念归纳一下。

I'd like to see a show of hands. How many of you have ever [experienced something]?

I'd like to see a show of hands. How many of you have ever lost your temper when dealing with complaints?

我想做个调查。在座的有多少人曾经在处理抱怨时失去耐心？

I'd like to see a show of hands. How many of you have ever dealt with difficult customers?

我想做个调查。在座的有多少人曾经处理过难缠的客户？

I'd like to see a show of hands. How many of you have ever been in charge of big campaigns?

我想做个调查。在座的有多少人曾经负责过大型活动？

MEMO

Chapter 5

Business Conference
商务会议

前言

　　职场上，不论您身在哪行或任职哪个职位，都一定会与上司、同事，甚至是客户开会讨论议题，表达意见。那么在办公环境中使用英语，便有"会议英语"会使用到的词汇与语句。当主席的会有主席这个角色会使用到的语句，比方说为控制时间，请与会者要精简说明，主席便可以提醒"We don't have much time left. Can you be brief, please?"（我们所剩时间不多了。你可以讲重点吗？）或是与会者想要插话，便可以说"May I come in here?"（我可以插个话吗？）诸如此类的。身在职场的员工，对基本会议的流程、话题掌握、表达意见、倾听别人、分析利弊、做出结论等技巧，的确是需要好好学习与熟悉的。

　　讨论到会议英语，通常会分为三个阶段：

1. **事前准备 / 主席开场**：开会时间（When）与地点（Where）的确认与通知、与会者（Who）有谁、议题（What）的讨论方向与议程（Agenda）应如何进行（How）等细节的准备，都是在会议前需确认好的。且在会议开始时，主席的责任便是要确认上述细节的准备，以便跟与会者报告需讨论的议题、时间掌控、发言顺序和所想要达成的目标等。

2. **会议中的讨论**：到这个阶段，与会者便会针对所需讨论的议题产生出"正 / 反"两面的意见了。同意提案的与会者除了表态之外，也需说明支持提案的确切理由原因。同样的，反对提案的与会者除了反对之外，也应说明原因，并提出其他的替代办法（alternatives）。

3. **做结论**：开会的目的是就某问题讨论出解决方案，因此会议终了，主席便会根据讨论的内容让与会者达成共识。有可能是当场就有结论，也有可能需要再安排会议讨论。主席可依照实际的状况来给予指示。

　　不同的会议情境，或在会议中不同角色可以现学现用的用语，都将在以下章节内详细讨论。

会议开场／结束
Beginning / Ending the Conference

开场跟结尾

首先，我们就"主席"（chairperson）这个角色的任务来讨论。主席最主要的任务是在会议开始时做开场，介绍议题。讨论当中要串场或控制（讲题／时间等）。会议结束时要做个结束、下结论，或交代后续事项等。

主席的开场白部分，通常会包括以下几个小要点：

1. 通知开始

> 例 Shall we begin now?
> 我们可以开始了吗？

若与会者陆续进会议室，或还在讨论其他事情，主席开口通知算是提醒大家。

2. 欢迎参与

> 例 Welcome to today's meeting.
> 欢迎大家来参加今日的会议。

此"欢迎词"可视会议的正式度而调整。若是在公司内三五个熟同事开会，那么就自然地说：

> 例 Welcome, guys.
> 欢迎呀。

但若是较为正式的会议，那可以转换一下说法：

> 例 I'd like to start by welcoming everyone.
> 首先我要欢迎大家的参与。

Unit 1 会议开场/结束

3. 引出主题

> 例 Our objective today is to discuss new marketing strategies.
> 我们今天主要讨论新的营销策略。

主席要负责告知与会者开会的目的和主题。

4. 介绍议程

> 例 As you can see from the agenda, we'll discuss... first, and then...
> 如同议程上列出的，我们会先讨论……，再讨论……

除了了解会议的目的之外，与会者也应明白讨论议题的顺序。通常都是按照 agenda（议程）上的步骤来进行的。

5. 会议记录

> 例 John will be the minute-taker.
> 约翰是今天的会议记录者。

主席也要指派一位做会议记录的人。

6. 会议时间

> 例 The meeting is scheduled to finish by 3 p.m.
> 此会议会在三点前结束。

一场高效会议的重要因素之一是时间的掌握。主席要有时间掌控的概念，而非让大家随心所欲地讨论下去。

7. 正式开始

> 例 All right, now let's start with Betty.
> 好的，就请贝蒂开始发言吧。

上述的会议细节都交代清楚之后，就可以开始议程，让与会者发言了。

主席的角色就是在会议刚开始时，将这些细节对与会者说明。将上述的细节综合起来，便可得出一段完整的开场讲稿。以下便列出两个开场的参考范例。

EXERCISE

1. 以下何者〔不是〕会议主席的主要任务？
  A. 欢迎参与
  B. 介绍议程
  C. 掌控时间
  D. 帮忙倒茶

答案：D

2. 以下哪句话可能是一场会议的主席所讲的话？
  A. 请玛丽负责将今日会议结论整理出来。
  B. 您想喝咖啡、茶还是水？
  C. 我完全不同意你，你的意见对我们没帮助。
  D. 不好意思，我今天有事无法参与会议。

答案：A

Unit 1 会议开场／结束

扩充人力讨论会议

Chairperson:

Good morning, everyone. All right, so our objective today is to discuss whether we need to recruit more engineers in our technical support division. I am sorry but Vincent won't be able to join us because he is on a business trip to Japan. But he has told me that he supports the idea of increasing the size of the after-sales service team. I'd also like to hear what everyone thinks before we make a final decision. The meeting is scheduled to finish at 3 p.m., so let's make a start now. Let's start with Jack.

扩充人力讨论会议 ▶ 中译

主席：

大家早安。好的，我们今天的目的是要讨论我们是否应该招募更多工程师到技术支持部门。不好意思，文森今天无法出席，因为他去日本出差了。但他已经跟我说，他是支持这个扩大售后服务部门提案的。在做出最终决定之前，我也想听听每个人的看法。我们的会议会在三点结束，所以我们赶紧开始吧。杰克，就由你开始。

---

objective [əb'dʒektɪv]
n 目的，目标

recruit [rɪ'kruːt]
v 招募

technical ['teknɪkl]
a 技术的

division [dɪ'vɪʒn]
n 部门

increase [ɪn'kris]
v 增加

schedule ['skedʒuːl]
v 安排、订时间

163

营销策略动脑会议

Chairperson:
All right. Let's get down to business. First, thank you for attending today's meeting. I've called this meeting because I want all of our team members to brainstorm ideas for more effective marketing strategies. I've got a few ideas, and I'd like to raise them first, and then we'll go around the table and hear more ideas from each participant here. Our time is limited, so please try to be brief. Also, I've asked Linda to take minutes for the meeting. So, first of all, I'd like to talk about some traditional marketing strategies we've been using...

营销策略动脑会议 ▶ 中译

主席：
好的，来谈正事吧。首先，谢谢大家来参加今天的会议。我发起这个会议是为了让大家脑力激荡，想些更有效的营销策略。我会先讲一些我已经想到的点子，然后我们会轮流发言，听每位参与者的意见。我们时间有限，所以每人都尽量精简。另外，我已请琳达做会议记录。好，首先，我就先讲一些我们所用的传统营销方式……

---

attend [əˈtend]
v 出席

brainstorm [ˈbreɪnstɔːrm]
v 脑力激荡

effective [ɪˈfektɪv]
a 有效的

strategy [ˈstrætədʒi]
n 策略

raise [reɪz]
v 提出

participant [pɑːrˈtɪsɪpənt]
n 参与者

limited [ˈlɪmɪtɪd]
a 有限的

brief [briːf]
a 简明的

minute [ˈmɪnɪt]
n 会议记录

traditional [trəˈdɪʃənl]
a 传统的

Unit 1 会议开场 / 结束

在经过与会者积极地参与讨论之后，可能会出现场面很热烈、与会者发表意见欲罢不能的状况，但在时间有限的状况下，不管大家讨论得多热烈，主席还是有责任要做好收尾、下结论，或指派后续任务的工作。

如同开场一般，主席在会议结束下结论时，也应包括以下几个要点：

1. 要点结论

例 All right, let me summarize what we have discussed.
好的，让我归纳一下我们讨论到的要点。

会议终了，主席应整合一下与会者所讨论到的重点。

2. 行动指示

例 We've decided to take three actions.
我们已决定要采取三个行动。

会议中讨论的结果，还是要通过实际采取行动才会发挥作用。因此，主席也应分派一下后续的任务。

3. 其他议题

例 Is there any other business?
还有其他事要讨论吗？

为避免与会者还有其他事项想讨论或有遗漏的议题，主席应再询问确认一下。

4. 会后感谢

例 Thank you for your contributions. You've provided wonderful ideas.
谢谢大家的贡献。你们都提供了很棒的点子。

会后再度感谢与会者的参与。

5. 会议结束

> Wonderful. If there are no further points, we can finish here.
> 很棒，若没其他要点，那我们就结束吧。

主席收尾，告知会议结束。

将这些要素整合起来之后，便可以得到一小段完整的说词。接着请参考以下的两段范例。

EXERCISE

1. 主席开始一场会议的开场白可能是什么？
　　A. 欢迎各位来参与今日的讨论。
　　B. 大家都安静地听我说就好。
　　C. 请各位翻到课本第四百页。
　　D. 有人准备好十分钟演讲了吗？

答案：A

2. 主席可以如何结束一场会议？
　　A. 你再不讲重点，我要离开了。
　　B. 谢谢大家今天的参与。
　　C. 谁想来一杯柳橙汁？
　　D. 我想看看你家猫咪的照片。

答案：B

Unit 1 会议开场 / 结束

 发想会议

Chairperson:

All right, thank you for providing so many brilliant ideas. I wish we had more time to brainstorm new ideas, but we're running out of time. So for today, I'll just bring this point to a close. I'd like to ask Karen to type up the outline from the minutes first, and then I'll schedule another meeting to discuss which ones to implement and which ones to reject. You should have a copy of the minutes by this Friday. And I'll confirm the date and location of our next meeting by next Wednesday. Okay, thank you again for your contributions.

 发想会议 ▶ 中译

主席：

　　好的，谢谢大家提供这么多好点子。我真希望有更多时间可以多想些主意，但时间可能不够了。那么，今天我们就讨论到此。我想请凯伦先将今天讨论的架构打出来，然后我会再约另一个会议讨论哪些点子可以执行，哪些要舍弃。你们应该在本周五前会收到会议记录。我下周三之前会跟大家确认下一次会议的时间和地点。好了，再次谢谢大家今天的贡献。

---

brilliant ['brɪliənt]
a 聪慧的

brainstorm ['breɪnstɔːrm]
v 集思广益

run out of
ph 用尽，缺乏

outline ['aʊtlaɪn]
n 大纲

schedule ['skedʒuːl]
v 安排，预定

implement ['ɪmplɪmənt]
v 执行

reject [rɪ'dʒekt]
v 反对，舍弃

confirm [kən'fɜːrm]
v 确认

contribution [ˌkɑːntrɪ'bjuːʃn]
n 贡献

办公室空间更新会议

Chairperson:

All right, that basically covers everything I wanted to accomplish at this meeting. Just to summarize, we've decided to redesign our current offices rather than moving into new buildings. Linda will contact three interior designers and ask them to provide quotations for redesigning our office settings. And Jack, will you contact the bank and check how they can help us cover the expenses. Okay, so our next meeting will be on Friday, May 6th at 3 p.m. It's been a productive meeting. Thanks for your active participation this afternoon.

 办公室空间更新会议 ▶ 中译

主席：

好的，我在这会议中想讨论的事项大抵都讨论到了。整理一下，我们已经决定要重新设计我们的办公室空间，就不要搬去其他新办公大楼了。琳达会跟三家室内设计公司接洽，并请他们针对重新设计我们的办公室做报价。另外，杰克，你要去找银行，问他们可否贷款支持我们的花费。好的，我们下次会议是五月六日，周五下午三点。今天讨论很有效率。谢谢大家下午的参与。

---

provide [prə'vaɪd]
v 提供

basically ['beɪsɪkli]
ad 基本地

cover ['kʌvər]
v 涵盖

accomplish [ə'kɑːmplɪʃ]
v 达成

summarize ['sʌməraɪz]
v 总结

redesign [ˌriːdɪ'zaɪn]
v 重新设计

current ['kɜːrənt]
a 目前的

interior [ɪn'tɪriər]
a 室内的

quotation [kwoʊ'teɪʃn]
n 报价

expense [ɪk'spens]
n 花费

productive [prə'dʌktɪv]
a 生产力高的

active ['æktɪv]
a 活跃的

Unit 1 会议开场 / 结束

实用句型 例句 搭配开场范例学习句型。

1. Our objective today is to discuss whether we should [do something] (or not).

Our objective today is to discuss whether we need to recruit more engineers in our technical support division.

我们今天的目的是要讨论我们是否应该招募更多工程师到技术支持部门。

Our objective today is to discuss whether we should expand our product lines.

我们今天的目的是要讨论我们是否应该扩展产品线。

Our objective today is to discuss whether we should cut costs.

我们今天的目的是要讨论我们是否应该降低成本。

2. I've called / scheduled / conducted / held / arranged this meeting because I want to [do something].

I've called this meeting because I want all of our team members to brainstorm ideas for more effective marketing strategies.

我发起这个会议是为了让大家脑力激荡，想些更有效的营销策略。

I've scheduled this meeting because I want to discuss ways to boost team moral.

我安排这个会议是因为我想讨论提振团队士气的方法。

I've arranged this meeting because we need to discuss details of the annual marketing conference.

我安排这个会议是因为我想讨论年度营销大会的细节。

3 I wish we had more time to [do something], but we're running out of time.

I wish we had more time to brainstorm new ideas, but we're running out of time.
我真希望有更多时间可以多想些主意，但时间可能不够了。

I wish we had more time to discuss details, but we're short of time.
我希望我们有更多时间讨论细节，但时间不太够。

I wish we had more time to talk about budgets, but I am afraid we don't have time left.
我希望我们有更多时间讨论预算，但恐怕没时间了。

MEMO

主持会议
Hosting a Meeting

> 主席的任务

主席除了开场的介绍之外，另一项主要的任务是，在会议讨论当中串场、指导发言、控制时间等。当然，要有能力做到掌握议题讨论成效、鼓励引导发言和人员时间的控制，主席必须对议题本身有深入的了解。以下，我们便列出和讨论十种需要主席特别关注的情境：

1. 议程细项

虽说可能与会者每人手上都有一份议程了，主席还是可以提点一下要讨论的项目内容，比方说：Firstly..., secondly..., finally...（首先……、第二……、最后……）让与会者大概知道要讨论的要点是什么。

2. 询问意见

主席在完成开场的任务之后，接着就是要请与会者发言了。可以询问与会者意见、邀请提问或轮流发表看法等。此时可以使用实用说法来询问他人的意见：

> 例 What do you think, Lily?
> 莉莉，你认为呢？

> 例 What is your opinion about this?
> 你对此事的意见是什么？

> 例 I'd like to hear what Linda has to say.
> 我想听听琳达的说法。

> 例 Sam, would you like to comment on this?
> 山姆，你要说一下看法吗？

3. 鼓励参与

会议中通常会有些人不太发表意见，此时若主席可以稍加鼓励，邀请参与，便可以激荡出集思广益的效果。鼓励参与的说法有：

例 We haven't heard from you yet, Mark. Would you share your thoughts with us?
马克，我们还没听到你的意见。你可以分享一下看法吗？

例 Sandra, you're a bit quiet back there. I'd like to know what you think.
珊卓，你在后面有点安静。我想知道你是怎么想的。

4. 控制时间

在时间有限的状况下，要讨论很多议题，便要将时间做有效的分配。若某议题的讨论已占用过多时间，主席便要提醒与会者对时间的掌控。比方说：

例 We don't have much time. Let's just move on.
我们时间不多。我们讨论下个题目吧。

例 We agreed ten minutes per item. Now it's twenty minutes on this already. Let's move on.
我们同意每个议题讨论十分钟。现在这个议题已经讨论二十分钟了。我们讨论下个题目吧。

5. 控制主题

会议中大家讨论到后来就离题了，也是常发生的状况。此时主席也应提醒与会者会议的主要目的，并将话题拉回来。比方说：

例 I am not sure if that is relevant. Can we return to the main topic?
我不确定这是否有关。我们回到主题上可以吗？

例 This is outside the scope of our meeting. We'd better stick to the agenda please.
这超出今天会议的范围了。我们最好照着议程讨论，谢谢。

6. 临时动议

虽说会议通常会照着议程进行，还是有可能临时出现新的提议或意见。为避免有所遗漏，主席可以决定是否讨论临时动议。比方说：

例 Let's digress for a minute. I think employee training should also be considered.
我们岔开话题一下。我认为员工培训也应加以考虑。

例 It's not on the agenda, but we should also discuss the budget issue.
虽说是没在议程内，但我们也应该讨论预算事宜。

7. 询问问题

会议中与会者发表各种意见，有可能仅是提个大概，其他听者不太能确认其真正的意思。此时主席可以请发表意见者再多做些解释，比方说：

例 Linda, you mentioned market expansion. Could you elaborate on that a bit?
琳达，你提到市场扩张。你可以再详细说明一下吗？

例 Bob, can you give an example to make your point clearer?
包柏，你可以举个例让你的要点更清楚吗？

8. 做出结论

多数上班族会认为会议没效率的原因之一是"讨论了半天也没结论"。的确，开会讨论议题的目的就是要有结论，因此主席有责任提醒与会者就已讨论的内容归纳出结论（conclusion）和行动项目（action items）。就算是讨论一次尚未有决定，主席也可以提醒将议题纳入下一次会议的讨论：

例 We need more information on this issue. We'll have to leave this until the meeting next week.
针对此议题，我们需要更多信息。我们要将此事留待下周的会议讨论了。

例 We need more time to make a decision on this.
我们需要多点时间才能做决定。

9. 会议结尾

在会议告一段落之后，主席通常还会预定下一次会议的细节或提醒会议记录者发会议报告给与会者等。此时可使用的实用语句包括：

例 Our next meeting has been set on May 8th. I'll confirm the location next week.
我们下次会议设在五月八日。我下周会与大家确认会议地点。

例 Jack, please make sure you send a copy of the minutes to all participants this afternoon.
杰克，请确认下午要将会议记录发给每位与会者。

10. 问题讨论

通常会议结束之后，有可能有与会者还有其他问题要找主席讨论的。或许问题不是一时半刻就可得到解决，但也可以持保留的态度，表示要持续性地观察。

例 We'll need to monitor the problem to see if it gets worse over time.
我们要监测问题是否每况愈下。

接着，以下列出针对这十种流程设计出不同情境可能使用的对话与实用的说法。

Unit 2 主持会议

 确认议程

Chairperson: I assume all of you have a copy of the agenda, right? Good. As you can see from the agenda, there are three items that we need to discuss today.

Mary: Yes, we need to discuss new product strategies, budgets, and marketing activities.

主席：我想所有人都有一份议程了，对吗？很好。如同大家看到的，我们今天要讨论三个项目。
玛丽：是的，我们要讨论新产品策略、预算和营销活动。

assume [ə'suːm]
v 预设，假定
agenda [ə'dʒendə]
n 议程
budget ['bʌdʒɪt]
n 预算

 询问意见

Chairperson: The management is considering expanding our product lines. What are your thoughts about this, Mary?

Mary: I think it's a fantastic idea. Expanding product lines could really help sales.

主席：管理层正考虑拓展产品线。你有何看法，玛丽？
玛丽：我认为那是个很棒的主意。拓展产品线对销售有帮助。

management ['mænɪdʒmənt]
n 管理层
expand [ɪk'spænd]
v 扩大
fantastic [fæn'tæstɪk]
a 极好的

175

难以置信的实用职场英语

鼓励参与／回答

Chairperson: Linda, you're very quiet back there. Would you like to comment?

Linda: Sure. Ah, I am afraid I can't agree to that. Instead of spending money on advertising, I think we should focus more on providing excellent customer service.

主席：琳达，你在后面显得很安静。你想发表一下意见吗？
琳达：当然。恐怕我无法同意。与其花钱在广告上，我认为我们应该专注在提供良好的客户服务上。

quiet ['kwaɪət]
a 安静的
comment ['kɑːment]
v 发表意见
focus ['foukəs]
v 聚焦于
excellent ['eksələnt]
a 杰出的

控制时间

Chairperson: We're pretty short of time now. Let's move on to the next item.

Mary: Yeah, so the next item on the agenda is budgeting.

主席：我们时间不太够了。我们赶紧讨论下个议题好了。
玛丽：是呀，那议程中下个议题是预算。

pretty ['prɪti]
ad 相当，很
budget ['bʌdʒɪt]
n 预算

控制主题

Chairperson: Mary, I think you're getting side-tracked. The main question here is whether we should enter the Japanese market or not.

Mary: Oh, sorry. Let's skip the culture part for now.

主席：玛丽，我认为你离题了。我们主要的问题是是否该进入日本市场。
玛丽：不好意思。那我们现在就先跳过文化的部分好了。

side track
ph 迂回，走偏
main [meɪn]
a 主要的
culture [ˈkʌltʃər]
n 文化

 临时动议

Chairperson: Oh, Mark has raised his hand. Would you like to add something, Mark?

Mark: Yes, I just want to point out that the customer satisfaction rate is also an important indicator of our service.

主席：马克举手了。你是想要补充什么吗，马克？
马克：是的。我想要指出客户满意度也是我们服务的重要指标之一。

raise [reɪz]
v 提出，举起
satisfaction [ˌsætɪsˈfækʃn]
n 满意度
indicator [ˈɪndɪkeɪtər]
n 指示，指标

询问问题

Chairperson: Hold on, Mary. Could you explain a bit more about the "relationship building" point you just mentioned?

Mary: Sure. I mean we need to deal with clients on a more personal level.

主席：等等，玛丽。你可以针对你刚提的"关系建立"多做些解释吗？

玛丽：当然。我的意思是说我们要多跟客户建立个人化的关系。

explain [ɪkˈspleɪn]
v 解释

relationship [rɪˈleɪʃnʃɪp]
n 关系

mention [ˈmenʃn]
v 提及

deal with
ph 处理，应付

client [ˈklaɪənt]
n 客户

personal [ˈpɜːrsənl]
a 个人的

 下结论

Chairperson: All right, I think that covers everything. Are you guys ready to make a final decision?

Mary: Sure. We're all in favor of the proposal.

主席：好的，我认为该讨论的都讨论到了。大伙准备好要做最终结论了吗？

玛丽：当然。我们都支持提案。

in favor of
ph 支持

proposal [prəˈpouzl]
n 提案

Unit 2 主持会议

 会议结尾

Chairperson: All of you should have a copy of the minutes by this Friday. All right, let's call it a day.

Mary: So see you at the next meeting on July 9th!

主席：所有人在周五前都会收到一份会议记录的副本。好的，今天就讨论到这吧。
玛丽：下次会议七月九日见！

copy ['kɑ:pi]
n 副本

 问题讨论

Chairperson: Well, we're still facing the deadline problem. We'll discuss it at our next meeting.

Mary: Yeah, the problem won't be solved any time in the near future anyway.

主席：我们仍面临期限的问题。我们就下次会议再讨论。
玛丽：是呀，那问题也不是马上就可以解决的。

deadline ['dedlaɪn]
n 期限

solve [sɑ:lv]
v 解决

搭配情境对话学习句型。

1 The management is considering [doing something]. + [问意见]的句型。

The management is considering expanding our product lines. What are your thoughts about this, Mary?	管理层在考虑拓展产品线。玛丽，你对此有何想法？
The management would like to recruit more staff. What do you think, Jack?	管理层在考虑招聘更多员工。杰克，你觉得呢？
The management is planning to enter Japanese market. Do you support the idea, Linda?	管理层在规划进入日本市场。琳达，你认为可行吗？

2 [提醒时间不够]的句型。

We're pretty short of time now. Let's move on to the next item.	我们时间所剩不多了。我们赶紧讨论下个议题吧。
We're running out of time. Let's leave this item to our meeting next week.	我们时间有限。这议题就留待下周再讨论吧。
We don't have much time left. Let's continue discussing tomorrow.	我们没时间了。就明天继续讨论吧。

3 [要求他人多做解释]的句型。

Could you explain a bit more about the "relationship building" point you just mentioned?	你可以再解释一下你刚提及的"关系建立"那部分吗？
Could you explain a bit more about the budget plan?	你可以再解释一下关于预算计划吗？
Could you explain a bit more about how you want to approach the client?	你可以针对你想如何接触客户方面再讨论些细节吗？

列出议程
Agenda Listing

重要的议程

接着，不管是主席或是与会者，被通知要开会，当然最基本的议程（Agenda）便不可少。否则连最基本的讨论议程都不清楚，会议很难有效率及生产力。一份议程内要详细地将会议细节列出，包括日期、时间、地点、与会人员、角色、主题、讨论项目（条列出）、预期结果等项目。如此，让主席和与会者都有重要的指标可以遵循。否则若让与会者无目的地讨论下去，不会产生有效的结论，那就仅仅是浪费时间了。

EXERCISE

1. 以下哪一项（不属于）一份议程的内容？
  A. 与会人员
  B. 老板的生日
  C. 讨论项目
  D. 日期及地点

答案：B

2. 为什么开会前须列出议程？
  A. 工作不多，要找事做
  B. 主席有强迫症
  C. 这是一条既有的法律
  D. 让与会者有讨论方向可以遵循

答案：D

软件示范操作

Software Demonstrations		
Sun Convention Center, October 5th 2017 *All software demonstration sessions will be held in the Sun Room*		
Time	**Topic**	**Speaker**
9 a.m. — 10 a.m.	SQL Database application in Manufacturing Industry	Phil Wilson, Consultant, Data Systems Inc.
10 a.m. — 11 a.m.	Big Data Analysis — The Latest Trend	Mary Legg, Analyst, Core Analytics Inc.
11 a.m. — 11:15 a.m.	Coffee Break	
11:15 a.m. — 12:15 p.m.	Customizing ERP Solutions	Mark Black, Engineer, Best ERP Inc.
12:15 p.m. — 2 p.m.	Luncheon	

… Unit 3 列出议程

议程范本 范例一
软件示范操作 ▶ 中译

软件示范操作		
太阳会议中心，2017 年 10 月 5 日 所有的软件示范操作都会在"太阳会议室"举行		
时间	主题	演讲者
9 点～10 点	SQL 资料库在制造业的应用	菲利·威尔森，顾问，资料系统公司
10 点～11 点	大数据分析——最新趋势	玛丽·雷格，分析师，核心分析公司
11 点～11 点 15 分	中场休息	
11 点 15 分～12 点 15 分	定制化 ERP 解决方案	马克·布雷克，工程师，最佳 ERP 公司
12 点 15 分～2 点	午餐飨宴	

demonstration [ˌdemənˈstreɪʃn]
n 示范，展演

convention [kənˈvenʃn]
n 会议

session [ˈseʃn]
n 讲习会

application [ˌæplɪˈkeɪʃn]
n 应用

manufacturing [ˌmænjuˈfæktʃərɪŋ]
n 制造业

industry [ˈɪndəstri]
n 产业

consultant [kənˈsʌltənt]
n 顾问

analysis [əˈnæləsɪs]
n 分析

trend [trend]
n 趋势

customize [ˈkʌstəmaɪz]
v 定制化

solution [səˈluːʃn]
n 解决方案

luncheon [ˈlʌntʃən]
n 午餐宴会

每月营销会议

Meeting Agenda – Monthly Marketing Meeting

Meeting Information
* Date: 12/1/2017
* Time: 10 a.m. — 11:30 a.m.
* Venue: Conference Room 203, Building A
* Attendees: Paul Smith, Linda Chen, Jack Wilson, Luke Liu, Mary Worth

Action Items from Previous Meeting
* Email blasting — Paul Smith
* New advertisement design — Jack Wilson

Agenda Items
* Review results of marketing activities held in November
* Plan marketing strategies for Q1 2018
* Arrange marketing campaigns for Model 888 laptop product
* Design leads generation programs

每月营销会议 ▶ 中译

会议议程——每月营销会议

会议信息
* 日期：2017年12月1日
* 时间：上午10点到上午11点30分
* 地点：A栋大楼，203会议室
* 出席者：保罗·史密斯、琳达·陈、杰克·威尔森、路克·刘、玛丽·华滋

前期会议办理事项
* 电子邮件寄发宣传——保罗·史密斯
* 新版广告设计——杰克·威尔森

讨论事项
* 检讨11月举办营销活动的结果
* 为2018年第一季规划营销策略
* 为888型号笔记本电脑产品安排营销活动
* 设计找到潜在客户的活动

---

agenda [əˈdʒendə]
n 议程

monthly [ˈmʌnθli]
ad 每月地

venue [ˈvenjuː]
n 场地，场所

attendee [ˌætenˈdiː]
n 出席者

previous [ˈpriːviəs]
a 之前的

blasting [ˈblæstɪŋ]
n （电邮）广发

advertisement [ˌædvərˈtaɪzmənt]
n 广告

strategy [ˈstrætədʒi]
n 策略

campaign [kæmˈpeɪn]
n 活动

generation [ˌdʒenəˈreɪʃn]
n 产生

 部门会议

International Development Group
Monday, April 30, 2018, 10 a.m. — 12 noon
Digi Meeting Room

Chairperson: Linda Smith
Minute-taker: William Lin

Time	Activity	Facilitator
10 a.m. — 10:10 a.m.	Review of agenda	Linda Smith
10:10 a.m. — 10:40 a.m.	Updates on Japanese market	Helen Robert
10:40 a.m. — 11:10 a.m.	Plan for international goal	Edward Kim
11:10 a.m. — 11:40 a.m.	Set up budget plan	Vivian Good
11:40 a.m. — 12:00 noon	Demand generation events	Mark Jerry
12:00 noon	Adjourn	

议程范本 范例三 — 部门会议 ▶ 中译

国际发展事业部

2018 年 4 月 30 日,周一,上午 10 点~中午 12 点
迪吉会议室

主　　席:琳达·史密斯
会议记录:威廉·林

时间	活动	主讲
10 点~10 点 10 分	议程检视	琳达·史密斯
10 点 10 分~10 点 40 分	日本市场状况更新	海伦·罗博特
10 点 40 分~11 点 10 分	国际市场目标设定	爱德华·金
11 点 10 分~11 点 40 分	预算规划	薇薇安·古德
11 点 40 分~12 点	促成客户需求的营销活动	马克·杰瑞
12 点	会议结束	

---

development [dɪˈveləpmənt]
n 发展

chairperson [ˈtʃerpɜːrsn]
n 主席

minute-taker [ˈmɪnɪt ˈteɪkər]
n 会议记录者

facilitator [fəˈsɪlɪteɪtər]
n 讲者,主持人

update [ˌʌpˈdeɪt]
n 更新

budget [ˈbʌdʒɪt]
n 预算

demand [dɪˈmænd]
n 需求

adjourn [əˈdʒɜːrn]
v 休会,结束

执行议程
Acting on Agenda

> 同意与反对

会议的进行，在主席开场致词之后，最主要的部分便是与会人的提议讨论、表达同意意见、表达反对意见和在衡量利弊之后所做的最终决定了。如果一组团队的成员对议题看法完全一致，不需过多讨论就可以很快做出决定，那当然是很好。但通常在一个团体内，所有人的看法完全相同是不太可能的，一定或多或少有人会提出相左的意见、反对的声音。

有人提出与我们意见相左的看法并非坏事，若反对者可以提出合理的理由、事实和论述，反而会给人一种"真的是这样！我当初怎么没想到这点呢"的感觉，进而可能产生对反对者提出不同角度看法的感谢之心，"是呀！幸亏你提出不同层面的看法了，否则我恐怕错失这方面的考虑呢！"因此，在一个团队中开会，就是要听取"正／反"两方面的声音与意见才有意义，若仅一面倒大家都同意某事，不愿多运用批判思考的能力来考虑其他因素，那么便也失去"要大家开会集思广益"的作用了。

由此可见，会议中与会者所提出的"同意看法"和所提出不同角度的"反对看法"同等重要，所有参与会议的主席和与会者都要有仔细倾听他人意见、包容不同角度看法的雅量。接着我们便先讨论要表达"同意"和"不同意"分别可使用的英语表达法。

表达同意的方式

强烈语气

> 例 I am convinced that we should cut costs.
> 我确实认为我们应降低成本。

> 例 I hold the belief that we should recruit more staff.
> 我坚信我们应该招募更多员工。

Unit 4 执行议程

中等语气

例 I feel that we should invest more in R&D.
我觉得我们应该增加在研发上的投资。

例 My view is that we should expand the Japanese market.
我的看法是要拓展日本市场。

例 It seems to me that we should provide more training to employees.
我看我们应该为员工提供更多的培训。

温和语气

例 I tend to think that we should improve productivity.
我建议我们应改善生产力。

例 I would suggest that we should reduce costs.
我建议我们应该降低成本。

例 It might be better if we could postpone the meeting.
若我们将会议延后可能会更好。

表达同意，除了强弱的程度差别之外，有时也可通过声调或表情来加强呈现。若发言的人嘴上说的是"I totally agree with you."（我完全同意你）。但声音语调确是平淡的，这会让人怀疑发言的人是否真心同意？反之，若发言的人说的是"Well, I partially agree..."（嗯，我同意一部分……）。而语调上却是热心兴奋地，也会让听者摸不着头绪。

最佳的状况是，所讲出的话和语调、表情要搭配。强烈地表示同意的话，语气与表情要坚定热情。若仅是部分同意的话，声调就可以弱化，并将焦点放在"部分不同意"的要点上，说明"不同意的部分"的原因、应如何改进等。东方人生性较为保守不喜出头，因此倾向少提出自己的不同看法。但欧美人士刚好相反，他们不会因为你"完全同意"他们的意见而感到高兴。他们喜欢听取不同的声音，或参考由各种不同角度提出来的点子。因此，与欧美人士的会议中，若不是非常认同某些意见，还是勇敢地表达出不同的看法吧！

难以置信的实用职场英语

表达反对的方式

强烈语气

例 I totally disagree with you.
我完全无法同意你。

例 I can't support that idea at all.
我完全不支持那样的论点。

中等语气

例 I am against that because expanding into a new market might be risky.
我反对，因为拓展新市场可能会有风险。

例 I am afraid I can't agree to that.
恐怕我无法同意那样的点子。

例 I hold a different opinion.
我抱持不同的看法。

温和语气

例 I see what you mean, but there might be some potential problems.
我了解你的意思，但那可能有潜在风险。

例 You may be right, but you overlooked the budget issue.
你或许对，但你忽略了预算的问题。

表达反对意见"I completely disagree with you."的本身已有"负面敌对"的意味了，语气上便不要过于激动，肢体与表情上也不适宜再产生冲突感了。先前提到过，欧美人士通常不在意有人提出相反意见，因此他们听到"I don't agree with you."（我不同意你的意见。）时会认为很正常。但重点是，不要只为了反对而反对，不同意没关系，那你可以提出的具体看法、宝贵意见或解决方案又是什么呢？提出反对之后，应立即将要点放在不同意的理由、缺乏什么、可行的解决办法上，以说服他人。若提出的新意见有道理，还会让对方有"这点我还真的没想到过呢！谢谢你即时提出来。"的感觉。因此，表达反对无妨，更应该后续要提出自己认同的角度与确切做法来说服别人，这才是要点。

接着，清楚地表达自己"同意"或"不同意"的看法之后，更重要的是提出自己之所以会这么认为的"明确理由、原因、例证"来使人信服。可以说服他人的例证事实可能会是：自己的观察、和客户互动的经验、市场的调查数据、客户的意见回馈和产品的实际销售状况等。在开会之前就应该针对议题，将所需的资料准备好，以便在开会时随时可以提出明确的例证来支持自己的论点，进而说服别人同意我们。以下，我们便通过三则会议讨论的范例，来学习一下开会时"提出同意看法"和"提出反对看法"的语句使用情境。

EXERCISE

1. 以下哪项为举办会议的意义？

A. 大家工作量太少

B. 工程师有事情要宣布

C. 与会人针对议题提议，并交换意见

D. 训练自己要有接受他人批评的雅量

答案：C

2. 哪项为（不恰当）的表达反对意见的方式？

A. 我不认为扩大业务会有风险。

B. 我认为你的意见太愚蠢了。

C. 我完全无法同意你。

D. 恐怕我无法认同你的想法。

答案：B

难以置信的实用职场英语

 讨论业绩状况

Chairperson: So is everybody here? All right, everyone, thank you for
(Mr. Chen) attending our sales meeting. Mary is going to review our
recent sales performance. Over to you, Mary.

Mary: Thank you, Mr. Chen. Well, our sales performed well in
the last quarter. I think this was mainly due to the launch
of our new laptop model.

Jack: Can I come in here, please? Although Mary just
mentioned that the overall sales performance was good,
when I looked at individual sectors, I found that some
didn't do well as expected.

Chairperson: Yeah, that's a good point Jack. Take a look at this chart.
(Mr. Chen) Sales performed poorly in pharmaceuticals. Mary, could
you explain why?

Mary: Well, the pharmaceutical market is still a bit depressed,
and we haven't done good planning on our part either.

Jack: All right, I see your point. Well, later we might need to
discuss strategies to generate more sales leads in the
pharmaceutical sector.

Unit 4 执行议程

讨论业绩状况 ▶ 中译

主席（陈先生）：大家都到了吗？好的，先谢谢各位来参加今天的业务会议。玛丽会检讨一下最近的业绩状况。先交给你，玛丽。

玛丽：谢谢，陈先生。好的，上一季我们业绩表现亮眼。我认为这主要是因为推出新型号笔记本电脑的原因。

杰克：我可以插个话吗？虽然玛丽提到的整体业绩是不错的，但我在看个别领域时发现，一些领域的表现不如预期。

主席（陈先生）：是的，杰克，说得有道理。看看这张图表，医药领域方面的业绩做得不太好呀。玛丽，你可以解释一下吗？

玛丽：嗯，医药市场还有点衰颓不振，而我们自己也没有做好规划。

杰克：好的，我了解你的意思。我们之后可能要讨论一下在医药业多创造潜在销售机会的策略了。

---

review [rɪ'vjuː]
v 回顾，检视

recent ['riːsnt]
a 最近的

perform [pər'fɔːrm]
v 表现

quarter ['kwɔːrtər]
n 一季

mainly ['meɪnli]
ad 主要地

due to
ph 由于

launch [lɔːntʃ]
n 上市，发行

model ['mɑːdl]
n 型号

mention ['menʃn]
v 提及

overall [,ouvər'ɔːl]
a 整体的

individual [,ɪndɪ'vɪdʒuəl]
n 单独，个人

sector ['sektər]
n 部分，领域

expect [ɪk'spekt]
v 预期

chart [tʃɑːrt]
n 图表，表格

poorly ['pʊrli]
ad 不佳的

pharmaceutical [,fɑːrmə'suːtɪkl]
a 医药的

explain [ɪk'spleɪn]
v 解释

depressed [dɪ'prest]
a 衰颓，不振

generate ['dʒenəreɪt]
v 产生

sales leads
ph 潜在客户名单

拓展国际市场

Chairperson: All right, Mary and Jack, thank you both for joining
(Mr. Chen) the discussion today. I would like to have this meeting with you two to follow up on our conversation on the phone last Friday. As I mentioned, the management is considering to expand our international market to China, Japan, and Korea. I want to collect more feedback from you guys.

Mary: Well, I suggest we start from doing some market research. Before taking proper action, we need to understand the market, don't we?

Jack: Yeah, exactly. I totally agree with Mary. Perhaps I should start looking for a local research firm in China. What do you say, Mr. Chen?

Chairperson: Well, I guess we could do that. But the management
(Mr. Chen) would also consider how much and how long it's going to take to do the market research.

Mary: The market in China is certainly very big. How about we start from Japan?

Jack: Absolutely. I can speak some Japanese. I will talk to some local market research firms in Japan and tell them our needs.

Unit 4 执行议程

拓展国际市场 ▶ 中译

主席（陈先生）：好的，玛丽和杰克，谢谢你们今天参与讨论。我召开这个会议是想接着讨论我们上周五在电话中讨论到的议题。如同我说的，管理层在考虑要拓展国际市场到中国、日本和韩国。我想听听你们的意见。

玛丽：嗯，我建议可以先从做市场调查开始。在采取任何行动之前，我们应先了解市场，不是吗？

杰克：的确是。我同意玛丽所说的。或许我应该在中国找些当地的市场调查公司。陈先生，你觉得呢？

主席（陈先生）：也可以。但管理阶层也会考虑到做市场调查的花费和要花多久的时间。

玛丽：中国市场太大了。我们何不从日本开始做呢？

杰克：是呀！我会说日语。我可以先从日本当地找些市场调查公司开始，再跟他们讲我们的需求。

---

conversation [ˌkɑːnvərˈseɪʃn]
n 对话

collect [kəˈlekt]
v 收集

feedback [ˈfiːdbæk]
n 意见回馈

research [rɪˈsɜːrtʃ]
n 研究

proper [ˈprɑːpər]
a 恰当的

certainly [ˈsɜːrtnli]
ad 确实地

absolutely [ˈæbsəluːtli]
ad 的确地，完全地

firm [fɜːrm]
n 公司

将营销案外包

Chairperson: All right. Here is the proposal on the table whether we
(Mr. Chen) should outsource our marketing management to the Best
Marketing Group. So Mary, do you agree that we should
go ahead with the proposed outsourcing?

Mary: Absolutely. I think it's a wonderful idea. It's clear that
it'll allow us to concentrate more on our core business
instead of spending time and efforts on marcom.

Jack: Well, I can't go along with Mary. Don't you think
outsourcing causes too many communication problems?
It's not a good idea for us to give up the control of
marketing our own products.

Chairperson: What about you, Linda? What is your position on this?
(Mr. Chen)

Linda: Well, I personally support Jack's aspect. Marketing
management is essential for us, and outsourcing such an
important aspect to another company, well, is something
we have to consider very carefully.

Chairperson: All right, thank you for your feedback. We need some
(Mr. Chen) more time to think it over. I would like to collect more
information from other team members before we can
take further actions.

Unit 4 执行议程

将营销案外包 ▶ 中译

主席（陈先生）：好的。我们有个提案说要将营销管理外包给"好佳在营销集团"。玛丽，你同意我们采取外包行动吗？

玛丽：很棒呀！我认为那是个好点子。外包之后我们就可以专注在核心业务上，而非花时间和精力做市场沟通。

杰克：嗯，我和玛丽持不同看法。你不觉得外包会产生很多沟通问题吗？我们放弃营销自己产品的控制权，这听起来不好吧！

主席（陈先生）：那你认为呢，琳达？你的立场如何？

琳达：嗯，我个人支持杰克的看法。营销管理对我们来说是很重要的，且要将这么重要的事情外包给其他公司，我们的确要仔细考虑。

主席（陈先生）：好的，谢谢大家的意见。我们要再花点时间考虑。在采取更进一步行动前，我会再从其他团队成员那里收集些意见。

---

wonderful ['wʌndərfl]
a 很棒的

concentrate ['kɑːnsntreɪt]
v 集中精神，专心注意于

core [kɔːr]
a 核心的，主要的

effort ['efərt]
n 精力

cause [kɔːz]
v 引起

position [pəˈzɪʃn]
n 立场，位置

aspect ['æspekt]
n 方面，角度

197

难以置信的实用职场英语

搭配情境对话学习句型。

1 **Our [something happened] [sometime]. I think this was mainly due to [reason].**

Our sales performed well in the last quarter. I think this was mainly due to the launch of our new laptop model.

我们上季的业务表现很好。我认为这主要是因为推出新型号笔记本电脑的关系。

Our customer satisfaction rate increased in the last month. I think this was mainly due to high stability of our product.

我们上个月的客户满意度上升。我认为这主要是因为产品稳定度高的关系。

The seminar attendance rate was not as high as expected. I think this was primarily due to the bad weather condition.

研讨会的出席率不如预期。我认为这主要是因为天气状况不佳。

2 **It's clear that we should [do something] instead of [something].**

It's clear that we should concentrate more on our core business instead of spending time and efforts on marcom.

很清楚地,我们应该专注在核心业务上,而非花时间和精力在做市场沟通上。

It's clear that you should concentrate more on your school work instead of spending too much time on playing games.

很清楚地,你应该多专注在学校课业上,而非花太多时间打游戏。

It's clear that we should concentrate more on fulfilling customers' needs instead of spending resources on advertising.

很清楚地,我们应该专注在满足客户的需求上,而非把资源花在做广告上。

Unit 4 执行议程

3. Before [doing something], we need to understand [something], don't we?

Before taking proper actions, we need to understand the market, don't we?

在采取适当的行动之前,我们应该先了解市场,不是吗?

Before designing new products, we need to understand customers' demands, don't we?

在设计新产品之前,我们要先了解客户的需求,不是吗?

Before planning marketing strategies, we need to understand competitors' next move, don't we?

在规划营销策略之前,我们要先了解竞争对手的下一个动态,不是吗?

MEMO

Unit 5 讨论技巧
Discussion Skills

> 注意及避免

根据前几个章节所讨论的，读者应对"会议"的大概架构和可使用的"英语表达法"有初步的概念了。

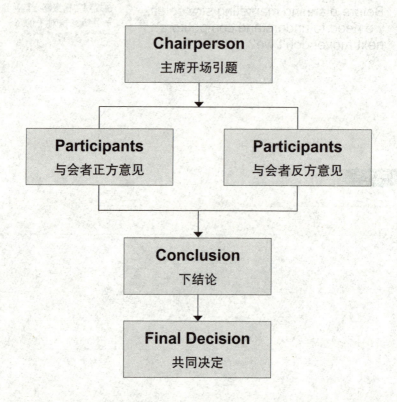

在主要的架构之下，会议中可能还是会有一些需应付的小状况或插曲，比如说：请人重述意见、接受他人说服、提出额外看法等状况。针对额外的会议状况与实用说法，补充在下列"情境对话"部分。

最后，我们将一些重要的会议讨论技巧做个归纳整理，让大家更明确地了解会议的"DOs & DON'Ts"（应注意的和该避免的事项）有哪些。

主席：

DOs

- 会议前应确认所有会议相关的"人／事／时／地／物"，包括部门人员、讨论议题、时间、地点、所需设备等。
- 会议开始时要先跟与会者说明议题、前因后果和所预期的会议成效。
- 会议中要尽量邀请所有与会者多发言多参与，以发挥更多集思广益的效果。
- 对会议的时间、人员、议题等，要做有效的掌控，确保每人都有机会在时间内发言。
- 会议后要做出有效的结论。

DON'Ts

- 对"人／事／时／地／物"等细节掌握不够。若跟其他部门人员开会，有可能不知道与会者姓名时，便需要准备名牌，或开会时间稍长，便有可能要准备茶点等。
- 独自占着麦克风发言，而忽略其他与会者的感受。
- 若有人发言离题，或占用过多时间发言，主席没有导回正题。
- 会议后没有下结论，或下的结论过于轻率。

与会者：

DOs

- 会议前先详阅议程，并将所需的报告、图表、文件都准备好。
- 表达意见时音量要够大、表达语句要够清楚，以利其他与会者明白意思。
- 支持其他与会者的看法，若遇到不同角度的意见，也应予以尊重，从不同角度学习。
- 仔细听其他与会者的发言，不要一直存有先入为主的观念，而忽视其他人所说的话。

- 表达意见要明确、直接、有道理。使用明确有实际例证的事实，取代模棱两可的概念。
- 努力与他人达成共识。共识是要对团队或公司有利的，而非对个人本身有利的。

DON'Ts

- 会议中途玩手机、接电话或被其他杂事打断。
- 过多插话，一直打断别人发表意见。
- 对其他与会者所提的意见，依个人喜好判定。
- 表达时使用艰涩难懂的用字或文绉绉的句子。
- 假装了解其实不明白的事物。不探究事情前因后果，仅凭自己片面的感觉做决定。
- 会议尚未结束，没有听到结论之前就先行离席。

同意观点

Chairperson: I think we should allocate more budget on marketing activities.

Sherry: I entirely agree with you.

 同意观点 ▶ 中译

主席：我认为我们应该分配更多预算在营销活动上。

雪莉：我完全同意。

 同意观点 ▶ 其他说法

- **You're definitely right.**
  你完全说对了。
- **That's exactly what we should do next.**
  那的确是我们接下来该做的。
- **That's just how I feel.**
  我也是这么觉得。
- **Exactly.**
  的确是。
- **That makes a lot of sense, doesn't it?**
  那很有道理，对吧！

---

allocate ['æləkeɪt]
v 分配

budget ['bʌdʒɪt]
n 预算

marketing ['mɑːrkɪtɪŋ]
n 营销

activity [æk'tɪvəti]
n 活动

entirely [ɪn'taɪərli]
ad 全然地

definitely ['defɪnətli]
ad 确实地

exactly [ɪɡ'zæktli]
ad 的确地

make sense
ph 有道理

难以置信的实用职场英语

 情境对话 场景二 不同意观点

Chairperson: Perhaps we should outsource our IT services?

Jack: I totally disagree.

 情境对话 场景二 不同意观点 ▶ 中译

主席：或许我们应该把信息科技服务管理外包？

杰克：我完全不同意。

 实用例句 不同意观点 ▶ 其他说法

- **It's not realistic at all.**
  这完全不切实际呀。
- **You must be kidding.**
  你是在开玩笑吧。
- **I am afraid I can't agree with that.**
  恐怕我无法同意你。
- **Well, I don't think it's a good idea.**
  我不认为那是个好主意。
- **I am against the proposal.**
  我反对此提案。

---

perhaps [pərˈhæps]
ad 或许，可能

outsource [ˈaʊtsɔːrs]
v 外包

disagree [ˌdɪsəˈgriː]
v 反对，不同意

realistic [ˌriːəˈlɪstɪk]
a 实际的

kidding [ˈkɪdɪŋ]
a （口）开玩笑

proposal [prəˈpoʊzl]
n 提案，建议书

Unit 5 讨论技巧

 提案

Chairperson: Well, we need to choose an endorser for this product. What do you think?

Mary: I've got a suggestion. We could use a movie star. I think it's worth trying.

 提案 ▶ 中译

主席：我们要为产品找个代言人。你认为呢？

玛丽：我有个建议。我们可以找电影明星。我认为值得一试。

 提案 ▶ 其他说法

- Perhaps we should use a famous movie star.
  或许我们该找个有名的电影明星。
- It's just an idea, but what about using a famous movie star?
  我提个意见，何不就找个有名的影星呢？
- Shall we try to look at this from customers' perspective?
  我们要试着从客户的角度看吗？
- Well, one possibility is to use a famous movie star.
  有个可能性是找个有名的影星。
- What if we use a famous movie star to catch people's attention?
  若我们找个有名的影星来吸引人们的目光呢？

---

endorser [ɪnˈdɔːsə]
n 背书人，代言人

suggestion [səˈdʒestʃən]
n 建议

worth [wɜːθ]
a 值得的

famous [ˈfeɪməs]
a 有名的

perspective [pərˈspektɪv]
n 观点，洞察力

possibility [ˌpɑːsəˈbɪləti]
n 可能性

catch attention
ph 引起……注意

难以置信的实用职场英语

 接受提议

Chairperson: The management would like to hire more sales representatives.

Mary: That's not a bad idea at all.

 接受提议 ▶ 中译

主席：管理层想聘雇更多销售代表。
玛丽：那也是个不错的主意。

 接受提议 ▶ 其他说法

- **Yes, I think it would really work.**
  是的，我认为那可行。
- **A brilliant idea.**
  聪明的点子。
- **Okay, let's go ahead and do that.**
  好的，就照这么办吧。
- **Good suggestion.**
  好建议。
- **Yes, that might be worth trying.**
  是的，值得一试。

---

hire ['haɪər]
v 雇用

representative
[ˌrɛprɪˈzɛntətɪv]
n 代表

at all
ph 一点都不

brilliant ['brɪliənt]
a 聪明的

go ahead
ph 先走

suggestion [səˈdʒɛstʃən]
n 建议

worth [wɜːrθ]
a 值得

try [traɪ]
v 试试看

不接受提议

Chairperson: The management is considering to expand our market internationally.

Mary: Well, sounds good. But to be honest, I could see a few problems with that.

不接受提议 ▶ 中译

主席：管理层在考虑要拓展国际市场。

玛丽：听起来不错。但老实讲，我认为会有些问题。

不接受提议 ▶ 其他说法

- **I am not too sure about that.**
  我可不太确定。

- **Do you really think it would work?**
  你真的认为那会成功？

- **Frankly speaking, I don't think it's a good strategy.**
  坦白说，我不认为那是个好策略。

- **I suggest you think twice.**
  我建议你再多想一下。

- **There might be some risks.**
  可能会有些风险。

---

consider [kən'sɪdər]
v 考虑

expand [ɪk'spænd]
v 扩大

honest ['ɑːnɪst]
a 诚实的

frankly ['fræŋkli]
ad 坦白地

strategy ['strætədʒi]
n 策略

think twice
ph 多想一下

难以置信的实用职场英语

 确认意思

Chairperson: The numbers for this month are not pretty at all.

Mary: Let me make sure I understand what you mean. You're saying that the sales performance is not good, right?

 确认意思 ▶ 中译

主席：本月的数字不太好看。

玛丽：让我确认一下你的意思。你的意思是说业绩表现不佳，没错吧？

 确认意思 ▶ 其他说法

- Let me get this straight. You mean the sales performance is not good enough, right?
  让我确认一下。你是指业绩不够好，是吗？

- What do you mean by that?
  你是什么意思？

- I don't exactly understand what you mean when you say "numbers are not pretty."
  我不是很了解你说"数字不漂亮"是什么意思。

- I am not quite sure what you mean by "numbers are not pretty."
  我不是很确定你说"数字不漂亮"是什么意思。

- Sorry, I am not with you. Could you please explain what you mean?
  不好意思，我不了解你的意思。你可以多解释一下吗？

---

performance [pərˈfɔːrməns]
n 表现

straight [streɪt]
ad 直接地

sale [seɪl]
n 出售

exactly [ɪgˈzæktli]
ad 确切地

quite [kwaɪt]
ad 完全地

explain [ɪkˈspleɪn]
v 解释

Unit 5 讨论技巧

 打断 / 插话

Chairperson: All right, so now let's move on to our next item on the agenda.

Mary: Hold on a second. Let me just confirm one point.

 打断 / 插话 ▶ 中译

主席：好的，那我们现在就讨论议程上的下个议题吧。
玛丽：等一下。我要先确认一个要点。

 打断 / 插话 ▶ 其他说法

- **Can I just come in here?**
  我可以插个话吗？

- **Mr. Chen, I would just like to add one point.**
  陈先生，我想先补充一点。

- **Excuse me for interrupting, but can I add a few words on that topic?**
  不好意思我要打断一下，我可以针对那主题再做些补充吗？

- **Please allow me to raise some different perspectives.**
  请容我提出一些不同角度的看法。

- **I think you're forgetting one important point: expenses.**
  我认为你忘了一个要点——开支。

---

item [ˈaɪtəm]
n 条款；项目

agenda [əˈdʒendə]
n 代议事项

confirm [kənˈfɜːrm]
v 确认

point [pɔɪnt]
n 要点

interrupt [ˌɪntəˈrʌpt]
v 打断

topic [ˈtɑːpɪk]
n 主题

perspective [pərˈspektɪv]
n 角度

expense [ɪkˈspens]
n 开支

采取行动

Chairperson: All right. We've all agreed that we will establish a new branch office in Japan.

Mary: Let's just go ahead and do it.

采取行动 ▶ 中译

主席：好的。我们都同意要在日本开设分公司了。

玛丽：就这么办吧！

采取行动 ▶ 其他说法

- **Let's make it happen.** 让我们实现它吧。
- **Let's take action.** 采取行动吧。
- **I've got faith in you.** 我对你有信心。
- **We'll do our best.** 我们会尽全力的。
- **We're going to succeed.** 我们一定会成功。

---

agree [əˈgriː]
v 同意

establish [ɪˈstæblɪʃ]
v 建立

branch [bræntʃ]
n 分部

action [ˈækʃn]
n 行动

faith [feɪθ]
n 信念，信任

succeed [səkˈsiːd]
v 成功

Unit 5 讨论技巧

 搭配情境对话学习句型。

1 I think we should allocate more [something] on [something].

I think we should allocate more budgets on marketing activities.
我认为我们应该分配更多预算在营销活动上。

I think we should allocate more time on internal training.
我认为我们应该分配更多时间在内部培训上。

I think we should allocate more resources on customer service.
我认为我们应该分配更多资源在客户服务上。

2 We need to choose a [someone] for [something].

We need to choose an endoser for this product.
我们要为此产品选个代言人。

We need to choose a leader for this project.
我们要为此项目选个专案领导人。

We need to choose a chairperson for this meeting.
我们要为此会议选个主席。

3 We've all agreed that we will [do something].

We've all agreed that we will establish a new branch office in Japan.
我们都同意要在日本开设个分公司了。

We've all agreed that we will plan more marketing activities.
我们都同意要规划多点营销活动了。

We've all agreed that we will design more innovative products in order to meet customers' needs.
我们都同意要多设计创新的产品以满足客户的需求。

211

难以置信的实用职场英语

MEMO

Negotiation
协商及谈判

前言

　　商业环境中，企业通常不会在市场上单打独斗，而是常有机会跟其他公司建立买卖关系，或合作关系等。但每个公司背景、产品、立场都不同，要建立起良好的商务合作的关系，就要靠持续地沟通协调，以达到双方各自想要的目标。比方说，各个企业在商务协商谈判中在意的点各不相同，可能是 good payment terms（好的付款条件）、good relationship（良好的关系）、short delivery time（快速交货）、discount on large quantities（大量购买的折扣）、product quality（产品品质）、flexibility（灵活弹性）等。因而通常在商务谈判中，企业在乎的也多跟这些主题有关。

　　接着，跟厂商或商业伙伴在协商谈判的过程当中，有可能花了很多时间讨论，到最后却不了了之，或甚至于没有结论。为了避免这种情况，且要让协商谈判有效率又有效果，那么就要设定 "S.M.A.R.T." 的目标了。

　　Specific（明确）：协商谈判前要设立好明确的目标，看自己确实想要达成的目的是什么。

　　Measurable（可衡量性）：目标要是可衡量的，而非模棱两可的。

　　Achievable（可达成的）：设定的目标要实际可达成，不要不切实际，强人所难。

　　Relevant（恰当，有意义的）：谈判结果仅对一方有好处并无意义，重要的是让双方达到 win-win（双赢）的局面。

　　Timed（时效性）：要设定确切可行的时间点，而非遥遥无期地拖延下去。

　　由此可看出，要和背景／需求不同的企业协商谈判，要顾及的要点的确不少，也真是一门学问。本章节将就谈判的准备、切入要点与协商技巧做深入的讨论。

Unit 1 谈判礼仪
Negotiation Etiquette

> 做好万全准备

如同前言提到的，商务类的协商谈判，对象通常会是与自己公司背景、产品、需求等各不相同的企业。要说服对方认同我们的观点，达成自己想要的目的，还要让对方也获得利益，达到双赢的局面，可以说这些是要有技巧的，而非像在夜市买东西讨价还价一般。

而此处所说的"技巧"并非在协商谈判当中才展现就好，而是指从协商会议前的铺垫、联络与准备就开始的。一流的企业在协商会议前的准备，从秘书打电话联络、议程的规划、与会人的邀请、书面资料的准备和电子邮件的往来，就可以让人感觉到其专业程度。

因此，此章节的"谈判礼仪"便包括从"约定会议""协商前的准备""对方背景了解"，到"见面寒暄""开场介绍"与"导入正题"等各细节。

1. 约定会议

要约协商谈判总会有个目的。因此，会前可先说明目的，便可以用这些说法开头：

- 例 The reason for this meeting is...
  开此会议的目的是……

- 例 We need to / We require...
  我们要做……

- 例 We want / We would like...
  我们想要……

- 例 It's time for us to discuss...
  我们是时候讨论一下……了

Unit 1 谈判礼仪

例 We call this meeting because...
我们召开这一次会议是因为……

2. 协商前准备

此处的准备包括 Who、What、When、Where、Why、How，即谁会参与、何时、何地、讨论主题、议程、如何进行等项目，都要明确并详细地列出。

3. 双方背景了解

所谓"知己知彼，百战百胜"，协商谈判的目的不仅是达到自己的目的，也要顾及对方的利益。因此，协商前先做点功课，了解对方的背景，在意的点，想达成的目标是什么……这有助于协商的进行。若对对方的立场不太明白，可以直接询问：

例 For you, this is a good opportunity to...
对您来说，这是个……的机会……

例 The most important point for you is payment terms, right?
付款条件对您是最重要的点，对吗？

例 As I understand it, you would like higher discount. Is that correct?
据我了解，您想要更高折扣。没错吗？

4. 见面寒暄

不要误认为协商会议就是要对立或是剑拔弩张，而应该从刚开始就建立起和谐的气氛。问候对方：

例 How are you doing? / How's everything?
您好吗？

或

例 Would you like some coffee or tea?
要喝点咖啡或茶吗？

都可以先创造出缓和平静的氛围。

5. 开场介绍

协商会议的一开始就导入话题，会让人感到摸不着头绪。最好是先铺垫一下讨论的议题与顺序。

6. 导入正题

寒暄与介绍讨论主题后，接着便可进入正题的讨论。一开始可以先表明自己的立场，比方说：

> 例 In our opinion...
> 我们是认为……

> 例 We are confident that...
> 我们很确定……

> 例 From our point of view...
> 由我们的观点来看……

> 例 We are of the opinion that...
> 我们的看法是说……

以下，就让我们将上述六个要点带入情境之中吧。

Unit 1 谈判礼仪

 约定时间

Mr. Thomson: Hello, Thomson Corp. Sam Thomson speaking.

Mary: Hello, Mr. Thomson. This is Mary Ford from Best Software here. From our sales record, we've learned that your software subscription will expire this year. It's time for us to discuss the renewal issue.

Mr. Thomson: I see. We're considering renewing our software agreement as well. But we will sign the new agreement only if you agree to lower the technical support fee.

Mary: Well, I suggest we arrange a meeting to discuss this matter.

Mr. Thomson: Sure. How about this Friday, 13th of March, at 10 a.m.? Is that okay with you?

Mary: Yes, that should be fine. We'll meet in your boardroom at Thomson Corp. I'll also send you the agenda via email as soon as possible.

 约定时间 ▶ 中译

汤姆森先生：你好，汤姆森企业。我是山姆·汤姆森。

玛　　丽：汤姆森先生，你好。我是最佳软件公司的玛丽·福特。从我们的销售记录看来，贵公司的软件订购今年就要到期了。现在是要讨论续订的事宜。

汤姆森先生：我了解。我们也正在考虑要更新软件合约的事呢。但你们要调降技术支持费用，我们才会续约。

玛　　丽：嗯，我建议我们约个时间讨论此事。

汤姆森先生：当然。那本周五，三月十三日的早上十点可以吗？你方便吗？

玛　　丽：可以的，那时间方便。我们就在汤姆森企业的会议室见了。我会尽早将议程用电邮寄给您。

---

subscription [səbˈskrɪpʃn]
n 订购，订阅

renewal [rɪˈnuːəl]
n 更新，续订

agreement [əˈɡriːmənt]
n 合约

boardroom [ˈbɔːrdruːm]
n 会议室

agenda [əˈdʒendə]
n 议程

协商准备

Mary: We've got an agreement negotiation coming up this Friday, Jack. Would you like to sit in to see the procedure?

Jack: Sure. I am available this Friday. So who's the other party in this negotiation?

Mary: It's one of our clients, Thomson Corp. They want to renegotiate the software agreement that we initially signed with them.

Jack: I see. But what kind of deal are they looking for?

Mary: Well, the client mentioned that they will only extend their agreement with us if we agree to lower the technical support fee.

Jack: Right. So the agenda of the negotiation will then include bargaining on the new fee.

 协商准备 ▶ 中译

玛丽：杰克，我们本周五有个合约协商会。你想进来听，顺便看一下流程吗？
杰克：当然好呀。我本周五有空。那是要跟谁谈呢？
玛丽：那是我们的一个客户，汤姆森企业。他们想再次跟我们谈原本签的软件合约。
杰克：了解。但他们想要什么样的条件呢？
玛丽：客户说若我们同意降低技术支持的价格，他们才会跟我们续约。
杰克：是的。所以协商的议程就会包括讨论新的价格事宜了。

---

negotiation [nɪˌgouʃi'eɪʃn]
n 谈判，协商

procedure [prə'siːdʒər]
n 程序，步骤

initially [ɪ'nɪʃəli]
ad 最初地，原始地

extend [ɪk'stend]
v 延长，续约

bargain ['bɑːrgən]
v 讨价还价

Unit 1 谈判礼仪

 背景了解

Jack: Mary, in order to prepare for the negotiation with Thomson Corp., I'd like to learn more about Mr. Thomson and his company.

Mary: Sure. What would you like to know then?

Jack: Has Thomson Corp. had a long-term relationship with our company?

Mary: Well, originally Ms. Anderson was their account manager and sold them 100 software licenses three years ago.

Jack: Wow, 100 software licenses, that's a big order! I certainly expect the negotiation to turn out as a win-win settlement.

Mary: Yeah, and Mr. Thomson is a pretty rational and articulate manager. I am sure we can come up with a mutually beneficial agreement.

 背景了解 ▶ 中译

杰克：玛丽，为了要准备跟汤姆森企业的协商，我想多了解关于汤姆森先生和他公司的事。

玛丽：当然。你想知道些什么呢？

杰克：汤姆森企业跟我们有长久的业务关系了吗？

玛丽：最初安德森小姐是他们的业务经理，也是在三年前卖给他们一百个软件授权。

杰克：哇，一百个软件授权，那可是个大单呢！我真的很希望协商是个双赢的局面。

玛丽：是呀，汤姆森先生是个很理性又能言善辩的经理。我很确定我们可以讨论出双方都互利的合约。

---

originally [əˈrɪdʒənəli]
ad 起初，最初

settlement [ˈsetlmənt]
n 解决，处理

rational [ˈræʃnəl]
a 理性的

articulate [ɑːrˈtɪkjulɪt]
a 能说善道，说话清楚的

mutually [ˈmjuːtʃuəli]
ad 双方地，互相地

见面寒暄

Mary: Good morning, Mr. Thomson. I am glad to see you again. May I introduce Jack Black, a colleague of mine? Jack will be sitting in on our negotiations.

Mr. Thomson: I am delighted to meet you, Jack.

Jack: Nice to meet you, Mr. Thomson.

Mr. Thomson: Thank you. So, Mary, will Ms. Anderson also participate in our agreement negotiation today?

Mary: Well, Ms. Anderson left sales already, so now I am in charge of your software agreement extension.

Jack: All right, since we've got a full agenda today, why don't we get started now?

见面寒暄 ▶ 中译

玛　　丽：汤姆森先生，早安。很高兴又见到您。容我跟你介绍我的一位同事，杰克·布来克。杰克会加入我们的讨论。

汤姆森先生：很高兴见到你，杰克。

杰　　克：很高兴见到你，汤姆森先生。

汤姆森先生：谢谢。那么，玛丽，安德森小姐会加入我们今天的讨论吗？

玛　　丽：这个，安德森小姐离职了，因此现在由我来负责您的软件合约。

杰　　克：好的，我们今天要讨论的议程颇多，现在就开始吧？

---

introduce [ˌɪntrəˈduːs]
v 介绍

colleague [ˈkɑːliːɡ]
n 同事

delighted [dɪˈlaɪtɪd]
a 高兴的，欣喜的

participate [pɑːrˈtɪsɪpeɪt]
v 参与

in charge of
ph 负责

开场介绍

Mary:	All right. To begin with, I think we should first agree on a procedure for our negotiation.
Mr. Thomson:	Certainly. Let's just run through the procedure.
Mary:	Sure. So we could begin by outlining our position, and then we could hear your presentation. After that we'll have a question and answer session. How does that sound?
Mr. Thomson:	That sounds fine. We've drawn up some agreement terms of our own. So after we both run through the proposals, we can just focus on the areas that we don't agree on.
Mary:	That's right. Oh, and Jack is also sitting in on our negotiations, so he'll take minutes for us.
Jack:	Okay, no problem.

开场介绍 ▶ 中译

玛　　丽：	好的。一开始，我想我们应该先同意今天协商的顺序。
汤姆森先生：	当然。让我们了解一下步骤。
玛　　丽：	好的。那我们可以以表明我们的立场开始，然后听听您的意见。之后再来个问答讨论时间。这样听起来如何？
汤姆森先生：	可以呀。我们自己也拟定了一些合约的条件。那在听了双方的提议之后，我们可以专注讨论分歧之处。
玛　　丽：	是的。对了，杰克也参与今天的讨论，所以他会帮我们做会议记录。
杰　　克：	可以，没问题。

---

certainly [ˈsɜːrtnli]
ad 当然，的确

outline [ˈaʊtlaɪn]
v 概括，列大纲

presentation [ˌpriːzenˈteɪʃn]
n 表达，陈述，简报

term [tɜːrm]
n 条款，条件

proposal [prəˈpoʊzl]
n 提议，提案

难以置信的实用职场英语

 导入正题

Mary: Mr. Thomson, as you may also be aware, your 3-year software licenses will expire this year. We believe it's time for us to discuss the license extension issue.

Mr. Thomson: Basically, we'd like to extend the software licenses, but we think the technical support fee is too high.

Mary: I understand your viewpoint, Mr. Thomson. But let me raise a question, please. How important is technical support to you?

Mr. Thomson: Well, technical support is certainly very essential for us as our manufacturing processes must be continuously running, and we cannot tolerate any application downtime.

Mary: Exactly, and I'd like to stress that Best Software is the only software company on the market who provides clients with 24/7 technical support service. And in order to offer our customers excellent service, we recruit only talented and experienced engineers. We do all these for your benefit.

Mr. Thomson: I understand, but there are other factors needing consideration on our end as well.

 导入正题 ▶ 中译

玛　　丽：汤姆森先生，您可能也已经知道，贵公司三年软件授权将在今年到期了。我们相信现在就是要讨论授权续约的事宜了。

汤姆森先生：基本上我们会延续软件授权，但我们觉得技术支持费用实在太高了。

玛　　丽：我明白您的观点，汤姆森先生。但请先容许我问个问题。技术支持对贵公司有多重要呢？

汤姆森先生：嗯，技术支持是很重要，因为我们的生产过程是持续运作的，且我们无法忍受任何软件的停止运作。

玛　　丽：的确，且我要强调"最佳软件"是市面上唯一一家会提供全年无休的技术支持服务的软件公司。而为了给客户提供最好的服务，我们只请有能力且有经验的工程师。我们做这些都是为了您好。

汤姆森先生：我了解，但我们还是有其他因素要考量。

---

viewpoint ['vju:pɔɪnt]
n 观点，看法

essential [ɪ'senʃl]
a 重要的，关键的

tolerate ['tɔ:ləreɪt]
v 忍受，忍耐

talented ['tæləntɪd]
a 有才能的

consideration [kən,sɪdə'reɪʃn]
n 考虑，深思

Unit 1 谈判礼仪

搭配情境对话学习句型。

1

They will [only do something] if we agree to [do something].

They will only extend their agreement with us if we agree to lower the technical support fee.	若我们同意降低技术支持的价格，他们才会跟我们续约。
They will place the order if we agree to offer higher discount.	若我们同意给多点折扣，他们才会下订单。
The vendor will offer 8.5% discount if we guarantee an order of 1,000 units.	若我们保证订一千件，供应商才会给 8.5% 的折扣。

2

[Someone] is a pretty [adj.] and [adj.] manager.

Mr. Thomson is a pretty rational and articulate manager.	汤姆森先生是一个颇理性和能言善辩的经理。
Ms. Anderson is a rather polite and flexible negotiator.	安德森小姐是一个颇礼貌和懂得变通的谈判者。
Bob is a very firm and competent executive.	鲍勃是个很坚定又能力强的执行者。

3

I'd like to stress that [company] is the only [company] on the market who provide clients with [some unique benefits].

I'd like to stress that Best Software is the only software company on the market who provides clients with 24/7 technical support services.	我要强调"最佳软件"是市面上唯一一家会提供全年无休的技术支援服务的软件公司。
I'd like to stress that Good Taste is the only restaurant on the market who provides clients with fresh seafood from Japan.	我要强调"好味道餐厅"是市面上唯一一家提供日本新鲜海鲜的餐厅。
I'd like to stress that ABC Company is the only publisher on the market who provides online eBooks for clients to download.	我要强调"ABC 公司"是市面上唯一一家会提供线上电子书给客户下载的出版商。

Unit 2 切入重点
Cut to The Point

> 协商阶段

经过见面、问候寒暄、了解谈判目的之后,接着登场的就是主题谈判协商的重头戏了。一般来说,主题谈判协商包括六个阶段,以下便针对此六个主要阶段做详细的说明。

1. 确认双方立场(Clarifying positions)

本章开始时讨论过,商业协商的谈判目的不是得到自己想要的结果就好,而是要尽力达到双方都满意的结果,各取所需,也就是"双赢局面"(win-win situation)。因此,谈判刚开始就要确定双方的立场是什么。除了讲述自己的需求之外,也要仔细聆听了解对方的要求与立场。

2. 提议与回应(Making and responding to proposals)

双方立场都确定了之后,就可以进入协商了。当然,一方会针对讨论议题先提出可行的方案,看对方是否可以接受。若对方认为不合理或还需再讨论,那么便会再提出其他的方案来做回应。如此往返讨论,目的就是达到一个双方都可接受的方案。

3. 讨价还价(Bargaining)

通常来说,协商谈判的双方不会很快地马上接受对方所提的条件(若是马上无异议地接受所有条件,那也不用谈判了)。因此,待双方各自提出可行或可接受的方案之后,接下来可能就是要有一番讨价还价的过程了。通常在此时,最常听到的,也最实用的句型会是"We might be willing to [do something] if you can [do something]."(我们可能会……若你先……),以提出交换条件。

Unit 2 切入重点

4. 解决冲突（Handling conflicts）

若所交换的条件可以接受那最好，若不能接受的话，双方便有 conflicts（冲突），sticking points（胶着状态）产生了。这样的时候，双方继续坚持己见可能只会延宕谈判协商的时效。为了让协商更顺利地进行，双方便应专注于解决胶着的障碍点，并且认识到要"达到双方都满意的结果"比"仅一方大获全胜"更重要。因此，为了解决冲突，各退一步（make concessions）是有必要的。

5. 谈判尾声（Closing a negotiation）

解决了冲突或胶着点之后，若双方都认为条件可以接受，那便进入谈判的尾声了。但有可能还需收集更多信息才能决定，或是还需要安排下一次谈判会议让更高层的主管介入，如此，便应先做初步结论，并安排下一次的会议，例如：We'll prepare a summary and let's meet again next Monday to review this.（我们会先归纳要点，下周一再讨论。）

6. 达成协议（Reaching an agreement）

谈判的最终目的就是双方达成协议，并建立良好的合作关系，因此会后别忘了说声："We have a good deal and we look forward to our long-term relationship."（我们达成共识了，很期待我们的长远合作。）

以下我们便通过贴近现实的情境对话来了解上述六个协商阶段的实际应用吧。

确认双方立场

Mary: Ok, so Mr. Thomson, if I may summarize your company's position, you would require us to keep technical support fees low.

Mr. Thomson: That's correct. As you can see from the sales record, we've been deploying your software solutions since 2012. As a loyal client, we deserve more discount on technical support, don't we?

Mary: We are sympathetic to the position your company is in. However, providing excellent technical support is our major priority. If we cut costs on recruiting exceptional staff, we're afraid that the service standard will be hard to maintain.

Mr. Thomson: Well, effective support is equally essential to us. We still need to work on this to find a happy medium.

确认双方立场 ▶ 中译

玛　　丽：好的，那么汤姆森先生，让我归纳一下贵公司的立场，您想要我们降低技术支持的费用。

汤姆森先生：是的。你可以查一下销售记录，我们自2012年就开始部署贵公司的软件解决方案了。身为忠诚的客户，我们应该有更优惠的技术支持计划，不是吗？

玛　　丽：我们非常了解贵公司的立场。但是，提供优良的技术支持是我们公司的首要任务。若我们降低招聘的成本，就难以找到优秀的员工，恐怕服务的水准就无法维持了。

汤姆森先生：嗯，有效率的技术支持对我们也是很重要的。我们要讨论找出个折中的办法。

---

summarize ['sʌməraɪz]
v 归纳，做结论

deploy [dɪ'plɔɪ]
v 部署

sympathetic [ˌsɪmpə'θetɪk]
a 同情的，共鸣的

exceptional [ɪk'sepʃənl]
a 优秀的，非凡的

happy medium
ph 折中的办法

Unit 2 切入重点

提议与回应

Mary: Well, there are a couple of ways that we could work together. From our point of view, we maintain an excellent support reputation by offering clients 24/7 support service. In addition, we're confident that our service representatives are experienced and professional.

Mr. Thomson: I agree with that. But most importantly, it seems to me that all software applications are running so smoothly that we seldom require serious technical support from you. Thus we prefer not to allocate too much budget on it.

Mary: I understand your point, Mr. Thomson. Then may I suggest an alternative proposal. We would propose that, instead of paying for 24/7 support services, you just go with the normal support plan. You could call our service hotline during normal business hours, which are from 9 a.m. to 6 p.m., thus you could reduce the support budget by two-thirds.

Mr. Thomson: That sounds reasonable, so we might be able to do that.

提议与回应 ▶ 中译

玛　　丽：好的，我们可以朝其他几个方向进行。我们的看法是，我们就是因为提供客户全天候的技术支持服务才会得到优良的服务名声。另外，我们也对服务代表的经验和专业深具信心。

汤姆森先生：我同意。但最重要的是，在我看来所有的软件应用程序都使用得很顺畅，我们很少需要使用到技术服务来解决重大问题。因此，我们不希望分配太多预算在这上面。

玛　　丽：我了解您的立场，汤姆森先生。那我提个不同的建议。我们想说您可以不要买全天候无休的技术服务，而只要购买一般的服务计划就好。您可以在一般上班时间内，也就是早上九点到下午六点打支持热线。这样您就可以减少三分之二技术支持的支出了。

汤姆森先生：听起来合理，我们倒是可以这样做。

---

maintain [meɪnˈteɪn]
v 保持，维系

representative [ˌreprɪˈzentətɪv]
n 代表

seldom [ˈseldəm]
ad 鲜少

alternative [ɔːlˈtɜːrnətɪv]
n 额外选择，其他选项

reasonable [ˈriːznəbl]
a 合理的，可行的

227

讨价还价

Mary: All right. Mr. Thomson, so this time you will renew existing software licenses and purchase 40 more new licenses. Is that correct?

Mr. Thomson: That's right, well, what kind of discount could you give us on this new order? The thing is that we plan to increase 40 more licenses for now, and if the price is right, we'll probably be throwing some more business your way.

Mary: I see. How about this, if you order over 70 licenses, I can offer you a 10% discount off the list price. Why don't you consider combining your purchases for the future projects? Then we can discuss a bigger discount.

Mr. Thomson: We can agree to place an order of 75 new licenses on condition that you could provide us a 15% discount.

Mary: You drive a hard bargain!

Mr. Thomson: As you know, we're expanding rapidly, and we'll be placing more software orders in the future.

讨价还价 ▶ 中译

玛　　丽：好的，汤姆森先生，所以目前您就是要更新现有的软件授权，还要购买四十个新授权。这样没错吗？

汤姆森先生：是的，那么你们可以提供多少折扣呢？重点是，我们现在会先买四十个授权，要是价格可以的话，我们可能还会再追加。

玛　　丽：了解。那这样好了，若您订超过七十个授权，我就给您定价的九折。您何不考虑多买些授权，以便今后的项目使用呢？这样我们才能提供较高的折扣。

汤姆森先生：若你可以提供我们八五折的优惠，我们同意买七十五个授权。

玛　　丽：您真会杀价。

汤姆森先生：你知道的，我们拓展很快，未来还会再下更多软件订单的。

---

existing [ɪgˈzɪstɪŋ]
a 现有的

purchase [ˈpɜːrtʃəs]
v 购买

combine [kəmˈbaɪn]
v 合并

bargain [ˈbɑːrgən]
n 讲价

expand [ɪkˈspænd]
v 拓展，扩大

Unit 2 切入重点

解决冲突

Mary: Well, Mr. Thomson, after consulting with my managers, offering a 15% discount would probably be a bit tough for us. You see... competition is really fierce, and our margins are already very tight.

Mr. Thomson: Actually, we're also evaluating other software vendors.

Mary: Let me put it this way please, Mr. Thomson. You've been our long-term client and we truly value your business. I suggest that we provide you with a 10% discount and offer to install and configure the software applications for free. Do you think it's reasonable?

Mr. Thomson: To be honest, our technicians are experienced enough to install the applications by themselves already.

Mary: All right, the major obstacle at the moment seems to be the price issue.

Mr. Thomson: Let's take a break and hopefully we can come back with fresh ideas later.

解决冲突 ▶ 中译

玛　　丽：汤姆森先生，跟我们经理询问过后，要给八五折优惠对我们来说可能有点困难。您知道的……竞争非常激烈，我们利润已经很薄了。

汤姆森先生：事实上，我们也在评估其他的软件厂商。

玛　　丽：我这么说吧，汤姆森先生。您是我们长期的客户，我们很珍惜贵公司的生意。我们提供九折折扣，另外免费帮您安装和设定软件应用程序。这样您认为合理吗？

汤姆森先生：老实说，我们的工程师都有足够的经验可以自己安装。

玛　　丽：那么，目前最大的问题就是在价格问题上了。

汤姆森先生：让我们先休息一下，希望等会回来之后有些新的想法。

---

tough [tʌf]
a 困难的

fierce [fɪrs]
a 激烈的

evaluate [ɪˈvæljueɪt]
v 评估

configure [kənˈfɪɡjɚ]
v 设定

obstacle [ˈɑ:bstəkl]
n 障碍

 229

难以置信的实用职场英语

 谈判尾声

Mary: All right, Mr. Thomson, let's try something different. As per my understanding, you are expanding and recruiting more employees, right?

Mr. Thomson: You're right. 15 new employees will be on board next month.

Mary: As they will need to familiarize themselves with operation of the software package, we could offer a 6-hour training session for free. How does that sound?

Mr. Thomson: Sounds not bad. I think I can accept that.

Mary: Okay, great. So you will place a new order for 75 new licenses. We offer 10% discount off the list price and a free 6-hour training session. All right. It's a deal. I'll have the paperwork sent over later this week.

Mr. Thomson: Please also send me a detailed agreement by email.

 谈判尾声 ▶ 中译

玛　　丽：好的，汤姆森先生，让我们试试其他的办法。根据我的了解，贵公司在拓展且要招募更多员工，对吗？

汤姆森先生：是的。十五位新员工下个月就会上任了。

玛　　丽：那他们就要熟悉如何操作软件，我们可以提供六小时免费的培训。这样是否可以？

汤姆森先生：听起来不错。我想我们可以接受。

玛　　丽：好的，太棒了。那么您会下七十五个授权的订单。我们会提供定价的九折优惠和六小时免费培训。好的，就这么办了。我本周稍晚会将书面资料寄给您。

汤姆森先生：请另外用电子邮件将详细合约寄给我。

---

understanding
[ˌʌndərˈstændɪŋ]
n 理解

on board
ph 上任

familiarize [fəˈmɪliəraɪz]
v 使熟悉

operation [ˌɑːpəˈreɪʃn]
n 操作

detailed [ˈdiːteɪld]
a 详细的

Unit 2 切入重点

 达成协议

Mary: Thank you for your patience today, Mr. Thomson. I really appreciate it.

Mr. Thomson: No problem, Mary. We are generally satisfied with your software products and services.

Mary: I am really glad to hear that. So would you like to go through the points we discussed once more?

Mr. Thomson: No, not really. Please put all items we've discussed today into a written proposal. I'll sign the license renewal document if there is no problem.

Mary: Sure. We're confident that we can provide you with top quality products at a good value.

Mr. Thomson: I am happy that we eventually made progress to reach a final agreement.

 达成协议 ▶ 中译

玛　　丽：谢谢您的耐心，汤姆森先生。我很感激。
汤姆森先生：没问题，玛丽。我们对你们的产品和服务整体来说是很满意的。
玛　　丽：很高兴听到您这么说。那么您想要再看一下我们刚讨论的要点吗？
汤姆森先生：不用了。请将刚讨论的要点写成书面提案。若没问题我就签授权续约书。
玛　　丽：当然。我们对给您提供超值的好产品是深具信心的。
汤姆森先生：我很高兴最终可以达成协议了。

---

patience ['peɪʃns]
n 耐心

appreciate [ə'pri:ʃieɪt]
v 感激

written ['rɪtn]
a 书面的

eventually [ɪ'ventʃuəli]
ad 最终地

progress ['prɑ:gres]
n 进步，进展

搭配情境对话学习句型。

1. [Doing something] is our major priority / main consideration / primary issue.

Providing excellent technical support is our major priority.	提供优良的技术支持是我们的首要任务。
Fulfilling customers' demands is our main consideration.	满足客户的需求是我们的主要考量。
Resolving the sticking points is the primary issue.	解决胶着状态是主要议题。

2. We can agree to [do something] on condition that you [do something].

We can agree to place an order of 75 new licenses on condition that you could provide us a 15% discount.	若你们可以提供八五折优惠，我们就同意下七十五个新授权的订单。
We can agree to offer 5% discount on condition that your company would guarantee an order of 1,000 units.	若贵公司保证下一千件的订单，我们就同意帮您打九五折。
We can agree to place the order by the end of this month on condition that you reduce the price to $50 per unit.	若你降低价格至每件五十美元，那我们就愿意这个月月底前下订单。

3. The major obstacle at the moment seems to be the [something].

The major obstacle at the moment seems to be the price issue.	目前主要的障碍似乎是价格问题。
The major obstacle at the moment seems to be the payment terms.	目前主要的障碍似乎是付款条件。
The major obstacle at the moment seems to be the delivery date.	目前主要的障碍似乎是交货日期。

协商技巧
Negotiation Skills

> **轻松愉快**

讨论到谈判协商，不免会让人联想到"立场对峙""剑拔弩张"或"气氛严肃"等负面的状况。但事实上，商务协商会议的主要目的是双方合谐的合作，不必把谈判协商场面搞得很火爆或陷入僵局。为达到谈判协商的目的，双方都可有坚定的立场，也应有认知要腾出一些让步的空间，若再搭配使用温和并具说服力的遣词表达方式，便较有机会较轻松愉快地达成谈判协商的目标了。在此单元，我们便来了解一下在谈判协商会议的各个环节中，可以使用的更具说服力的明确表达方式。

> **EXERCISE**

1. 什么是谈判协商的主要目的？
  A. 帮助双方和谐地合作
  B. 与协商者立场对峙
  C. 为了垄断整个利益
  D. 提高客户满意度

答案：A

2. 什么方法有助于提高协商成功的概率？
  A. 解决冲突
  B. 占人便宜
  C. 花钱消灾
  D. 唯唯诺诺

答案：A

难以置信的实用职场英语

 解释立场与讲述原因

- Our aim is to get better conditions and payment terms as well as a discount on large quantities.

  我们的目标是谈到更好的付款条件和大量购买的折扣。

- We're an established company. The Hi-Tech Company was founded in 1998 and has always had a great reputation for product quality.

  我们是信誉卓著的公司。高科技公司创办于1998年并在产品品质上颇负盛名。

- In such a competitive market, price is certainly an important issue for us.

  在如此竞争激烈的市场,价格对我们来说是很重要的一环。

- I think we need to discuss pricing policy first, because we often need to cut prices dramatically to promote sales.

  我认为我们应该先讨论定价策略,因我们常需要通过大幅降价来促销产品。

- The initial offer you provided indicated an average production time of 10 working days for the IC chipsets. That seems to be a bit long for us.

  你们最初提供的IC芯片的平均制造时间是十个工作日。这对我们来说有点久。

- As a matter of fact, there are a number of vendors now contacting us for partnership opportunities.

  事实上,现在有一些供应商跟我们接触想建立合作关系。

---

reputation [ˌrepjuˈteɪʃn]
n 名声

competitive [kəmˈpetətɪv]
a 竞争的

dramatically [drəˈmætɪkli]
ad 引人注目地

indicate [ˈɪndɪkeɪt]
v 指出

production [prəˈdʌkʃn]
n 生产,制造

提议与回应

- **There is also the possibility of shipping the goods at intervals. What do you think of that?**
  另一个可能是分批交货。您认为如何?

- **Would it help if we offered to install and configure software applications for free?**
  若我们提供免费安装和设定软件程序会有帮助吗?

- **If we agreed to offer a 5% discount, would you find it more acceptable?**
  若我们同意给九五折优惠,您可以接受吗?

- **Would it be possible if you shorten the lead time?**
  请你们缩短交货时间是否有可能?

- **Well, I think it's a fair suggestion.**
  嗯,我认为这建议还算公平。

- **Unfortunately, a further discount of 2% cannot be done because of the high price for raw materials at the moment.**
  很不幸地,要多给九八折的优惠是不太可能的,因为现在原物料价格很高。

---

interval [ˈɪntɚvl]
n 间隔,区间

configure [kənˈfɪɡjɚ]
v 设定,安装

acceptable [əkˈsɛptəbl]
a 可接受的

fair [fɛr]
a 公平的

unfortunately [ʌnˈfɔːrtʃənətli]
ad 不幸地

提出反对意见

- **Frankly speaking, we're not satisfied with the offer on the table.**
  坦白说，我们对这提议不是很满意。

- **I am hoping for better prices. Honestly, I am not sure whether I can get my other team members to agree to this.**
  我是希望有更好的价格。老实讲，我不确定我是否有办法说服其他同仁同意此事。

- **I am afraid we couldn't agree to that. But why not offer us free training courses?**
  恐怕我们无法同意。那你们何不提供我们免费训练课程呢？

- **I am sorry, but offering a 20% discount is just out of the question.**
  很抱歉，但要给八折优惠是不可能的了。

- **I don't have the authority to give approval on that.**
  我没同意此事的权限。

- **The requirements seem a bit strict for us.**
  这些要求对我们来说太严苛了。

---

frankly ['fræŋkli]
ad 坦白地

out of the question
ph 谈不上，不可能

authority [ə'θɔːrəti]
n 权力

approval [ə'pruːvl]
n 批准，赞同

strict [strɪkt]
a 严格的

讨价还价

- **We'd be willing to offer a 20% discount provided that your company would guarantee an order of 1,000 units.**
  若贵公司保证会下一千件订单,那么我们愿意提供八折优惠。

- **Have you considered ordering 10 more copies? Then you could save on shipping.**
  您考虑多订十套吗?那就可以免运费。

- **Give us a better discount, and we will place a larger order.**
  给我们多点折扣,我们才会下较大的订单。

- **How about this... we can provide free delivery if you are willing to accept a later shipment.**
  那这样好了……若您愿意接受延期,我们就免费送货。

- **Well, providing free training might be possible, but we want something in return.**
  嗯,提供免费训练是可行的,但我们也想得到点回馈。

- **Sorry, but free shipping might be hard for us to do.**
  很抱歉,但免运费我们可能难以办到。

---

guarantee [ˌɡærənˈtiː]
v 保证,担保

consider [kənˈsɪdər]
v 思考

order [ˈɔːrdər]
n 订单

accept [əkˈsept]
v 接受

possible [ˈpɑːsəbl]
a 可能的

解决胶着点

- **I suggest we come back to the delivery issue after we've discussed payment terms.**
  我建议先讨论付款条件之后再回过头来讨论交货问题。

- **How about we look at this from another perspective?**
  我们何不从不同角度来看这件事？

- **Then please tell us what you think to be the reasonable solution.**
  那请告知我们您认为怎样才是合理的解决方案。

- **I hope you can appreciate our difficulties with this please.**
  我希望您可以了解我们这方面的难处。

- **If you have to be firm on the price, we'll have to look elsewhere.**
  若你们在价格点上如此坚持，那我们就必须要再找找其他厂商了。

- **Let's take a 15-minute break to have both sides cool down.**
  让我们休息十五分钟，让双方可以冷静一下。

---

delivery [dɪˈlɪvəri]
n 运送，寄送

perspective [pərˈspɛktɪv]
n 角度，洞察力

reasonable [ˈriːznəbl]
a 合理的

appreciate [əˈpriːʃieɪt]
v 领会，感受，感激

elsewhere [ˌɛlsˈwɛr]
ad 向别处，往其他地方

结论与收尾

实用句子 例句六

- It seems that we've found some common ground.
  看起来我们找出一些共通点了。

- Would you be willing to sign the license extension agreement right now?
  您现在愿意签延长授权合约吗？

- I am glad that we both are satisfied with this decision.
  我很高兴我们双方都满意这个决定。

- Mr. Jones, I'd like to confirm that you also agree to these terms, right?
  琼斯先生，我想确认您也同意这些条件，没错吧？

- I'll get all the discussed items in writing.
  我会将所有讨论过的事项写下来。

- Can I have your word that the after-sales software training will be provided free?
  你可以保证售后软件训练是免费提供的吗？

---

common ground ph 共同点

satisfied ['sætɪsfaɪd] a 满意的

confirm [kən'fɜːrm] v 确认

discuss [dɪ'skʌs] v 讨论

provide [prə'vaɪd] v 提供

难以置信的实用职场英语

搭配实用句子学习句型。

1

In such a competitive market, [something] is certainly an essential / important / vital / crucial / critical / significant issue for us.

In such a competitive market, price is certainly a critical issue for us.	在这样一个竞争激烈的市场上，价格对我们来说的确是很重要的。
In such a competitive market, product quality is certainly a vital issue for us.	在这样一个竞争激烈的市场上，产品品质对我们来说的确是很重要的。
In such a competitive market, customer service is certainly a significant issue for us.	在这样一个竞争激烈的市场上，客户服务对我们来说的确是很重要的。

2

I am sorry, but [doing something] is just out of the question.

I am sorry, but offering a 20% discount is just out of the question.	很抱歉，但是要给八折优惠是不太可能的。
I am sorry, but providing free shipping is just out of the question.	很抱歉，但是要免运费是不太可能的。
I am sorry, but arranging ten free training sessions is just out of the question.	很抱歉，但是安排十场免费训练课程是不太可能的。

3

Can I have your word that [something will happen]?

Can I have your word that the after-sales software training will be provided free?	你可以保证售后软件训练是免费提供的吗？
Can I have your word that the new contract will take effect on March 1st?	你可以确保新合约会自三月一日开始就生效吗？
Can I have your word that my pay will increase by 10% starting from next month?	你可以答应我自下个月开始，我的薪水就调高一成吗？

附录
Appendix

常用商务英语缩写、单词表

- 实义动词列表
- 常用商务英语缩写
- 全书单词总整理

实义动词列表

四百七十个 Action Verbs 列表

在撰写简历的时候使用动词都是有诀窍的。在英语中使用实义动词（Action Verbs）会让你的态度显得积极有活力。以下整理出了四百七十个动词，按照字母分列。通常简历会使用的动词都是已做过的事情，因此本附录直接提供这些动词的过去式。

A

abolished 废除，废止
abridged 缩短
absorbed 全神贯注
accelerated 促进
accommodated 使适应
accomplished 完成，实现
accumulated 累积，积聚
achieved 完成，实现
acquired 取得，获得
acted 做事，行动
adapted 使适合
adopted 采纳
addressed 称呼
adjusted 调节
administered 管理，掌管
advanced 推进，促进
advertised 为……宣传
advised 忠告
advocated 主张
affirmed 断言，申明
alerted 警觉
aligned 校准
allocated 分派，分配
altered 改变
analyzed 分析
anticipated 预期，期望
applied 申请
appointed 任命，指派
appraised 估计
approached 接近，靠近
approved 批准
arranged 筹备
articulated 明确有力地表达
aspired 向往
assembled 集合，召集
assessed 估算
assigned 分配，分派
assisted 协助
assured 担保
attained 达到
attended 出席
authored 著作，编写
authorized 授权给
automated （使）自动化
avoided 避开
awarded 授予

Unit 1 实义动词列表

B

balanced 平衡
benchmarked 基准
benefited 利益，好处
blended 混合，混杂
blocked 阻挡
boosted 促进
branded 印……商标于
broadened 变宽，变阔
budgeted 预算
built 建筑

C

calculated 计算
capitalized 用大写书写
captured 俘虏
carved 雕刻
categorized 将……分类
catalogued 登记，记载
cautioned 告诫
certified 证明
chaired 主持（会议）
challenged 挑战
championed 支持
charted 绘制……的图表
circulated 循环
clarified 澄清，阐明
classified 将……分类
cleared 清除，收拾
coached 训练
collaborated 合作
collected 收集
combined 结合
commanded 命令
commended 称赞
commenced 开始

commissioned 委任，委托
communicated 沟通，交流（想法）
compared 比较
compiled 编辑
completed 完成
complied 顺从，遵从
composed 构成
computed 估算
concentrated 集中
conceptualized 概念化
conducted 引导
configured 安装
confirmed 确定
confronted 面临
connected 连接，联结
conserved 保存，保护
considered 考虑
consolidated 联合，统一
constructed 建造，构成
consulted 商议，磋商
contacted 接触
continued 继续
contracted 缩小
contributed 捐献，捐助
controlled 控制
converted 转变，变换
conveyed 传达
convinced 说服
cooperated 合作
coordinated 协调，调节
corrected 改正，矫正
corresponded 符合，一致
counseled 商议
created 创造
critiqued 评论
cultivated 耕种，耕作

附 Appendix 常用商务英语缩写、单词表

243

customized 定做

D

dealt 处理
debated 辩论，争论
debugged 除去故障
decided 决定
decreased 减少
dedicated 献出
defined 解释
delivered 投递，运送
demonstrated 证明
deployed 展开
described 描写
designed 设计
detailed 详细说明
detected 发现，察觉
determined 决定
developed 发展
devised 策划
diagnosed 诊断
differentiated 区别，区分
directed 指挥
discovered 发现
discussed 讨论
dispatched 派遣
displayed 展出
distinguished 区别，识别
distributed 分配
diversified 多样化
divided 划分
documented 为……提供文件
doubled 加倍
drafted 设计草稿
drove 驾驶

E

earned 赚得
economized 节约，节省
edited 编辑，校订
educated 教育
effected 造成
elaborated 精心制作
elected 选举
eliminated 排除，消除
embraced 拥抱
emphasized 强调
empowered 授权，准许
enabled 使能够
encouraged 鼓励
enforced 实施，执行
engaged 吸引
engineered 设计，建造
enhanced 提高
enlisted 征募（兵）
enriched 使富裕
enrolled 注册
ensured 保证
entertained 招待，款待
equipped 配备
established 建立
estimated 估计
evaluated 评价
examined 检查，细查
exceeded 超过，胜过
executed 实施
exercised 锻炼
exhibited 展览
expanded 扩大
experienced 经历，经验
experimented 试验
explained 解释

Unit 1 实义动词列表

explored 探测
expressed 表达，陈述
extended 延长
extracted 抽出

F

facilitated 促进，帮助
familiarized 使熟悉
filed 归档
finalized 完成，结束
financed 筹措资金
fine tuned 协调
focused 聚焦
followed 跟随
forecasted 预测，预报
formed 形成，构成
formulated 使公式化
forwarded 发送，递送
fostered 养育
founded 创办，成立
framed 建造
fulfilled 达到（目的）
functioned as 起作用
furnished 装备

G

gained 获得
gathered 收集
generated 造成，引起
governed 管理
graduated 毕业
guaranteed 保证，担保
guided 带领

H

halved 将……对分

handled 操作
heightened 增高
hosted 主持
hypothesized 假设，假定

I

identified 识别
illustrated 阐明
implemented 履行
imported 进口
improved 改进，改善
improvised 即兴表演
included 包括
incorporated 包含
increased 增大，增加
indicated 指示，指出
influenced 影响，作用
informed 通知
initiated 创始
innovated 创新
inspected 检查，审查
inspired 鼓舞，激励
installed 安装
instructed 指示，命令
integrated 使结合
intensified 加强，增强
interacted 互动
interpreted 口译
interviewed 面谈，面试
invented 发明，创造
invested 投资
investigated 调查，研究
involved 牵涉
isolated 孤立

J

joined 参加
judged 审判
justified 辩解

L

launched 发射
lectured 授课
leveraged 手段，影响力
linked 连接
loaded 装载
located 定居

M

maintained 维持，保持
managed 管理，经营
manipulated 运用
manufactured（大量）制造
marketed 销售
mastered 制服，统治
maximized 达到最大值
measured 测量
memorized 记住，背熟
mentored 指导
merged（公司）合并
minimized 缩到最小值
mobilized 动员
moderated 使和缓
modified 更改，修改
monitored 监控
motivated 给……动机
multiplied 增加

N

navigated 航行
negotiated 谈判，协商

neutralized 抵销
nominated 提名
notified 通知，告知

O

observed 观察
obtained 获得
offered 给予，提供
operated 运作
optimized 持乐观态度
organized 组织
originated 发源
outlined 概述，略述
outperformed 胜过
overcame 战胜，克服
oversaw 眺望

P

packaged 包装
packed 捆扎，包装
participated 参加，参与
partnered 使合作
penetrated 穿过，刺入
perceived 察觉，感知
perfected 使完美
performed 履行，执行
persuaded 说服
photographed 拍照
pinpointed 使突出，使显著
pioneered 先驱
placed 放置，安置
planned 计划
praised 赞扬
predicted 预言
prepared 准备
prescribed 规定，指定

Unit 1 实义动词列表

presented 赠送，呈献
prevented 防止，预防
prioritized 按优先顺序处理
processed 处理，办理
produced 生产
profiled 描出……的轮廓
programmed 安排节目
progressed 前进
projected 计划
promoted 晋升
proofread 校对
proposed 提议，建议
protected 保护，防护
proved 证明
provided 提供
publicized 宣传
purchased 购买
pursued 追赶，追踪

Q

quadrupled 成为四倍
qualified 使合格
quantified 使量化
queried 询问
questioned 讯问

R

raised 举起，抬起，提出
ranked 排列
rated 评价
reached 抵达，到达
realized 领悟，了解
rearranged 重新整理
reasoned 推论
received 收到，接到
recognized 认出

recommended 推荐
reconstructed 重建
recorded 记载，记录
recovered 恢复
recruited 征募
redesigned 重新设计
redirected 使改方向
reduced 减少
referred 论及，谈到
refocused 重调焦距
registered 登记，注册
regulated 管理
rehabilitated 复兴
reinforced 增援
related 涉及
released 释放，解放
relieved 缓和
remained 剩下，余留
remodeled 改建
renewed 更新
reorganized 改组
repaired 修理，修补
replaced 归还
replied 答复
replicated 折叠
reported 报告
represented 描绘
reproduced 繁殖
requested 要求，请求
researched 研究
reserved 保存
resolved 解决，解答
responded 回应
restored 恢复
restructured 重建
retrieved 收回

247

reversed 倒转
reviewed 再检查
revised 修订
revitalized 使复兴
revolutionized 彻底改革
rewarded 报答

S

scanned 审视
scheduled 安排，预定
screened 掩蔽
sculptured 雕刻
searched 搜查
secured 保卫
seized 抓住
selected 选择
separated 分隔
sequenced 连续
served 服务
settled 安放，安顿
shared 分享
sharpened 削尖
shipped 船运
shortened 缩短
simplified 简化，精简
simulated 假装
sketched 速写
smoothed 使光滑
solidified 变坚固
solved 解决
sourced 获得
sparked 发动，点燃
spearheaded 当……的先锋
specialized 专攻
specified 详细指明
sponsored 主办

spurred 鞭策
standardized 使标准化
stimulated 刺激
streamlined 使现代化
strengthened 加强
stretched 伸直，伸出
structured 构造
submitted 屈从
succeeded 成功
suggested 建议，提议
summarized 总结
supervised 监督，管理
supplied 供给
supported 支撑
surpassed 胜过，优于
surveyed 俯视
symbolized 象征
synthesized 综合，合成
systemized 组织化

T

tabulated 列表显示
tackled 交涉
targeted 把……作为目标
tasted 尝，辨
teamed 合作
tempered 锻炼
tended 走向
terminated 结束，终止
testified 作证
topped 向高处升
totaled 合计
traced 跟踪
tracked 跟踪，追踪
trained 训练
transcribed 誊写

Unit 1 实义动词列表

transformed 改变，改观
transitioned 过渡
translated 翻译
transmitted 传送，传达
trimmed 修剪，修整
tripled 使成三倍
troubleshoot 故障处理

U

uncovered 揭露
underlined 在……下划线
underscored 在……下划线
undertook 试图
unearthed 发掘，掘出
unified 统一，联合
united 统一
updated 更新
upgraded 提高
urged 催促
utilized 利用

V

validated 使有效
verbalized 唠叨
verified 证明
visualized 想象
voiced 声音，嗓子
volunteered 自愿服务

W

weathered 风化，褪色
weighed 称起来（重量）
widened 加宽
withstood 反抗

Y

yielded 出产

Unit 2 常用商务英语缩写

缩写	全称	中文
@	at	在
#	number	数量，号码
a/c	account	账号
approx.	approximately	大概，约略
asap	as soon as possible	尽快
asst.	assistant	助理
Attn:	attention	注意
Bcc	blind copies to	密件副本
biz	business	生意
bkgd	background	背景
Bldg	building	大楼
BTW	by the way	顺道一提
Cc	copies	副本
CEO	chief executive officer	首席执行官
CFO	chief financial officer	首席财务官
CIO	chief information officer	首席信息官
CKO	chief knowledge officer	首席知识官
Co.	company	公司
COD	cash on delivery	货到付款
Conf. room	conference room	会议室
COO	chief operating officer	首席营运官
Corp.	corporation	企业，公司
CPA	certified public accountant	注册会计师
CTO	chief technology officer	首席技术官
CV	curriculum vitae	个人简历
Dept.	department	部门
Div.	division	部门
e.g.	for example	举例
edu	education	教育
etc.	and so on	等等
FAQ	frequently asked questions	常见问题

Unit 2 常用商务英语缩写

FYI	for your information	给您参考信息
FYR	for your reference	供您参考
gov	government	政府
HQ	headquarters	总部
i.e.	that is	意即
impt	important	重要客户
Inc.	Incorporated	组成公司
info	information	信息
Int'l	international	国际的
JD	job description	职责
L/C	letter of credit	信用状
Ltd.	limited company	有限公司
max	maximum	最大值
MBA	master of business administration	工商管理学硕士
mgr	manager	经理
N/A	not available	不可用 / 不适用
NG	no good	不佳
No.	number	号码
p.s.	postscript	附言
pls	please	请
PO	purchase order	订单
prep	preparation	准备
Q	quarter	一季，季度
Q&A	question and answer	问题讨论
R&D	research and development	研发
Re.	regarding	关于
rep	representative	代表
Rgds	regards	问候，致意
sub	subject	主题
Tks	thanks	谢谢
Typo	type error	打错字
VIP	very important person	重要客户
vs.	versus	对抗
w/	with	有
w/out	without	没有

Unit 3 全书单词总整理

简历面试

ability n 能力
- talent n 天才

accomplish v 达成
- accomplishment n 成就

accountable a 可信赖的
- reliable a 可靠的

achievement n 成就
- achieve v 达成

acumen n 聪明才智
- insight n 洞察力

additional a 额外的
- addition n 附加物

administration n 管理
- administer v 管理，施用

application n 申请
- applicant n 申请者

appreciate v 感激
- appreciation n 感谢，感激

appropriate a 恰当的
- agreeable a 宜人的

articulate a 能说会道的
- articulate v 清楚地表达

attached a 附件的
- attachment n 附件

attitude n 态度
- position n 立场

attribute n 特质，属性
- attribute v 归因于

avoid v 避免
- shun v 躲开

background n 背景
- experience n 经历

behave v 行为举动
- behavior n 行为

belief n 信念
- believe v 相信

brilliant a 聪明的
- brilliance n 才智，聪明

broaden v 拓展
- widen v 放宽，加大

candidate n 候选人
- applicant n 申请者

capable a 有能力的
- capability n 能力

capacity n 能力
- capable a 有能力的

career n 职涯
- vocation n 行业

characteristic n 特质，特性
- quality n 品质

clever a 聪慧的
- cleverly ad 聪明地

comfort n 安逸，舒适
- comfortable a 舒服的

commitment n 承诺
- commit v 允诺

competence n 能力
- competent a 能力强的

Unit 3 全书单词总整理

competitive a 有竞争力的
- competition n 竞争

compliment n 恭维，赞赏
- complimentary a 赞许

concentrate v 专心于
- concentration n 注意力

considerable a 大量的
- considerably ad 相当地，非常地

constant a 固定的，不变的
- constantly ad 一致地

contribute v 贡献
- contribution n 贡献

convey v 运送，搬运
- conveyable a 可传达的

convince v 说服
- convincing a 具说服力的

create v 创造
- creative a 有创意的

cultivate v 耕耘
- cultivation n 耕种

curious a 好奇的
- curiosity n 好奇心

customer n 顾客
- client n 客户

decisive a 决定性的
- decision n 决定

decline v 回绝
- turn down v 拒绝

department n 部门
- division n 处，课

designer n 设计师
- design v 设计

determination n 决心
- determine v 决定

develop v 发展
- development n 发展

devote v 将……奉献给
- devotion n 奉献

differentiate v 差异化
- difference n 不同点

dignity n 庄严，尊贵
- dignitary n 显贵，要人

distinct a 有区别的
- distinction n 区别

distinguish v 分辨
- distinguishing a 引人注目的

diverse a 不同的，互异的
- diversify v 使多样化

earnings n 获利，收益
- earn v 赚取

education n 教育
- educated a 有教养的

emphasize v 强调
- emphasis n 强调，着重

ensure v 保证，担保
- assure v 向……保证

enthusiastic a 热心的
- enthusiasm n 热情，热忱

entrepreneur n 创业家
- entrepreneurial a 创业者的

estimate v 估算
- estimation n 价值，判断

evolution n 发展，进化
- evolutionary a 渐进的，发展的

example n 例子
- exemplify v 例示

excerpt v 摘录，引用
- extract v 选用

expectation n 期望
- expect v 预期

experience n 经验
- experience v 体验，经历

expertise n 专门能力
- **expert** n 专家

extend v 延伸，扩大
- **extension** n 延长，伸展

failure n 失败
- **fail** v 失败

faithful a 有信心的
- **faith** n 信仰

faultless a 完美的
- **fault** n 缺陷

fixed a 固定的
- **fix** v 使固定

foremost a 最前的，最先的
- **chief** a 为首的

freelancer n 自由作家
- **freelance** v 当自由作家

fulfilling a 能实现个人理想的
- **fulfill** v 满足

generate v 产生，发生
- **produce** v 生产，出产

graduation n 毕业
- **graduate** v 毕业

harmful a 有害的
- **harm** v 伤害

headhunter n 猎头公司
- **headhunt** v 物色

immigrant n 移民
- **immigration** n 移居

impact v 产生影响
- **impaction** n 压满，压紧

impression n 印象
- **impressive** a 印象深的

income n 收入
- **salary** n 薪资

industry n 产业
- **industrial** a 产业的

instinct n 本能，天性
- **instinctive** a 本能的

intelligence n 聪明才智
- **intelligent** a 聪明的

interest n 利息
- **interest** v 感兴趣

interview n 面谈
- **interviewer** n 面试官

intuition n 直觉
- **intuitional** a 直觉的

involve v 涉入，牵涉
- **involvement** n 涉及程度

leadership n 领导能力
- **lead** v 领导

logical a 有逻辑的
- **logic** n 逻辑

manpower n 劳动力
- **human resources** n 人力资源

mediocre a 普通的，平凡的
- **mediocrity** n 平凡，平庸

memorize v 记忆
- **memory** n 记忆

milestone n 里程碑
- **landmark** n 地标

multinational a 跨国的
- **global** a 全球的

multiple a 复合的，多样的
- **multiple** n 倍数

noticeably ad 引人注意地
- **notice** v 注意

offer v 提供
- **provide** v 提供

opening n 开始
- **opening** a 开头的

option n 选项
- **opt** v 选择

Unit 3 全书单词总整理

overcome v 克服
  beat v 打败，胜出
ownership n 拥有权
  owner n 持有人，物主
passion n 热情
  passionate a 有热情的
perceive v 觉察，感知
  perceivable a 可感知的
perk n 津贴，补助
  bonus n 奖金
physical a 身体上的
  physically ad 身体地
platform n 平台
  podium n 讲台
powerful a 有影响力的
  power n 能力
premier a 首位的，首要的
  premier n 首相
pressure n 压力
  stress n 压力，紧张
primary a 主要的，重要的
  elementary a 初级的
productivity n 生产力
  produce v 生产，产出
progress v 前进，进行
  progressive a 先进的，革新的
promotion n 推广，升迁
  promote v 提升，促销
prosperity n 繁荣，兴旺
  prosperous a 兴旺的，繁荣的
qualification n 资格
  qualified a 有资格的
raise v 升起
  boost v 举，抬
realistic a 现实的
  reality n 现实面

recession n 萧条，不景气
  slump n 暴跌，下降
redundancy n 过多，冗赘
  redundant a 多余的，过剩的
reimbursement n 补偿，退还
  reimburse v 偿还，归还
reliable a 可靠的
  reliability n 可靠度
reluctant a 不甘愿的
  reluctantly ad 勉强地
replace v 取代，代替
  replacement n 接替，取代
requirement n 需求，要求
  require v 要求
responsibility n 责任
  responsible a 负责的
retain v 保留，保持
  retainable a 可保留的
revolution n 革命，革新
  revolutionary a 革命的
satisfying a 令人满意的
  satisfy v 使满意
schedule n 行程
  agenda n 议程
scope n 范围，领域
  extension n 扩大
separate v 分隔，分离
  separation n 分开，分隔
shareholder n 股东
  investor n 投资者
shortage n 不足，缺乏之处
  shorten v 缩短，减少
simultaneously ad 同时地
  simultaneous a 同时的
slip v 下滑
  edge lower v 降低

附 Appendix

常用商务英语缩写、单词表

slogan n 口号
- expression n 表达

social a 社会的，社交的
- socialize v 交际，社会化

solve v 解决
- solvent a 有偿付能力的

specialty n 专长
- special a 特别的

sponsor n 赞助者
- sponsorship n 赞助，发起

stable a 稳定的
- stability n 稳定性

strength n 强度
- strengthen v 加强，强化

substantial a 大量的
- generous a 慷慨的

suggestion n 建议
- suggest v 建议

supplement v 补充
- supplementary n 补充物

tactic n 手段，策略
- strategy n 战略

temporarily ad 临时地
- temporary a 临时的

timesheet n 时间表
- schedule n 行程

treasure v 珍爱，珍视
- treasury n 库房，国库

undeniable a 不可否认的
- evident a 明显的，明白的

unexpected a 无预警的
- unexpectedly ad 无预期地

unsure a 无信心的，无把握的
- uncertain a 不确定的

variety n 多种类
- vary v 多变，变化

vendor n 供应商
- provider n 供应者

volunteer n 志愿者
- voluntary a 自愿的

warranty n 保固
- warrant v 授权，批准

workforce n 劳动力
- manpower n 劳动力

worthwhile a 值得的
- useful a 有用的

社交技巧

accompany v 伴随
- accompaniment n 附加物

addicted a 沉迷的
- addict n 入迷之人

admire v 钦羡
- admiration n 钦佩，赞美

allocate v 分配
- allocation n 分配，分发

anticipate v 期望
- anticipation n 预料，期望

apologize v 道歉
- apology n 歉意

approximate a 大约的
- approximately ad 约略地

attract v 吸引
- attractive a 吸引人的

available a 可获得的
- availability n 可得性

beneficial a 有益的
- benefit n 益处

burden v 负担
- burdensome a 累赘的

Unit 3 全书单词总整理

celebration n 庆祝
- celebrate v 庆祝

challenge v 挑战
- challenging a 有挑战的

charisma n 魅力
- charismatic a 有魅力的

cherish v 珍惜
- treasure v 珍爱，珍视

climate n 气候，氛围
- atmosphere n 气氛

commemorate v 庆祝，纪念
- commemoration n 纪念日

commodity n 商品，日用品
- goods n 商品

complain v 抱怨
- complaint n 抱怨

concept n 概念
- conceptual a 概念上的

congestion n 拥塞
- congest v 充满，塞满

consecutive a 连续的
- consecution n 连贯

conservation n 保存
- conserve v 保育，保存

consult v 咨询
- consultant n 顾问

contemporary a 当代的
- contemporaneous a 同时期发生的

courteous a 礼貌的
- courteously ad 谦和地

crave v 渴求
- require v 需要

crossroads n 十字路口
- intersection n 交叉口

cultural a 文化的
- culture n 文化

delighted a 愉悦的
- delight v 欣喜，愉悦

dependable a 可靠的
- depend v 依赖

destination n 目的地
- destine v 命定，注定

difference n 差异
- different a 不同的

diplomatic a 外交的
- diplomacy n 外交

direction n 方向
- direct v 指引

disappointment n 失望
- disappointed a 失望的

disguise v 隐藏
- veil v 掩饰，遮盖

display v 陈列
- showcase v 玻璃陈列柜

distance n 距离
- distant a 远离的

disturb v 打扰
- disturbance n 扰乱，打扰

division n（公司）部门
- department n 部门

drastic a 激烈的，猛烈的
- drastically ad 激烈地

drawback n 缺点
- shortcoming n 缺点，短处

dynamic a 动力的
- dynamically ad 充满活力地

edition n 版本
- version n 译本

electronic a 电子的
- electricity n 电力

elegant a 优雅的，漂亮的
- elegantly ad 优美地

emotion n 情绪
- emotional a 情绪化的

empathy n 同感
- empathic a 移情作用的

energetic a 充满活力的
- energy n 精力，精神

enjoyable a 有乐趣的
- enjoy v 享受

enrich v 使富裕
- enrichment n 致富

entertain v 取悦
- entertainment n 娱乐

establish v 创建
- establishment n 建立，创办

excellent a 极好的
- excellence n 完美

exceptional a 非凡的
- exceptionally ad 优异地

express v 表达
- expression n 表达

extremely ad 极度地
- extreme n 极端

factor n 因素
- element n 要素

familiar a 熟悉的
- familiarity n 知晓

fashionable a 流行的
- fashion n 流行物

favorable a 赞同的，有利的
- favor v 赞同

fiction n 小说
- drama n 剧本

flourish v 繁茂，茂盛
- flourishing a 兴旺的

fluently ad 流利地
- fluent a 流利的

foreign a 外国的
- foreigner n 外国人

forgive v 原谅
- forgiveness n 谅解

foster v 培养，促进
- advance v 推进

fragrant a 芳香的
- fragrance n 香味

freedom n 自由
- free a 自由的

frequently ad 经常地
- frequent a 经常的

friendly a 友善的
- friendship n 友谊

glamorous a 有魅力，迷人的
- glamorously ad 迷人地

gorgeous a 极美的
- awesome a 太棒的

gossip n 八卦
- chitchat n 闲谈

gourmet n 美食家
- critic n 评论家

graceful a 优雅的
- grace n 优美，优雅

grateful a 感谢的
- gratefully ad 感激地

greed n 贪心，贪婪
- greedy a 贪心的

greeting n 问候
- greet v 问候

historical a 古迹的，历史的
- history n 历史

humble a 谦和的
- humbly ad 谦逊地

hygiene n 卫生
- hygienic a 卫生的

Unit 3 全书单词总整理

imply v 暗喻
- implication n 牵涉，卷入

indicate v 指出
- indication n 表示

individual n 单独的，个体的
- individually ad 个人地，单独地

inferior a 低等的，下级的
- inferior n 部属，属下

inhabitant n 居住者，居民
- inhabit v 栖息于，居住于

inherit v 继承
- inheritance n 继承

innermost a 最深处的
- deepest a 深的

innocent a 清白的
- innocently ad 无辜地

inspiration n 灵感，鼓舞人心之事
- inspire v 激励

interact v 互动
- interaction n 互动

invaluable a 无价的
- valuable a 有价值的

invite v 邀请
- invitation n 邀请函

irresponsible a 不负责任的
- irresponsibly ad 不可靠地

itinerary n 行程
- itinerant a 巡游的

jealousy n 妒忌
- jealous a 妒忌的

landmark n 界标
- milestone n 里程碑

landscape n 风景
- scene n 景色，景象

leisure n 空闲
- leisure a 闲暇的

limit v 限制
- limitation n 限制

literature n 文学
- literal a 照字面的

lounge n 休息室
- lobby n 会客室

luggage n 行李
- baggage n 行李

magazine n 杂志
- magazine n 弹药库

manner n 态度，行为
- behavior n 行为

marvelous a 非凡的，不可思议的
- marvelously ad 非凡地

memory n 记忆
- memorize v 记忆

mental a 精神的
- mentally ad 精神上地

mild a 温和的
- soft a 柔软的

minor a 小的，少数的
- minor n 未成年人

modern a 现代的，近代的
- modern n 现代人

motivate v 激励
- motivation n 激励，鼓舞

native a 天生的
- native n 本国人

negative a 负面的
- negatively ad 负面地

occasionally ad 时常地
- occasion n 场合

onstage ad 上场，上台
- onstage a 台上演出的

optimistic a 乐观的
- optimism n 乐观主意

orchestra n 管弦乐队
- band n 乐团

original a 原始的
- originally ad 起初，原来

outstanding a 突出的
- outstand v 突出

overwhelm v 压倒，征服
- overwhelming a 势不可当的

passenger n 旅客
- traveler n 旅行者

pedestrian n 行人
- pedestrian a 步行的

perform v 表现
- performance n 表现

pessimistic a 悲观的
- pessimist n 悲观主义者

pitiful a 令人同情的
- pity n 同情，怜悯

postpone v 延后，推迟
- put off ph 拖延

potential a 有潜力的
- potential n 潜力

present v 呈现
- presentation n 简报

previous a 先前的
- previously ad 先前地

probation n 试用，检验
- trial n 试验

productive a 有生产力的
- produce v 生产，产出

promptly ad 迅速地
- prompt a 及时的

protect v 保护
- protection n 警戒，保护

pursue v 追求
- pursuit n 追寻

questionnaire n 问卷
- form n 表格

quota n 配额
- quotation n 行情，报价

reassure v 使放心
- reassured a 使消除疑虑的

recently ad 最近地
- recent a 近期的

refuse v 拒绝
- decline v 婉拒，谢绝

region n 地域
- area n 场地

rehearsal n 预演
- tryout n 试演

reminder n 提醒
- remind v 提醒

reputation n 名声
- reputable a 名声好的

resign v 辞去
- resignation n 放弃

response n 回应
- respond v 回应，回复

review v 复审，再检查
- reviewer n 评论者

revise v 修正，修改
- revised a 经过修改

sacrifice v 牺牲，献出
- sacrifice n 牺牲的行为

scientific a 科学的
- science n 科学

seemingly ad 表面上
- seeming a 表面上的

sentimental a 多愁善感的
- sentiment n 感情，心情

sheltered a 被保护的
- shelter n 栖息处

Unit 3 全书单词总整理

shorten v 缩短
- short a 短的

significant a 有意义的，深长的
- significance n 重要性

skeptical a 存疑的
- skeptic n 怀疑者

slump v 下滑，下降
- slump n 不景气

soar v 高涨
- soaring a 高耸的

specialist n 专员
- expert n 专家

specialize v 专长于，擅长于
- specialty n 专长

stabilize v 趋缓
- stable a 稳定的

straightforward a 直白的
- direct a 直接的

strategy n 策略
- strategic a 策略的

stunned a 令人咋舌的
- stunning a 令人震撼的

sufficient a 足够的
- sufficiently ad 充裕地

tackle v 应付
- deal with ph 处理

talent n 才华
- talented a 有才干的

temperature n 温度
- heat n 温度

translator n 译者
- translate v 翻译

transportation n 交通
- transport n 运输

understanding n 理解
- understand v 了解

unknown a 不知名的
- nameless a 匿名的

unstable a 不稳定的
- changeable a 易变的

utility n 实用，效用
- utilize v 利用

various a 多样的
- variously ad 不同地

vital a 重要的
- essential a 必要的

workable a 可行的
- practical a 实践的

gridlock n 交通堵塞
- traffic jam ph 堵车

讯息沟通

absolute a 完全的，绝对的
- absolutely ad 当然地，必然地

access v 取得
- accessible a 可取得的

accuracy n 正确性
- accurate a 正确的

advertisement n 广告
- advertiser n 广告主

alertness n 警醒
- alert a 警觉的

annual a 每年的
- annually ad 每年地

assign v 指派
- assignment n 任务

auction n 拍卖
- sale n 特价

bonus n 红利
- benefit n 利益

难以置信的实用职场英语

boom v 激增
- boomer n 激增潮

brochure n 目录
- booklet n 小册子

cancel v 取消
- cancellation n 取消

category n 类别，种类
- categorize v 将……分类

charitable a 慈善的
- charity n 慈善机构

colleague n 同事
- co-worker n 同事

collect v 收集
- collection n 收集品

commission n 抽成
- commission v 委托，委任

commonplace n 司空惯见之事
- prevalence n 普遍，广泛

communication n 沟通
- communicate v 沟通

confirm v 确认
- confirmation n 确认

congratulate v 恭贺
- congratulation n 恭喜

conscious a 有知觉的
- consciousness n 清醒，意识

conserve v 保存，节省
- conservation n 保存

consideration n 考量
- consider v 考虑

consistent a 前后一致的
- consistently ad 始终如一地

consultant n 顾问
- consulting a 顾问的

coordinator n 协调者
- coordinate v 协调

correspondence n 符合，一致性
- correspond v 符合，配合

criticize v 批评
- criticism n 批评

currency n 货币
- legal tender ph 法定货币

decorate v 装潢
- decoration n 装潢

deposit v 放置，储存
- deposit n 押金

describe v 描述
- description n 描述

devastating a 致命的
- devastate v 破坏，蹂躏

directory n 电话簿
- yellow pages ph 电话簿，黄页

disappear v 消失
- disappearance n 失踪，消失

discover v 发现
- discovery n 发现

dispatch v 发送，快递
- transmit v 传送，传达

distract v 使分心
- distraction n 注意力分散

distribute v 分配，发派
- distribution n 分派，分送

download v 下载
- load v 载入

durable a 耐用的
- enduring a 持久的，耐久的

dweller n 住户
- dwell v 居住

effect n 结果，后果
- effective a 有效果的

emerge v 出现
- emergency n 突发状况

262

Unit 3 全书单词总整理

employ v 雇用
- employee n 雇员

enquiry n 询问
- query n 质问

environment n 环境
- environmental a 环境的

estate n 地产
- residence n 居住，住宅

exceed v 超越，超过
- excessive a 过度的

excessively ad 过度地
- excessive a 过多的

exclusive a 独家的
- exclusively ad 独家地

exhibition n 展览
- exhibit v 展出

expenditure n 花费
- expensive a 很贵的

export v 出口
- exporter n 输出国

fame n 名声
- famous a 有名的

feature n 特性
- quality n 特性

finance n 金融
- financial a 金融的

foresee v 预见，预测
- forecast v 预报

format n 格式
- style n 种类，式样

forward v 转交
- deliver 投递，传送

frame n 框架
- frame v 建构

fraud n 诈欺
- scam n 骗钱；诈取

freight n 货物
- shipping n 运输

funding n 补助，款项
- fund n 款项

gadget n 小玩意
- appliance n 器具，用具

genuine a 真正的，真诚的
- authentic a 可信的

gigantic a 巨大的
- giant a 巨大的

growth n 成长
- growing a 生长的，增大的

guarantee v 保证
- guaranteed a 肯定的

hazardous a 危害的
- hazard n 危险

hesitate v 踌躇，犹豫
- hesitation n 踌躇，犹豫

household n 家庭，一户
- home n 家

improve v 改善
- improvement n 进展

incentive n 刺激，鼓励
- motivation n 刺激

inconvenience n 不便
- inconvenient a 不便的

independent a 独立的
- independently ad 独立地

ingredient n 成分，原料
- element n 要素，成分

initial a 最初的，开始的
- initial n 首字母

inquiry v 询问
- inquire v 询问

install v 安装
- installation n 安装

insurance n 保险
- **insure** v 为……投保

introverted a 内向的，不爱交际的
- **introvert** n 内向的人

invoice n 出货单，付款明细
- **bill** n 账单

irrelevant a 无关的
- **irrelevance** n 不恰当

isolated a 孤立的
- **isolation** n 孤立

journey n 旅途
- **traveler** n 旅客，游客

knowledge n 知识
- **know** v 明白，知道

lecture n 演说，讲课
- **speech** n 演说，演讲

magnificent a 雄伟的，宏大的
- **magnificently** ad 壮观地

mainstream n 主流
- **current** n 趋势

masterpiece n 杰作，名作
- **classic** n 名著

material n 教材，材料
- **materialize** v 使具体化

meaningful a 有意义的
- **meaning** n 意义

measure v 测量
- **measurement** n 测量

membership n 会员制
- **member** n 会员

message n 信息
- **messenger** n 信差

miracle n 奇迹
- **marvel** n 令人惊奇的事物

mistake n 错误
- **error** n 错误

misuse v 误用
- **waste** v 滥用

modify v 修改
- **modified** a 已修改的

necessary a 必要的
- **necessarily** ad 必然地

observe v 观察
- **observation** n 观察力

obvious a 明显的
- **obviously** ad 显然地

ongoing a 进行的，不间断的
- **current** a 当前的，现在的

orientation n 方针，介绍状况
- **direction** n 方向

outcome n 结果，后果
- **result** n 结果

outpace v 赶过，胜过
- **outrun** v 超过，超出

overhear v 无意中听到
- **listen in** ph 收听，监听

overview n 概要，综述
- **analysis** n 分析，分解

partnership n 伙伴关系
- **partner** n 伙伴

payment n 款项
- **pay** v 付款

penalty n 刑罚
- **penalize** v 处刑

perspective n 洞察力
- **viewpoint** n 观点，见解

polish v 磨光，磨亮
- **varnish** v 装饰，修饰

positive a 正面的
- **positively** ad 肯定地

possession n 拥有物
- **possess** v 持有

Unit 3 全书单词总整理

precious a 珍贵的
　cherished a 珍爱的
precise a 精准的
　precisely ad 精确地
proactive a 主动的
　proactively ad 积极地
procedure n 程序，步骤
　process n 过程，进程
profound a 深刻的
　profoundly ad 深刻地
prohibit v 禁止
　prohibition n 禁令
promise v 答应，允诺
　promising a 前景看好的
properly ad 恰当地
　proper a 恰当的
purpose n 目的
　purposely ad 故意地
rarely ad 很少地
　rare a 稀少的
rate n 概率
　ratio n 比例
reasonable a 合理的
　reason n 理由
rebound v 弹回，跳回
　bounce back ph 恢复原状
recovery n 恢复
　recover v 回复
refund v 退款
　refundable a 可退款的
regional a 地方的
　region n 地区
relevant a 有关系的
　relevance n 关联性
renovation n 恢复，更新
　renovate v 更新

reproduction n 再生，再制
　reproduce v 再生
reservation n 预约
　reserve v 预约，预定
resignation n 辞职
　resign v 辞去
retailer n 零售商
　retail v 零售
rival n 竞争者，敌手
　rivalry n 对抗行为
safeguard n 保卫，安全措施
　safeguard v 保护，防护
secure a 安全的，无危险的
　security n 安全性
selection n 选项
　select v 选择
severe a 严重的
　severity n 严格，严厉
sharply ad 急剧地
　sharp a 激烈的
shrink v 缩小
　shrinking a 缩小的
skyscraper n 摩天大楼
　high-rise n 高楼
solution n 解决方案
　quick fix ph 权宜之计
spiral a 螺旋状的
　spiral v 成螺旋形
spirit n 精神，士气
　spiritual a 精神的
stimulate v 激发
　stimulation n 刺激
stock n 股票
　share n 股份，股票
struggle v 奋斗
　struggler n 挣扎的人

submit v 递交
- hand in ph 提出，缴交

superb a 宏伟的，华丽的
- first-rate a 极好的，很棒的

sympathy n 同情心
- sympathize v 同情

tangibly ad 明白地，可触知地
- tangible a 有形的

thrive v 兴旺，成功
- thriving a 繁荣的

transfer v 转移
- transferable a 可转移的

transport v 运输
- transportation n 交通运输

truthful a 诚实的，坦然的
- truth n 真相

underperformer n 表现不佳者
- underperform v 表现不如预期

unique a 独一无二的
- one-of-a-kind a 独一无二的

upset v 扰乱
- upset a 心烦的，苦恼的

vacancy n 空缺
- vacant a 空着的

vibrant a 栩栩如生的
- energetic a 精力旺盛的

warning n 警告
- warn v 警告

wonderful a 极棒的
- wonderfully ad 精彩地

yield n 产量
- production n 产量

drop v 下跌
- plunge v 下降

简报演说

abundant a 充裕的
- affluent a 富裕的

accent n 口音
- stress n 重音

accommodate v 容纳下
- accommodation n 房间，空间

acquire v 取得
- acquisition n 获取

advantage n 优点
- advantageous a 有好处的

anxiety n 焦虑
- anxious a 焦急的

apparently ad 显然地
- apparent a 明显的

arrangement n 安排
- arrange v 安排

attention n 注意力
- attentive a 注意的

award n 奖品
- award v 授予，给予

balance n 平衡
- balanced a 平衡的

boost v 增强
- surge v 激增

brand n 品牌
- character n 特性

campaign n 活动，战役
- activity n 活动，活动力

celebrity n 名流
- figure n 名人

ceremony n 庆祝会
- ceremonial a 仪式的

chronic a 慢性的
- chronological a 按时间顺序的

Unit 3 全书单词总整理

coherent a 协调的
  coherence n 一致性
community n 社区，群体
  communal a 自治的，共有的
commuter n 通勤者
  commute v 通勤
compensate v 补偿
  compensation n 报酬
complete v 完成
  completion n 完成
comprehensible a 可理解的
  comprehension n 理解力
concise a 简要的
  concisely ad 扼要的
consensus n 一致
  unity n 统一
consumer n 消费者
  consume v 消耗
contradict v 反驳
  contradiction n 矛盾
corporate a 法人的
  corporation n 法人公司
counselor n 顾问
  counsel v 商议
creativity n 创造力
  create v 创造
current a 目前的
  present a 现在的
deadline n 最后期限
  period n 时期，期间
decade n 十年
  ten years ph 十年
decrease v 减少
  downsize v 裁减
demand n 需求
  demanding a 苛求的

departure v 启程
  exit v 离去
description n 叙述
  describe v 描述
discount n 折扣
  rebate n 折扣
divide v 划分
  dividend n 红利，股息
economize v 节约
  economical a 节省的
efficient a 有效率的
  efficiently ad 有效率地
elaborate v 详细计划
  elaboration n 精巧
element n 要素，因素
  factor n 因素
elementary a 基本的
  fundemental a 基础的
encourage v 鼓励
  encouragement n 鼓舞
enhance v 增强
  upgrade v 升级
enterprise n 企业
  organization n 机构
entrance n 入口
  access n 入口
equipment n 设备
  equip v 配备
evaluation n 评估
  evaluate v 评估
exchange v 交换
  swap v 交换
experimental a 实验的
  experiment n 实验
explanation n 解释
  explain v 解释

附 Appendix 常用商务英语缩写、单词表

extravagant a 夸张的
　　excessive a 过度的
fabricate v 组装，伪造
　　fabrication n 组建，捏造
famous a 有名的
　　renown a 名声
fascinated a 着迷的
　　fascinatedly ad 如痴如醉地
feedback n 意见反馈
　　opinion n 意见，见解
finite a 有限的
　　limited a 有限的
flaw n 缺失
　　fault n 缺点
fluctuate v 波动
　　fluctuation n 振荡，摆荡
fortunate v 幸运的
　　fortune n 好运
fulfillment n 满足
　　achievement n 达成，完成
fundamentally ad 基本地
　　basically ad 在根本上
generally ad 一般地
　　general a 一般的
gimmick n 花招
　　device n 手段，谋略
gradually ad 逐渐地
　　gradual a 渐渐的，平缓的
gratifying a 满意的
　　pleasant a 令人愉快的
guidance n 指引，指导
　　guide v 引导
heighten v 增高，增多
　　enhance v 提高，增加
hierarchy n 阶层
　　pecking order ph 长幼尊卑制度

hypothesis n 假定
　　guess n 猜测
illustration n 举证
　　illustrate v 举实证
impeccable a 无懈可击的
　　perfect a 完美的
inaugurate v 就职，开幕
　　inauguration n 就职，开幕
increase v 增加
　　rise v 上升，上涨
influence n 影响
　　influence v 影响
initiative a 主动的，创始的
　　initiative n 主动，提议
innovation n 创新
　　innovate v 革新，创新
inspection n 检验
　　inspect v 检查
integrate v 整合
　　integration n 整合
invention n 发明（物）
　　invent v 发明
journal n 日记，期刊
　　journalist n 记者
keynote n 主题演讲
　　speech n 演说，演讲
launch v 上市，推出
　　introduce v 提出，推行
legend n 传奇
　　legendary a 传奇的
liberty n 自由
　　freedom n 自由
lower v 下降，放低
　　decrease v 减少
maintain v 维护
　　maintenance n 维持，保持

Unit 3 全书单词总整理

manual n 手册
- manual a 用手的，手工的

manuscript n 手稿
- writing n 笔迹

maximum n 最大值
- maximum a 最大的，顶点的

mention v 提及
- mentionable a 值得提的

minimum n 最低限度
- minimum a 最低的

misleading a 误导的
- mislead v 把……带错方向

morale n 士气
- spirit n 气魄，气概

mutually ad 双方地
- mutual a 互相的

normally ad 正常地
- normal a 一般的

obtain v 取得
- obtainable a 能得到的

official a 官方的
- officially ad 官方地，正式地

ordinary a 平常的，通常的
- common a 普通的，常见的

outdated a 过时的
- old-fashioned a 旧式的

overlook v 忽视，忽略
- ignore v 不理会，忽略

overtime v 使超过时间
- extra a 额外的，外加的

partially ad 一部分地
- part n 部分

passively ad 被动地
- passive a 被动的

penetration n 渗透
- penetrate v 渗入

permission n 允许，准许
- permit v 许可，允准

plentiful a 充足的，富足的
- plenty n 丰富，大量

pollution n 污染
- pollute v 弄脏

practical a 实际的
- practice v 实践，实施

preliminary a 初步的，预言的
- preliminary n 初步，开端，预备

presentation n 简报
- present v 呈现

prevent v 预防
- preclude v 防止，杜绝

principle n 原理，原则
- standard n 标准，水准

produce v 制造，生产
- producer n 制造商

professional a 专业的
- professor n 教授

proposition n 提议，建议
- propositional a 建议的

publish v 出版
- publication n 出版物

randomly ad 随机地
- random a 随机的

reaction n 反应
- react v 反应

reap v 收割
- gain v 收获

recharge v 再充电
- renew v 更新，恢复

reduction n 减少
- reduce v 降低，减少

regular a 平时的
- regularly ad 定期地

rejuvenate v 重新注入活力
  refresh v 使得到补充
rephrase v 排演，排练
  dry run ph 排演，练习
representative n 业务代表
  represent v 代表
reschedule v 改期
  hold off ph 延期
resolve v 解决
  settle v 安排，料理
restore v 恢复
  restoration n 恢复，复位
reward n 报答
  rewarding a 有益的
sanitary n 卫生的
  sanitation n 公共卫生
scrutiny n 仔细观察
  scrutinize v 细看
security n 安全性
  secure a 安全的
sensitive a 敏感的
  sensitively ad 神经过敏地
seriously ad 严重的
  serious a 严重的
signature n 签名
  sign v 签名
sincerely ad 诚心地
  sincere a 诚心的
socialize v 参与社交
  society n 社会
specification n 规格
  specific a 特定的
spokesman n 发言人
  spokesperson n 发言人
spread v 使延伸，传播
  stretch out v 延长

standard n 标准
  standardize v 标准化
stretch v 延伸
  stretchable a 能伸展的
subsidiary a 辅助的，次要的
  subsidiary n 附带物
suitable a 合适的
  suit v 配合，搭配
supply v 供应
  supplier n 供应商
tedious a 冗长烦人的
  tediously ad 沉闷地
terminal a 末端的，终点的
  terminal n 航空站
transaction n 交易
  transact v 处理，交易
treatment n 疗效
  treat v 医治，对待
uncertainty n 不确定性
  uncertain a 不确定的
unfamiliar a 不熟悉的
  unfamiliarity n 陌生
unwilling a 不甘愿的
  unwillingly ad 不甘愿地
valuable a 有价值的
  value n 价值
venue n 集合地，场所
  location n 位置，所在地
voucher n 优惠券
  coupon n 优惠券
wisdom n 智慧
  wise a 有智慧的
workload n 工作量
  tasks at hand n 手头上的工作

商务会议

emergency n 意外，突发状况
- emerge v 浮现，出现

absence n 缺席
- absent a 缺席的

accelerate v 加速
- speed up v（使）加速

adequate a 充分的
- sufficient a 足够的

adjourn v（使）休会
- suspend v 使中止

advertise v 登广告
- advertisement n 广告

agenda n 议程
- schedule n 行程

analysis n 分析
- analyze v 分析

anxious a 急迫的
- anxiously ad 焦急地

appointment n 约会
- date n 约会

association n 协会，联盟
- associate n 有关联性的事物

atmosphere n 气氛
- climate n 气候

authorization n 委任，批准
- authorize v 授权

barter v 以物易物
- trade n 贸易

boast v 夸耀，自吹自擂
- brag v 吹牛，自夸

brainstorm v 集思广益
- ponder v 仔细考虑

breakthrough n 突破
- development n 发展

Unit 3 全书单词总整理

breathtaking a 令人赞赏的
- breathtakingly ad 令人透不过气地

calculate v 计算
- calculation n 计算

caution n 小心翼翼
- cautious a 谨慎的

certainty n 确定性
- certain a 确定的

circulate v 发行
- circulation n 发行量

clarify v 确认
- clarification n 澄清，说明

coincide v 同时发生
- coincidence n 巧合

command v 命令
- commander n 指挥官

comment n 评语
- commentary n 评论

committee n 小组
- board n（政府的）部，局，会

component n 组成成分
- constituent n 组成要素

comprehension n 理解力
- comprehend v 理解

conclude n 结论
- conclusion n 结论

conduct v 处理
- conductor n 领导人

conference n 会议
- conference call 电话会议

confidential a 机密的
- confide v 信任

connection n 关联性
- connect v 连接

contemplate v 仔细思量
- consider v 考虑，细想

convention n 会议
  ⊙ conference 会议
cutting-edge a 最前线，尖端
  ⊙ state-of-the-art a 最先进的
deficiency n 不足，缺乏
  ⊙ deficient a 有缺点的
define v 定义
  ⊙ definition n 定义
delegate v 委派……为代表
  ⊙ assign v 分配，分派
demanding a 苛求的
  ⊙ demand n 需求
demonstration n 展示，示范
  ⊙ demonstrate v 示范
designate v 标出，表明
  ⊙ indicate v 指示，指出
disadvantage n 缺点
  ⊙ disadvantageous a 不利的
disagree v 不同意
  ⊙ disagreement n 反对意见
discussion n 讨论
  ⊙ discuss v 讨论
downsize v 缩编
  ⊙ reduce v 减少
duration n 持续时间
  ⊙ durable a 经久的，耐用的
effective a 有效果的
  ⊙ effectiveness n 有效力
endorsement n 背书
  ⊙ endorse v 签署，认可
engage v 从事
  ⊙ engagement n 诺言
evidence n 证据
  ⊙ evident a 分明的，清楚的
exclude a 排除
  ⊙ exclusive a 排外的

expand v 扩大，拓展
  ⊙ expansion n 扩张
fantastic a 想象中的，奇异的
  ⊙ fantasy n 空想
fierce a 凶猛的，好斗的
  ⊙ fiercely ad 残酷地
figure n 数字
  ⊙ number n 数字
fiscal a 财政的，会计的
  ⊙ budgetary a 预算的
forecast n 预测
  ⊙ forecaster n 推测者
forum n 论坛
  ⊙ discussion n 讨论，商讨
function n 功能
  ⊙ functional a 机能的
gentle a 温和的
  ⊙ gentleman n 绅士
globalization n 全球化
  ⊙ global a 全球的
gratitude n 感恩，感谢之情
  ⊙ thank n 感谢，道谢
guideline n 指导方针
  ⊙ guide v 引导
headquarters n 总部
  ⊙ main office ph 总部
horizon n 地平线
  ⊙ horizontal a 水平的，横的
identical a 同一的
  ⊙ identically ad 相同地
imagery n 意象，比喻
  ⊙ image n 形象
implement v 实行，实施
  ⊙ implementation n 履行，完成
inadequate a 不足的
  ⊙ inadequately ad 不充足地

Unit 3 全书单词总整理

incredible a 无法置信的
　unbelievable a 令人难以置信的
industrial a 工业的
　industry n 工业
inevitable a 不可避免的
　unavoidable a 不可避免的
inflation n 通货膨胀
　boom n（商业的）景气，繁荣
insight n 见解
　insightful a 有见解的
instruction n 教导，命令
　instruct v 指导，下指令
intensify v 增强，加强
　intense a 强烈的
interpret v 口译
　interpretation n 口译
interrupt v 打断
　interruption n 中止
inventory n 库存
　backlog n 存货
invest v 投资
　investment n 投资
label v 贴标签于
　label n 标记
laboratory n 实验室
　lab n 实验室
landslide n 山崩，滑坡
　landslip n 山崩
lease v 租赁
　lessor n 房东
lend v 借出
　loan v 借出
lucrative a 有赚钱的
　profitable a 赢利的
majority n 多数
　major a 主要的

manipulate v 操纵
　handle v 操作
manufacture v 制造
　manufacturer n 制造商
margin n 边缘，余裕
　marginalize v 被边缘化
marketing n 营销
　market n 市场
marketplace n 市场，市集
　forum n 讨论会
meltdown n 溶解
　crash n 撞击，砸碎
million n 百万
　million a 百万的
mission n 任务
　missionary n 鼓吹者，传教士
moderate a 中等的，普通的
　medium a 中间的
morality n 伦理，品性
　moral a 道德上的
nominate v 提名
　nomination n 任命
numerous a 许多的，很多的
　several a 许多的
objective n 目标
　object n 宗旨，标的
obstacle n 阻碍
　hurdle n 障碍，困难
offset v 补偿
　offset n 抵消，补偿
operator n 操作员
　operate v 操作
organize v 整理
　organization n 企业
ornament n 装饰品
　ornament v 美化

outgoing a 外向的
- open a 打开的

overpriced a 费用过高的
- costly a 代价高的

participate v 参与
- participant n 参与者

patience n 耐心
- patient a 有耐心的

pending a 悬而未决的
- undecided a 未决定的

persistence n 固执
- persistent a 坚持不懈的

pinpoint n 确定目标
- spotlight n 聚光灯

plummet v 骤降
- tumble v 跌倒，滚下

possibility n 可能性
- possible a 有可能的

predict v 预言
- foresee v 预见，预知

pretend v 佯装
- pretended a 假装的

priority n 优先顺序
- prioritize v 按优先顺序处理

procrastination n 拖延
- procrastinate v 耽搁

proficiency n 精通，熟练
- proficient a 熟练的

proposal n 提议案
- propose v 提出

punctual a 准时的
- punctuality n 严守时间

quality n 品质
- nature n 性质

rapidly ad 迅速地
- rapid a 迅速的

rational a 理性的
- rationalize v 合理化

recognize v 识别，认出
- recognizable a 可辨认的

recruit v 招募
- recruitment n 招聘

reform v 转变
- reformation n 改革，革新

register v 登记，注册
- registration n 登记

relation n 关系
- relationship n 关系

remain v 剩余，保有
- remaining a 剩下的

renown n 名声，名望
- renowned a 有名的

research v 研究
- researcher n 研究员

resolution n 决心，决定
- resolute a 不屈不挠的

restrict v 限制
- restriction n 限制

revenue n 营业额
- turnover n 交易额

rhythm n 韵律
- rhythmic a 按节拍的

salary n 薪资
- wages n 代价，报偿

scheme n 计划，方案
- strategy n 战略

sculpture n 雕像
- carving n 雕刻

seminar n 研讨会
- conference n 讨论会

session n 讲习
- seminar n 研究班

Unit 3 全书单词总整理

signal v 发出信号
　alert v 使警觉
sketch n 速写，速描
　drawing n 素描
society n 社会
　community n 社区
sophisticated a 世故的
　sophisticate v 使复杂
spectator n 观赏者
　spectate v 出席观看
splendid a 光彩的
　gorgeous a 灿烂的
statistics n 数据
　data n 数据
striking a 引人注目的
　noticeable a 值得注意的
subscriber n 订阅者
　subscription n 订阅
summarize v 做总结
　summary n 结论
supervisor n 领班
　supervise v 领导，监督
surge v 飙升
　soar v 升腾
target n 目标
　objective n 目标
theme n 主题
　subject n 主题
trademark n 商标
　brand n 商标
triumph v 成功
　triumphant a 胜利的，成功的
tumble v 坠落
　plummet v 笔直落下
undermine v 暗中破坏
　hurt v 造成损失

unforgettably ad 无法忘怀地
　unforgettable a 难以忘怀的
update n 更新
　renew v 更新
valid a 有效的
　validate v 使有效
vast a 广大的
　vastly ad 宽阔地
verbal a 言辞的
　verbalize v 以语言表述
wage n 薪资
　income n 收入
welcome v 欢迎
　welcoming a 受欢迎的
wholesaler n 批发商
　distributor n 批发商
workplace n 工作场合
　organization n 组织工作

协商谈判

insult v 羞辱
　insulting a 无礼的
afford v 负担得起
　affordable a 负担得起的
aggressive a 进取的
　aggressively ad 激进地
alternative n 其他的选择
　alternate a 交替的
ambiance n 气氛，氛围
　atmosphere n 气氛
ambitious a 有野心的
　ambition n 雄心，抱负
approach n 方式
　method n 方法

难以置信的实用职场英语

argument n 争执
　　argue v 争论
assume v 假设，认为
　　assumption n 假设，假定
authentic a 真正的
　　actual a 实际的
bankruptcy n 破产
　　bankrupt v 倒闭
bargain n 讨价还价
　　bargaining n 谈判
bilingual a 双语的
　　bilingualism n 能使用双语
bombard v 疲劳轰炸
　　attack v 进攻，袭击
budget n 预算
　　budget v 编预算
circumstance n 情况，状况
　　situation n 形势，情况
claim v 宣称
　　state v 声明
collaborate v 协同合作
　　collaboration n 合作
comparison n 比较
　　compare v 比较
compelling a 强制的
　　compel v 强迫
competitor n 竞争对手
　　compete v 竞争
complicated a 复杂的
　　complex a 复杂的
compromise v 妥协
　　compromising a 让步的
concern n 担忧之事
　　worry n 烦恼，担心
concession n 让步
　　surrender n 投降，屈服

conclusive a 决定性的
　　conclusion n 结论
condition n 情况
　　conditional a 有条件的
confidence n 信心
　　confident a 有信心的
conflict n 冲突
　　conflicting a 冲突的
consequence n 后果
　　result n 结果
constraint n 限制，约束
　　confinement n 限制
continuously ad 连续地
　　continuous a 连续的
contract n 合约
　　agreement n 协定，协议
controversial a 有争议性的
　　contradictory a 矛盾的，对立的
cooperate v 合作，协作
　　cooperation n 合作
crisis n 危及，转折点
　　trouble n 困难，困境
damage n 破坏
　　damage v 破坏
deadlock n 死结，僵局
　　plight n 困境，苦境
debate v 辩论
　　argue v 争论，辩论
challenge v 挑战
　　challenging a 有挑战的
deliberately ad 蓄意地
　　deliberate a 故意的
detailed a 细节的
　　detail n 细节
dialogue n 会话
　　conversation n 会话

Unit 3 全书单词总整理

diligent a 勤奋的
　◉ hard-working a 勤勉的
dimension n 尺寸
　◉ dimensional a 大小，空间
discipline n 自律
　◉ disciplinary a 训练的
discrimination n 不公平待遇
　◉ discriminate v 歧视
dispute v 争论，反驳
　◉ disputable a 有讨论余地的
diversity n 差异
　◉ diverse a 互异的
dominate v 支配，控制
　◉ control v 支配，控制
duplicate v 复制
　◉ duplication n 复制品
eliminate v 排除，消去
　◉ remove v 去掉，消除
embarrassed a 丢脸的，没面子的
　◉ disgraced a 失宠的，遭贬谪的
encounter v 遭遇
　◉ confront v 遭遇
enormous a 巨大的
　◉ enormously ad 庞大地
essential a 重要的
　◉ essence n 精髓
eventually ad 最终地
　◉ eventual a 最终的，结果的
exception n 例外
　◉ exceptional a 非凡的，杰出的
exhausted a 极累的
　◉ exhaust v 耗尽
explore v 探索
　◉ search v 搜查
extensive a 广大的
　◉ extensively ad 广泛地

fair a 公平的
　◉ fairness n 公正
festival n 节庆，节日
　◉ holiday n 节日，假日
finalize v 最后确认
　◉ final a 最后的
flexibility n 弹性
　◉ flexible a 有弹性的
force n 力量
　◉ forceful a 强有力的
focus n 焦点
　◉ spotlight n 聚光灯
frustration n 沮丧
　◉ frustrated a 丧气的
gallery n 画廊
　◉ corridor n 走廊，回廊
gather v 聚集
　◉ gathering n 集会
generous a 大方的
　◉ generosity n 慷慨
genius n 天资，才华
　◉ intelligence n 情报工作
greenback n 美金
　◉ US dollar 美金
handle v 处理，应付
　◉ deal with ph 处理
harvest n 收成
　◉ harvest v 采收
hurdle n 障碍物
　◉ barrier n 障碍物
identify v 视别，验明
　◉ identity n 身份，特性
imagination n 想象力
　◉ image n 想象
immediate a 立即的
　◉ immediately ad 马上地

implication n 牵涉，卷入
  - implicated a 有牵连的
impulse n 冲动
  - impulsive a 一时冲动的
incomplete a 不完整的
  - partial a 不完全的
indeed ad 的确地
  - certainly ad 无疑地
infinite a 无限的
  - infinitely ad 无穷地
insightful a 有见解的
  - insight n 见解
inspire v 激励
  - inspiration n 刺激
integrity n 正直
  - integral a 整体的
intention n 意图
  - intend v 意指
investigation n 调查
  - investigate v 调查
leap v 跳跃
  - jump v 跳跃
license n 授权
  - licensed a 获得许可的
luxury n 奢侈
  - luxurious a 奢侈的
management n 管理
  - manage v 管理
massive a 大量的
  - massively ad 大量地，巨大地
merger n 合并
  - merge v 合并
miserable a 痛苦的
  - unhappy a 不开心的
misjudge v 判断错误
  - mistake v 错误

navigation n 航行
  - navigate v 驾驶，操纵
negotiation n 谈判
  - negotiator n 谈判者
obligation n 义务
  - duty n 责任
omission n 省略，删除
  - omit v 省去
opposite a 相对立的
  - opposition n 反抗，对抗
outline n 大纲
  - organization n 组织
oversee n 监视
  - supervise v 监督
particularly ad 尤其地
  - especially ad 格外地
pattern n 样式，格局
  - design n 设计，构思
personality n 人格
  - personal a 个人的
persuade v 劝服
  - convince v 说服
pioneer n 拓荒者
  - pioneering a 先锋的
plunging a 突进的
  - plunge v 猛跌
praise v 赞扬
  - compliment v 恭维
prescription n 处方
  - prescribe v 开药方
prevalent a 普遍的
  - common a 普遍的
privacy n 隐私
  - private a 私人的
profitability n 获利（状况）
  - profitable a 有利可图的

Unit 3 全书单词总整理

progressive a 先进的，革新的
 progress n 进展
prosperous a 繁荣的
 prosperity n 兴旺
purchase v 购买
 purchaser n 买方
quantity n 数量
 quantify v 以数量表示
rapport n 和谐
 agreement n 一致
realize v 了解到
 reality n 现实面
recommend v 建议
 suggest v 建议
reference n 参考
 refer v 论及，交付
release v 释出，解放
 dismiss v 解散，遣散
relocate v 重新安置
 move v 移动，离开
remarkable a 可圈可点的
 remark v 评论
replacement n 更换，取代
 replace v 替换
resemble v 相像，类似
 resemblance n 相似
result n 结果
 outcome n 结果
retreat v 撤退
 withdraw v 撤退，撤离
reunion n 再会合
 reunite v 使重聚
ridiculous a 可笑的
 foolish 荒谬的
scenario n 情境
 plot n 情节

scholarship n 奖学金
 scholarly a 学者的
seasoned a 有经验的
 experienced a 有经验的
setback n 挫折
 defeat 挫败
sharpen 磨尖
 sharp a 尖锐的
skyrocket v 飙升
 soar v 高涨
sluggish a 懒散，呆滞的
 inactive a 怠惰的
solid a 实心的
 sturdy a 结实的
souvenir n 纪念品
 gift n 礼物
spending n 花费
 spend v 开销，花费
spotlight n 焦点目光
 limelight n 众人注目的中心
steady a 稳定的
 steadily ad 稳定地
structure n 结构
 structured a 条理清楚的
summit n 顶峰
 apex n 顶峰
superficial a 表面的
 superficially ad 表面地
survive v 生存
 survival n 残存，幸存
thoroughly ad 彻底地
 thorough a 彻底的
tolerance n 宽容，容忍
 tolerant a 忍受的，容忍的
traditional a 传统的
 tradition n 传统

难以置信的实用职场英语

trivial a 琐碎的
- trivia n 琐事

underestimate v 低估
- underestimation n 过低之估价

uniform n 制服
- uniform a 相同的，一致的

upscale a 高档的
- well-to-do a 富有的

version n 版本
- adaptation n 改编

visibility n 能见度
- visible a 可看见的

warehouse n 仓库
- depot n 仓库

widespread v 广为流传
- boundless a 无穷的，无限的

workshop n 研究会，专题讨论会
- session n 开会，会议

MEMO

版权专有　侵权必究

图书在版编目（CIP）数据

难以置信的实用职场英语 / 薛咏文著.—北京：北京理工大学出版社，2019.7
ISBN 978-7-5682-7209-4

Ⅰ.①难…　Ⅱ.①薛…　Ⅲ.①英语—自学参考资料　Ⅳ.①H31

中国版本图书馆CIP数据核字（2019）第131326号

北京市版权局著作权合同登记号图字：01-2017-2405
简体中文版由我识出版社有限公司授权出版发行
难以置信的实用职场英文，薛咏文著，2015年，初版
ISBN：9789865785949

出版发行 / 北京理工大学出版社有限责任公司
社　　址 / 北京市海淀区中关村南大街5号
邮　　编 / 100081
电　　话 / （010）68914775（总编室）
　　　　　（010）82562903（教材售后服务热线）
　　　　　（010）68948351（其他图书服务热线）
网　　址 / http://www.bitpress.com.cn
经　　销 / 全国各地新华书店
印　　刷 / 天津久佳雅创印刷有限公司
开　　本 / 710毫米×1000毫米　1/16
印　　张 / 18.25　　　　　　　　　　　　　　　　　责任编辑 / 武丽娟
字　　数 / 425千字　　　　　　　　　　　　　　　　文案编辑 / 武丽娟
版　　次 / 2019年7月第1版　2019年7月第1次印刷　　责任校对 / 周瑞红
定　　价 / 56.00元　　　　　　　　　　　　　　　　责任印制 / 李志强

图书出现印装质量问题，请拨打售后服务热线，本社负责调换